The climactic death-throes of Soviet Communism during the 1980s included a last-gasp attempt at strategic franchise expansion in Southern Africa. Funneled through Castro's Cuba, the oil-rich Angolan armed forces (FAPLA) received billions of dollars worth of advanced weaponry including MiG 23 and Sukhoi fighter jets, SAM 8 missile systems and thousands of Armoured vehicles. Their intent – to eradicate the US-backed Angolan opposition (UNITA), and then push southwards into South Africa's protectorate SWA/Namibia, ostensibly as liberators.

1985 saw the first large-scale Mechanised offensive in Southern African history. Russian Generals planned and led the massive offensive but without properly accounting for the tenacity of UNITA (supported by South African forces – SADF) or the treacherous terrain typical in the sub-tropical rainy season. The '85 offensive floundered in the mud, FAPLA returned to their capital Luanda and the South Africans stood down, confident their 'covert' support for UNITA had demonstrated the folly of prosecuting a war so far from home and against Africa's military Superpower.

The South Africans were mistaken. Fidel and FAPLA immediately redoubled their efforts by strengthening fifteen Battalions with more Soviet hardware while Russian and Cuban specialists oversaw Troop training.

As Cuban and Angola fighter pilots honed their skills over the skies of Northern Angola, David Mannall, a 17-year old kid completing High School, was preparing for two years compulsory military service. Through a series of fateful twists over the following two years he found himself leading soldiers in a number of full-scale armoured clashes including the largest and most decisive battle on African soil since World War II.

This is the David and Goliath story that, due to seismic political changes in the region, has never been accurately recorded. Finally, the author lifts the hatch on his story of how Charlie Squadron, comprising just twelve 90mm AFVs crewed by 36 national servicemen, as part of the elite 61 Mechanised Battalion, engaged and effectively destroyed the giant FAPLA 47th Armoured Brigade in a single day – 3 October 1987. Their 90mm cannons were never designed as Tank-killers but any assurances they would never be deployed against heavy Armour were left in the classroom during the three-month operation, never more starkly so than at the decisive 'Battle on the Lomba River'. The Communist-backed offensive died that day along with hundreds of opposition fighters.

47th Brigade survivors abandoned their vehicles and fled north across the Lomba, eventually joining up with the 59th Brigade, a precursor to the wholesale retreat of over ten thousand soldiers back to their original staging point at Cuito Cuanavale.

The myth perpetuated by post-apartheid politicians goes something like this "…the SADF force that destroyed 47th Brigade on 3 October numbered 6,000 men and the hard yards were run by UNITA forces!" The inconvenient truth is; 61 Mechanised Battalion comprised less than 400 combat soldiers, and when lined up for battle, just 36 South African boys held the frontline that day, superbly supported by their unit brothers. This is my account of their story.

Born in Dorset, England in 1968, the author's family immigrated to South Africa later that same year. The sub-tropical climate of KwaZulu Natal ensured a childhood spent mostly outdoors building forts in nearby pine-forests or swimming in the Indian Ocean.

Like most conscripts, David joined the army because he was required to do so by law, the alternative, four years in the Police Force or jail for conscientious objectors, held little appeal. His two year 'call-up' could've been postponed by tertiary study but, without any clear direction, he joined thousands of boys in 1986 to 'do his bit' for the good of his country.

Selected for Armoured Corps Officer training he excelled in most areas of military life, except perhaps discipline. Demoted for going off-base during training he attracted the ire of commanders who despatched him to a remote border outpost Omuthiya for 13 months. His experiences with 61 Mechanised Battalion shaped his view on the world and on the true potential of humanity, for good and evil alike.

Following his wartime experiences David embarked on a destructive journey of 'self-discovery', constantly questioning status-quo, re-examining life and societal norms through the hardened eyes of a government-trained and 'legally' sanctioned killer.

25 years after the guns fell silent he finally began to confront the experiences by recounting his memories of National Service and Operation Modular.

David and his wife Andrea live in London, England and have two children, Jessica and Luke.

I dedicate this book to my loving family, my wife Andrea, daughter Jessica and son Luke who've recently endured me rehashing old war stories and my many hours of absence while scribbling these words.

To Graham (Dad), Emma, Carol and Jenny for your support.

In memory of my loving mother Elizabeth Mannall.

To my nephew Tom, who showed such interest in his uncle's account of the war that he wrote his final year thesis on the subject, and my sister-in-law Robyn for proofreading the book. Tara O'Sullivan for expertly guiding me with my first big chapter.

Thanks to the brothers-in-arms who offered input and anecdotes, including Roland de Vries.

It would be remiss of me not to remember both the fallen and the survivors of all armed conflict, especially my SADF comrades. I hope that the content of this book honours their sacrifice and the sacrifice of those families who lost loved ones.

And finally, to the old boys of 61 Mechanised Battalion Group and particularly to the lads of Charlie Squadron, we were warriors.

I'm not a military historian, nor have I read other accounts for research, this is my story.

To Charlie, with Best wishes for your journey ahead. Dave

Battle on the Lomba 1987

The Day a South African Armoured Battalion Shattered Angola's Last Mechanised Offensive – A Crew Commander's Account

How good people are so easily misled...

David Mannall, MMM

David Mannall 5/12/14

Best 16 June 2019

Helion & Company

Helion & Company Limited
26 Willow Road
Solihull
West Midlands
B91 1UE
England
Tel. 0121 705 3393
Fax 0121 711 4075
Email: info@helion.co.uk
Website: www.helion.co.uk
Twitter: @helionbooks
Visit our blog http://blog.helion.co.uk/

Published by Helion & Company 2014. Reprinted 2014.

Designed and typeset by Bookcraft Limited, Stroud, Gloucestershire
Cover designed by Paul Hewitt, Battlefield Design (www.battlefield-design.co.uk)
Printed by Henry Ling Limited, Dorchester, Dorset

Text © David Mannall 2014 except Appendix © Maj Gen (Ret) Roland de Vries, SD, SM, MMM
Photographs © as individually credited
Maps © Johan Schoeman and George Anderson

ISBN 978 1 909982 02 4

British Library Cataloguing-in-Publication Data.
A catalogue record for this book is available from the British Library.

For details of other military history titles published by Helion & Company Limited contact the above address, or visit our website: http://www.helion.co.uk.

We always welcome receiving book proposals from prospective authors.

Contents

List of Photos

List of Plates

Some of Charlie's boys enjoying a few beers listening to U2. Just a typical night circa June 1987 at 61 Mech. (Photo Warren Adams).

Gunnery training at School of Armour. The 90mm turret atop the 'Noddy' car.

1st pass out after Basic Training. (Elizabeth Mannall)

Part way through Officer training. (Elizabeth Mannall)

Back home – Alive! (Graham Mannall)

LT Hind (call-sign 33) in command of King Tiger as our convoy hogs the highway. (Len M Robberts)

Owamboland desert convoy from the Sergeant Major's perspective. (Barry Taylor)

View from the 90mm turret as 53 Battalion Assault Pioneers (Storm Pioneer) mine one of the richest seams of sub-terrainian explosive material in the world. (Barry Taylor)

Innocent victim of Angola's long civil war. Ratels; 101 Battalion. (Barry Taylor)

UNITA fighters take up the lead in preparation for Battle Group Alpha's very first attack on FAPLA. (Len M Robberts)

UNITA 106mm recoilless anti-tank unit moving past us during a stop. (Len M Robberts)

Battle planning and operational update deep in Angola. (Len M Robberts)

Charlie Squadron on the move. (Len M Robberts)

Enemy logistics vehicle feels HEAT as Charlie Squad move into the Chambinga Highlands near Cuito Cuanavale. (Martin Bremer)

View through the commanders' cupola during an attack on 49th Brigade, the thick glass made target finding extremely challenging in the dense forest. (Len M Robberts)

Tired after a long day in the saddle. (Anthony de Robillard)

L/Cpl's Donald Brown, James Sharp with Trooper vd Merwe. (Martin Bremer)

Treacherous travelling through wet season conditions, note the vehicle column have cut deep furrows in the mud. (Len M Robberts)

The Brigade bell liberated from the 47th following their capitulation on 3rd Oct 1987. Fittingly, it now forms a centrepiece to the Hind Memorial at the Johannesburg Museum of War. (Martin Bremer)

31 Charlie destroyed and burned out following 8 October MiG strike. (Len M Robberts)

Charlie Squadron and the Assault Pioneer Platoon. This photo was hastily taken circa 10 October 'before we lost more guys'. (Len M Robberts)

Olifant tank joins the party in November. (Martin Bremer)

Gunner holds two 90mm rounds while being reminded the price of poor gunnery. (Barry Taylor)

This may be after drinking the Omuthiya Special. Cpl Venter and I getting chummy with Assault Pioneer LT Len Robberts standing on right. (Len M Robberts)

Survivor. Angolan grime scrubbed away on our final day at Omuthiya. Posing at the NCOs' tent, our bedroom on base. (Dave Mannall)

List of Maps

In colour section

Author's Note

Soldiers throughout the ages have engaged enemy forces in mortal combat on the field of battle, sometimes in small, insurgency type action, sometimes in much larger, more 'organised' battles.

Historians readily record details pertaining to most major conflicts while the public at large are understandably acquainted mainly with facts relating to world wars or those regional conflicts relevant to them.

Each war, battle or skirmish is doubtless peppered with amazing accounts of survival, commitment and bravery by participants from all tiers of the military food-chain, but the overwhelming majority of these exploits remain forever untold. I'm no historian and had no reason to believe my account of the war in Angola and exploits with Charlie Squadron, 61 Mechanised Battalion would ever be told. In fact, the historical account of Charlie Squadron's contribution, specifically to the destruction of the 47th Brigade, is sorely inadequate, recorded by people who, at best, were near, but not on the frontline that day.

Like most veterans, exposing battle scars doesn't come easily. As a young man in my 20's and 30's, I struggled to communicate my experiences and, quite truthfully, even to find an audience who took my story at face value. So I realise how difficult it is for the listener to comprehend a story about something remote to him but yet so vivid, real and painful for the storyteller.

By the time I hit my 40s I'd pretty much let the story go, and at most would mention to a new friend that I was once in combat in a country called Angola and worse, had lost comrades in battle. "Where is Angola?" was usually the only question asked before the conversation moved on to more current affairs.

And then, a number of things happened in 2011 that led to this publishing deal with Helion which has brought these words to your attention. It was a tumultuous year for my family. I was struggling to find employment as a civil servant in London following the global financial downturn and, to be completely candid, I'm not a very good 'yes man', preferring to take the most expedient course to achieve results rather than constraining myself too much with burdensome red tape.

In February, Mom and Dad called me from their home in Durban with some disturbing news. Mom was experiencing some form of paralysis in her right foot. I had been away from home for more than 20 years and the folks never once called to alert me of their ailments so I knew this one was serious. Mom had just turned 68 but had the energy of a woman half her age. Until recently, she'd been contemplating taking part in her fifth Comrades' Marathon, an ultra-distance race at almost 90km but well short of her longest marathon accomplishment, the gruelling 'Washie 100' – that's 100 miles!

Mom was scheduled for a battery of tests and scans, each in turn eliminating one of a list of ailments but at the same time leaving fewer, and more dreadful, possible diagnoses. Eventually we were confronted with an unvarnished and ugly bombshell – she had Motor Neurone Disease (MND), a condition for which there is neither a cure, nor known cause.

People often cite Oxford physicist Stephen Hawking as the most famous sufferer of MND: "he's lasted decades", they say. But the harsh reality is that Stephen survives by mechanically assisted respiration and most MND sufferers live typically only 2 to 5 years from the onset of the disease. Mom never wanted to be kept alive by mechanical means and got much less time, although I believe the disease had been eroding her motor neurone activity for at least a year before the formal diagnosis was made at the end of March. This was a devastating shock to Mom, as it must be for anyone afflicted with a terminal illness.

In April, I started hurting the credit card, booked a snap vacation for the family (a benefit of flexible unemployment) and made preparations, including a genuine attempt to relocate back to South Africa, to enjoy time with my folks and provide support in my mother's final years. Mom always said, "I sent my son to the army; he never came back." In many ways this was true and I really wanted to reconnect with her while there was still time.

Before leaving for South Africa, my wife Andrea began researching the heck out of MND while I tapped into my Civil Service contacts and procured a suit-case full of equipment and adaptations to assist Mom maintain her independence for as long as possible while the disease raced to shut down the neural pathways to her muscle fibres.

Explaining to Air France the need to transport a wheelchair, without incurring cost, was always going to be tricky, so for expediency I pretended to be tempo-rarily mildly disabled while in the airport, an act my family had to keep going longer than intended when our A380 failed to arrive from New York (due to a minor accident) which meant we had to stay overnight in a nearby hotel and fly the following morning.

While gathering equipment and information ahead of our trip home a friend, who also lost his mother to MND, told me that a great regret of his was that he'd never kept a record during his mother's five-year battle. "Make sure you get some video footage and hey, why don't you write a blog?" he suggested.

Michael's words struck a chord. I rushed out, bought a state-of-the-art 3D video camera and resolved to get writing a blog – something I'd never done before. The last time I kept a diary was when forced to do so during a six-week holiday to Europe as a fifteen-year-old kid in 1983.

Writing reports for local government had always been a drudge but in writing the blog, I relished the opportunity to offload some of the daily dread and disease milestones during the four-week trip to be with my mother. I named the blog 'A month with Mom' and received warm, positive feedback on my style of writing. This was something of a surprise.

I won't belabour the story of my dear mother's illness. She passed away peacefully less than seven months later on 1 November, but the journey, her passage from this world, was as gruelling a battle as any I had experienced in war, her final weeks a living hell.

My family were all deeply affected by the journey, none more so than my father, but during that time we had little choice but to get into the trenches to provide cover and relief from the invisible and merciless enemy.

One morning in early October, my wife Andrea and I made a disturbing discovery during our phone calls to SA. On learning that critical equipment Mom needed to assist her failing lungs was being held up by incompetence and red tape, I booked the next available flight to SA and within hours was *en route* Heathrow via Cairo. Unfortunately Egypt was having problems of its own and cancelled the onward flight, causing me a 24-hour delay. By the time I walked into my parents' home, Mom was gasping like a fish out of water and totally immobile with the exception of a weakened left hand.

With my sister Carol's assistance, I returned to combat for the first time in a quarter century; it really felt that intense. Mom needed round-the-clock care and as soon as we got the machine to support her lungs (not mechanical respiration) she began to drown in her own phlegm because she had become too weak to expectorate (cough). I was constantly on alert, suctioning machine at the ready. The ensuing combat-level exhaustion combined with adrenaline in a way that reminded me of the crazy days I had spent at war. Unfortunately I was also in the middle of a precious, time-limited work assignment and had only been able to take 10 days out before returning to complete the writing and presentation of some report or other.

The reality on the ground was that without my constant vigilance, Mom would not get a satisfactory level of care and furthermore, she had understandably grown fearful of drowning, so I asked Andrea to fly out and relieve me. Admirably, after juat a 24-hour handover, she stepped into the combat zone armed only with courage and a crash course in MND intensive care.

I said goodbye, fairly confident that I'd be back before the very end. The whole family was scheduled to be back in Durban just three-weeks later, on 11 November, for the folks' 45th wedding anniversary. It didn't work out like that. Two weeks later, following an urgent call from Andrea on 31 October I jumped on the first plane heading to SA. As the Virgin flight touched down in Johannesburg, I switched on my mobile phone. Within seconds it rang. It was Andrea. She asked me where I was and then said, "Say goodbye to your mom, we think she's going now."

Sitting as I was, among strangers who were rushing to gather bags from overhead lockers in that unique travellers' ritual where we rush to stand before waiting for the narrow aisle ahead to clear some minutes later, I whispered my goodbyes, unsure if Mom was cognisant. Then, about minute later, Andrea came back on the line: "She's gone Dave, I'm so sorry."

Admittedly I was a bit of a mess going through passport control and then when making a booking for an onward flight to Durban. Selfishly I'd imagined she'd be able to stay long enough to say 'totsiens' (goodbye) one more time.

Seven months and it was all over.

In a way, I was thankful that the dreadful ordeal ended sooner rather than later because incarceration in that disease-ravaged, broken body was a living hell from which Mom always knew that her untimely death was the only escape.

Witnessing my Mom's immense bravery, courage and faith throughout her illness inspired me to revisit my own ordeal at war in 1987 and so I joined a number of social media sites for South African Army veterans where I encountered a number of former comrades, notably Jaco Swanevelder. Jaco warmly welcomed me back into the brotherhood of 61 Mechanised Battalion, the unit I proudly served during my second year of National Service and with whom I joined battle deep into Angolan territory.

I took some comfort in reading others accounts of army training, experiences and days at war having never previously read a single account of the Angolan Conflict. And then I came across a photo that turned my blood cold. The image was of a guy standing in a bomb crater just in front of one of our bombed and burned-out Ratel 90 Armoured Personnel Carriers (APCs). The person who posted the photograph wanted to know if anyone had any background info. The scene captured by Len Robberts, a former comrade-in-arms, was exactly as I remembered it on that fateful day in October 1987 when most of Charlie

Squadron narrowly escaped death during an accurate aerial bombardment. Unfortunately we didn't all survive the bombing so the event itself is forever seared in my memory. Consequently, I was able to 'open up' and recount in fairly vivid detail the events leading up to that macabre scene.

My account of the incident stimulated a good amount of interest; people asked if I had more stories so I started writing about some of the other 'big bang' days (these social media groups are understandably sceptical of crazy war stories because it seems there are some guys out there willing to create stories of derring-do despite never having been in the combat area). I published a few chapters online and quite quickly people suggested that I should 'turn this into a book'. Someone offered the name of a British publisher with an interest in the Angolan 'Bush' War who agreed to publish this story.

It's staggering and surreal to have been afforded this opportunity and I'm deeply honoured to be able to tell my story; a rare privilege which I intend to respect throughout my account of Battle on the Lomba River in 1987.

That battle, and my involvement in it, didn't happen in isolation therefore I've taken the liberty of telling most of what I recall about the journey that delivered me and my comrades to that historic moment, and as much as I can remember of the dark weeks that followed when we chased a retreating enemy; when youthful exuberance was replaced by something different altogether and somewhat at odds with the views of mainstream society.

Unfortunately, I never maintained a journal during my National Service so the book focuses mostly on major events and actions augmented by anecdotes from a small number of fellow soldiers. I name individual contributors throughout, but primarily I tell this story as I remember it.

I'm sure there's much I've forgotten during the intervening years and absolutely certain there many individual stories or acts of valour, or craziness, not accounted for here. The nature of warfare is such that in the heat of battle an individual soldier can't know the detail of what each combatant is doing to stay alive, let alone the actions of other units. Equally, there are doubtless many amusing moments I've forgotten—and my recollections of many physically demanding or emotionally painful days have long-since paled into insignificance as the memory of the horror of war starved them of 'cranial air-time'.

I hope this book helps readers to better understand war from a soldier's perspective and that if he, or she, has a lost a loved one to conflict, this account helps them in some small way to deal with the psychological fallout.

David Robert Mannall, MMM

"Take a community of Dutchmen of the type of those who defended themselves for fifty years against all the power of Spain at a time when Spain was the greatest power in the world. Intermix with them a strain of those inflexible French Huguenots, who gave up their name and left their country forever at the time of the revocation of the Edict of Nantes. The product must obviously be one of the most rugged, virile, unconquerable races ever seen upon the face of the earth. Take these formidable people and train them for seven generations in constant warfare against savage men and ferocious beasts, in circumstances in which no weakling could survive; place them so that they acquire skill with weapons and in horsemanship, give them a country which is eminently suited to the tactics of the huntsman, the marksman and the rider. Then, finally, put a fine temper upon their military qualities by a dour fatalistic Old Testament religion and an ardent and consuming patriotism. Combine all these qualities and all these impulses in one individual and you have the modern Boer- the most formidable antagonist who ever crossed the path of Imperial Britain. Our military history has largely consisted in our conflicts with France, but Napoleon and all his veterans have never treated us as roughly as these bard-bitten farmers with their ancient theology and their inconveniently modern rifles. Look at the map of South Africa, and there, in the very centre of the British possessions, like the stone in a peach, lies the great stretch of the two republics, a mighty domain for so small a people. How came they there? Who are these Teutonic folk who have burrowed so deeply into Africa? It is a twice-told tale, and yet it must be told once again if this story is to have even the most superficial of introductions. No one can know or appreciate the Boer who does not know his past, for he is what his past has made him."

Sir Arthur Conan Doyle (author of Sherlock Holmes)

Introduction

THE BATTLE ON THE LOMBA 1987

"Charlie Squadron, we're holding for artillery 'ripple' bombardment. Close all hatches!" Captain Cloete's clipped command crackled simultaneously in each headset of the 12 crew commanders on the frontline.

I dropped into the turret quickly pulling the dome-shaped commander's hatch shut above my head. There was nothing more to do than wait at the ready, and pray that our artillery ordinance was on target.

We'd only once before used artillery at such close quarters. These guys were shooting from ten or fifteen clicks away, sometimes much further, so it had the potential to get a bit hairy, explosions so close to our lines we couldn't be certain if they were friendly or enemy bombs, but this was the nature of prosecuting close-quarters combat in such densely forested terrain. Not the ideal playground for Armoured Corps.

My crewmates and I waited in heavy silence for what seemed ages, but within two minutes…that familiar whistling of incoming ordinance, the unmistakeable flash of exploding munitions erupting no more than a few hundred metres ahead, and then the crump, crump, thump as countless kilo's of very high explosives detonated.

This was good!

Dead-eye mortar men, in concert with their long-range artillery and MRL (multiple rocket launcher) counterparts, released a well co-ordinated ripple of shock-and-awe onto enemy positions, like some kind of macabre fireworks display at its climax, lasting a good three or four minutes.

Then, as quickly as it started it was over. The forest fell silent once more; I opened and locked the hatch in the 90 degree 'up' position while re-evaluating the target area ahead. It seemed quite a lot of the forest foliage, beyond our immediate tree line, had been stripped bare, creating a sort of 'no-man's land' clearing across which opposing forces could operate.

A minute later, all 12 crew commander's headsets barked back to life with Cloete's unwelcomed command: "Charlie Squadron, move out in formation… may God be with you all."

"Okay boys this is it, let's move out. Gunner, prepare to fire."

Today, after 20 months of training, preparation, lesser battles and small skirmishes against a much larger, more powerful enemy, all the pieces of that monstrous mechanised jigsaw puzzle finally dropped into place. The stage had been set for The Battle on the Lomba, but of course we didn't know it at the time because, after a month in the hot zone, today's battle was expected to be similar to previous actions where contact was broken off within an hour due to difficulty with visibility or an enemy so well entrenched that digging them out would cost too many lives.

It wasn't always thus.

THE BEGINNING

At 17 and three quarter years old, I might've been described as a fairly scrawny, baby-faced 'late-developer' on the day I arrived for National Service.

In fact, at that stage of my life I was late for pretty much everything... late for school, late handing in homework, late getting dressed for church, late finding a girl for school final year [Matric] dance. Damn! The truth is that even puberty arrived embarrassingly late for me! At the age of 17, I'd only recently begun scraping sparse patches of wispy fluff off my baby face and my pube collection was more like semi-arid desert than the subtropical over-growth sported by some lads in my high school changing rooms. Fuck! How did I get left so far behind? It was bad enough that we were being shipped off to god-knows-where, worse still that some guys looked like men while I still looked very much a boy!

And I was still a virgin! My limited hands-on experience of close-quarters contact of the female kind was quite evidently, and woefully, inadequate in a man's world. If pushed into a corner about my sexual exploits I could bluff and obfuscate a little, but I knew my meagre knowledge of the female workings wouldn't withstand much probing by those who'd 'been there', I didn't want to get caught telling outright lies.

Finally—and this was perhaps my greatest shortcoming though thankfully I was not alone in this—I was an *Engelsman* (Englishman) and from Durban, probably the very worst combination of characteristics from an Afrikaaner army instructor's perspective. Afrikaaners were still a bit miffed at the arrogant British Empire and, by association, its subjects, for getting greedy in the 19th Century, reneging on land treaties, and then sending ship-loads of redcoats to take back land it had given away soon after the Crown realised just how valuable those gold-rich rocks are north of the Orange river in the area known as The Highveld.

Although this historic nastiness happened a century or so earlier, it had led to some rather brutal conflicts between the two sides, the establishment of concentration camps for wives and children of the less well equipped Boers—a colloquial Afrikaans word meaning 'farmer' by which the original Dutch settlers came to be known—some Afrikaaners seemed unable to let these bygones be bygones.

In fact, Afrikaaners pretty much ran and owned the modern South African military, it was in their DNA. So, upon my arrival into this modern day military machine I worried that my personal 'shortcomings' were like some unholy Trinity of flaws that increased my chance of being singled out, teased, humiliated or *opvokked* (fucked up) by the bellowing army instructors who'd just taken 'ownership' of us at the immaculately laid out, but intimidating, School of Armour [*Pantserskool*], one of a number of high profile units based at the South African Army's military complex at Tempe, Bloemfontein.

Bloemfontein [Flower-fountain], South Africa's fifth largest city, was as beautiful as it was conservative. Located in the heartland of Orange Free State Province, Bloemfontein was possibly the most Afrikaans place in the world. Certainly it was so in my limited experience.

The stunning scenery of the region belied potentially savage weather conditions. It is one of those areas that endure extreme summer heat, as you'd expect in Africa, but that also gets a very cold during a short winter. In fact, the coming winter (1986) would be my first African encounter of the formation of ice outside a domestic freezer. This kind of night-time cold was particularly unsuited to a Durbanite.

My concerns regarding my 'shortcomings' were not unfounded. One of the intimidating, muscular, and freakily moustachioed men singled me out for special attention. "*JY!*" (You!), he bellowed at me in Afrikaans.

Shit—clammy palm time! I realised with a shudder that the guy was shouting at me. What had I done wrong to get noticed so quickly? Had I moved a muscle while standing to attention, had I marched poorly, or was this the curse of my unholy Trinity of failings already blighting my two-year legally sanctioned National Service? Perhaps I'd just made the wrong kind of eye contact with him. "Uhm yes, yes sir" I squeaked nervously.

Moustache-man immediately swelled up like a Puffer Fish, rage etching deep fissures across his sun-hardened face. Obviously I had given the wrong answer! His volcanic reaction to my mumbled reply surely would not have been worse if

I'd just dropped my army-issue brown overalls and urinated on his magnificently polished size 10's!

He launched into a blistering tirade which went something like this…

"Hoekom praat jy met my in Engels piel-neus?" (Why are you talking to me in English, dick-nose?). I got the distinct feeling this wasn't meant as a compliment.

He went on, *"Lyk ek vir jou soos n sag-piel Officier, jou klein kak!?"* (Do I look like a soft-cock officer to you, you little shit?)

I felt the blood drain from my face as I desperately tried to calculate the magnitude of my mistake. If I'd had the magical powers of David Copperfield I would have frikkin-well vanished right out of there in a puff-o-smoke but the enraged beast was far from satisfied and I had nowhere to go. He continued, *"…ek is n Korporaal jou klein kak, sak en gee vir my 20 push-ups!"* (I'm a Corporal, you little shit, drop and give me 20 push-ups!).

I immediately dropped to the floor to perform the first of many thousands of punishment push-ups during the coming year on 'Junior Leader' (JL) training. The Corporal helpfully counted, in Afrikaans, demanding a quick, lactic-acid-inducing tempo. *"Een, Twee, Drie…negetien, twintig. Nou staan op."* (now stand up).

Breathing hard, sweat running down my back, I returned to standing at attention. Through the fog of embarrassment at being singled out, I figured there were a number of important lessons to be learned.

- One: The enraged beast's rank was that of Corporal and he needed, nay insisted, to be addressed thus, and only in Afrikaans language because, in truth, pretty much everything was conducted in Afrikaans – the army's first language but unfortunately, my extremely weak second language. Mom would say, "David your Afrikaans, at the age of four, when we lived in Port Elizabeth, was better then than it is now at the age of 17, why?" I'd had Afrikaans playmates back then, but since moving to a predominantly English city (Durban, AKA; The Last British Outpost) Afrikaans was another subject I'd never really troubled myself much with learning at school, but like everything else I'd encountered in the past week, it paid to learn lessons pretty damn quick if I were to improve my chances of surviving the strictly enforced 24-month call-up period unscathed – relatively speaking that is. But…
- Two: My understanding of spoken Afrikaans wasn't as bad as I'd previously thought though the business of learning to speak the language fluently would require a combination of both time and punishment.

- Three: My scrawny 7th team rugby physique could just about manage 20 push-ups, but my pride wasn't yet accustomed to the sense of shame at being singled out and watched by my peers as I wiggled my way through the last few reps. It seemed that I could've prepared myself a little better for army life, and…
- Four: The army-issue rule book we'd been given a week ago, which clearly stated that swearing or foul language would not be tolerated in the army, was just a little inaccurate, on that particular point at least. This begged the rather unsettling question: Which other rules would be so glibly disregarded during the next two years?

I rejoined Bravo Squadron, which consisted of 31 other boys who, like me, had just completed a taxpayer funded, 18-hour, overnight train journey to this place called Tempe, a sprawling military base the likes of which most of us had probably never imagined. It was like a town, and home of (amongst others) 1 South African Infantry (1SAI) and 1 Parachute Battalion. The School of Armour sat atop the hill at Tempe like a colossus looking down on the other Corps and city below, and it was to be our home for the next ten months, it was hard not to be a little proud of the place, the unit and especially the Corps. That is, if we didn't get RTU'd (returned to unit, for failing some part of JL training).

Corporal Moustache now seemed suitably satisfied that he'd impressed his significant authority upon me, but it's fair to say I was still *kukking* myself [bricking it] when he stepped forward, right up into my barely-started-shaving face, looked me up and down, and then shouted over to his fellow non-commissioned officers (NCOs), "*Haai, julle, die eene lyk soos* Trinity" [Hey, you guys, this one looks like Trinity.]

I was stunned! How could he have known about my unholy Trinity of 'flaws'?

He looked back at me, his eyes softening for an instant as he asked in pretty good, but thickly accented English, "Have you seen the movie 'They call me Trinity' starring Terrence Hill?"

Immediately I began trawling through my academically inferior memory bank but quickly returned with nothing!

"Nnnn nee Korporaal" I stammered, which was about all the Afrikaans I could muster with any confidence at that moment. I hadn't seen that movie, didn't know what Terrence Hill looked like then, nor what he looked like 15 years previously when he starred alongside Bud Spencer in that well known series of 'Spaghetti Westerns' that were so popular in the early 1970's.

Anyway, I had no idea why it should matter, nor if this apparent doppelganger was going to be an asset to aid my survival during JL training, or a painful millstone with which I'd be lumbered?

The Corporal called to his fellow NCOs, still in English, pointed at me and said, 'From now on this one will be known as Trinity!'

And with that, Corporal lost interest in me and began haranguing a fellow 'roofie' (derogatory nickname for new conscripts like us) for being a bit overweight, *"…en die eene is sewe maaltye voor en fyf kakke agter"* (…and this guy is seven meals ahead and five shits' behind) he barked, much to the amusement of his fellow instructors.

Admittedly I also found this acutely observed analysis quite amusing at the time but wouldn't have dared smirk or acknowledge the suffering of the chubby guy for fear of eliciting further unwanted attention from the instructors.

No, in the end, my first brush with our instructors could've gone far worse than it did, plus, the 7-meal/5-shits fat-gag firmly deflected attention onto the other guy…for a little while at least.

The Trinity nickname, coined by Corporal Moustache, stuck with me throughout JL's and into Angola and, secretly, I came to enjoy the reference to a frustratingly laid-back, gun-slinging, womaniser who regularly arrived late but often contributed to saving the day.

My name is David Robert Mannall; just one of hundreds of thousands of white boys conscripted to National Service during the 1960's, 70's, 80's and early '90's in defence of homeland security and the ever present threat of a Communist-backed takeover. Born in England, raised in Durban, I loved my carefree, barefoot, beach-boy type childhood. In the army, English speaking lads were 'affectionately' referred to as 'Soutie', or 'Soutpiel', which translates exactly as 'Salty' or 'Salt-Dick' – the reference to having one leg in England, the other leg in South Africa with our collective penises dangling in the Atlantic Ocean.

I grew up fairly apolitical, didn't pay much attention to current affairs but was aware that the differentiation of respect/rights for people based on colour (apartheid) wasn't fair, but like most white South Africans couldn't see a credible alternative that would ensure my country didn't follow the example of neighbouring Zimbabwe which had rapidly been transformed from the bread-basket of Africa, run by a racist white government (very bad), to one of Africa's notable basket-cases, run into the ground by a racist black government (much more acceptable to the international community).

At High School, as the date loomed when we became legally required to make ourselves available for National Service 'call-up', we heard rumour of some *okes* (guys) refusing to go on moral or religious grounds.

Some guys legitimately postponed service by starting tertiary education which had some real benefits because the army treated graduates more like grown-ups, sometimes even allowed them to gain experience in their chosen field if it suited army requirements (for example, Engineering and Medical degrees) and the army almost fell over itself in its rush to award these intellectual giants the highest possible rank attainable for a two-year conscript – 'two-pip' or full Lieutenant.

I had absolutely no idea what direction to follow as a future career, nor what I should study if I went to university. And then there was the not insignificant matter of privately funding my tertiary education to consider. It seemed unthinkable to blow my parents' modest savings on an expensive university education when I wasn't even sure what course to study. The options apparently available to me were either accountancy (boring) or law (not academically equipped) and if neither of these happened I'd end up a garbage collector or postman, or so the narrative went.

Draft dodgers spent four years in jail, which was, as it turned out, another great incentive for patriotism.

Dad's connections to the seafaring community meant that, with a few strings pulled, I probably could've joined the Navy but in a pique of teenage angst, I rejected his offer of assistance. Instead, I accepted the outcome of an IBM computer algorithm programmed simply to alter the course of many young lives, some irrevocably.

Truth is I could've 'legitimately' dodged the whole business of National Service by hitching a ride on a Boeing back to Heathrow because in '68, soon after my birth, my folks had immigrated to South Africa, partly because of our family connection to the country: my mom spent some of her childhood in King William's Town and my maternal grandma was South African going back a few generations.

My 'Old Man', displaced during the Second World War and permanently separated from his baby sister, had a childhood further blighted by the tragic loss of his young mother. Just as soon as legally able (aged 15), he joined the Merchant Navy working his way up the officer ranks on the 'mail-ships' between England and South Africa for Union Castle Line. By the mid 60's, Union Castle began taking advantage the lucrative passenger market by offering 'cruises', on the three-week journey between Cape Town and Southampton.

Luckily for my sisters and I, our mother's favourite aunty stumped up the cash (£21) for her to travel from SA via Southampton, England, and then on to Dumfries in Scotland to complete her midwifery training.

Once aboard the *Pretoria Castle*, the attractive 20-year old Elizabeth quickly came to the attention of a number of the sea-dog officers, including my dad, and as fate would have it, by the time the crew conducted the traditional 'rites-of-passage' ceremonies to mark Equatorial crossing, about 10 days into the journey, my parents' 47-year romance began taking its first fledgling footsteps. Within three years of crossing the Equatorial divide together, my parents were married. Shortly afterwards Baby Carol arrived with a second kid (me) hot on her heels. My younger sister, Jennifer, wouldn't make her appearance for another four years, by which time we were well settled into our Port Elizabeth home.

By the time I started school, Dad had taken promotion to become a ship's Pilot in Durban harbour.

My sisters and I were raised to be net-contributors to society, so it never really occurred to me to dodge National Service; back then it simply seemed the right and proper thing to 'do your bit for your country'. Without doubt, the IBM algorithm altered my life and it is certain that, had I done National Service as a 'swabby' in the Navy, it would've been tough in a few notably different ways.

True, I probably never would've found myself staring down the business end of a 100mm smoothbore fully operational Russian Main Battle Tank (MBTs) cannon but would've been taught to scuba-dive and face the ocean's MBTs, like hammerheads and ragged-tooth sharks which would've been a lot more fun.

For some boys the computer algorithm was a ticket to two years of 'living it up', for others, a death sentence. All that was, of course, unknowable to us then.

Toward the end of our final year at high school, guys started coming to class waving call-up papers naming places and bases previously unknown into my world. It was happening; letters were being sent out and it was only a matter of time until mine arrived, unless, somehow the papers went missing—there were stories of guys being overlooked by the system somehow!

No such luck for Private Mannall! Two days later, I came home to find a small, cheap brown window envelope propped up against the vase on the dining room table. My name and a long number were evident in the envelope window. With racing pulse, I unceremoniously tore the envelope open and whipped out the dreaded, dot-matrix-printed call-up papers.

My first reaction was excitement when I saw the unit name – 2 Special Services Battalion (2SSB). Despite knowing nothing at all about 2SSB, the name implied something quite important; 'special forces' perhaps? Scary, but at the same time it hinted at thrilling possibilities. The next thing that struck me was that 2SSB was located somewhere I'd hitherto never known of, a place called Zeerust!

"Mom, please grab the Atlas map of South Africa! Where, or what, is Zeerust?"

We easily found the name in the index – Zeerust was the very last name; the grid-reference located it close to the country's northern border.

I was deflated, "Jeez Ma", I moaned, "Could they have sent me any further from home, to a place so insignificant it was given the very last name available to the committee in charge of naming places?"

For a fun-loving free spirit, this Zeerust dump seemed like the arse end of nowhere, about as far as possible from family, friends, the ocean and modernity. Perhaps I had been a fool for spurning the possibility of a Navy deal.

Vasbyt boetie [Hold tight young brother], was the typical response to anything tough and army related – just get on with it, and do your bit like everyone else.

I reproached myself, why hadn't I been paying more attention? But it was too late for alternatives. The die was cast, my computer-gifted fate sealed. So, along with thousands of other boys around the country, I went shopping for irons, boot polish and padlocks.

I '*klaared-aan*' [checked-in] to the army January 1986, still aged 17.

On arrival at Natal Command we were strongly advised to remove any contraband and send it home with our families.

Saying goodbye to the folks wasn't as bad as I had expected, it helped being one of hundreds of other boys doing exactly the same thing. They say there's safety in numbers don't they?

Following a brief presentation by the unit commander, we were loaded onto Troop transport and taken to Durban's central train station where we embarked a sleeper train for the two-day journey to 2SSB.

As it turned out the 36 hour jaunt to Zeerust was actually quite a *jol* (fun), the officers and NCOs in charge were fairly *rustig* (chilled) and, with only one notable exception, mostly they left us alone to chat in our six-berth cabins.

Groups of guys who knew each other from school crammed the train's narrow corridors, others hung from windows whistling at anything remotely female, or hurling abuse as befit the encounter.

At about the same time, a guy called Jonas Savimbi, a rebel leader in Angola was meeting with US President Ronald Reagan requesting and receiving his support in UNITA's (National Union for the Total Independence of Angola) long running battle for power against an increasingly Communist-backed government.

This had no bearing on the young recruits in the narrow-gauge train as it slowly clattered its way into the night and into the following day. The journey reminded me of equally long childhood train trips to my Uncle John's farm in the Karoo and it was impossible not be awed as the landscape changed from one of mountainous grandeur to wide-open expansive escarpment with seemingly never-ending horizons as we rolled through some of South Africa's most stunning scenery.

Given the relatively benign surroundings on the train, and a growing sense of fate shared, the guys in the cabin quickly relaxed. Fledgling friendships formed and ribald teasing quickly followed. It became apparent that any perceived weakness would be pounced upon and exploited mercilessly, a bit like high school but with nowhere to run. Early on I was offered a great opportunity to enhance my credentials when some bloke asked me if I knew what it was like to 'trip on acid'.

As if I knew!! But to save face I proceeded to fabricate a cock-n-bull account of 'tripping' based only on snippets of anecdotal info acquired over the years. This guy, Wentzel, was so excited by my account that he decided he wanted to 'trip' right then and there. Not the brightest light on the train, he wondered if he could get acid directly from a torch battery. I'd never heard of it but simply agreed with him and then concocted this ridiculously convoluted idea that by sucking the positive terminal on a battery while holding an index finger to the opposite end, he could draw out acid and experience a 'trip'.

He bought it, hook, line and sinker! For about 20 minutes the crazy fool sucked on an AA battery!

When he still wasn't getting a buzz we suggested finding a larger battery. A quarter hour later, it still had no effect on him so I suggested, "the batteries must be flat", and he believed it!! Truth was I knew nothing at all about drugs really. Tripping on acid was way off my radar, I mean, I wouldn't even take a puff of a cigarette, let alone smoking dagga [marijuana] which a few mates had already tried.

No, in those days, I wanted nothing at all to do with drug-taking, except for occasional alcohol binges. Alcohol was my drug of choice during National Service, and that was cool, because pretty much everyone else did it.

After a couple of stops to scoop up more young boys on the Zeerust express, we finally arrived at the tiny town's rusty train station.

We were told to disembark, so we gathered up our small bags of belongings and jumped down onto the platform.

Then the shouting started.

We were ordered to stand to attention and barked at for what seemed like ages by some military heavyweight before eight large tarpaulin-covered Troop transport trucks arrived in convoy. Chocolate brown tailgates dropped open and for the first time we practised the technique of hurriedly clambering aboard without face-planting the deck or the unforgiving steel-tube benches. The prime seats at the rear of the Samil 50 were quickly snapped up but even from my seat deep inside the truck it was apparent that Zeerust had very little to offer a boy looking for fun.

Once again we were brought together in rather shabby formation and clearly some *okes* were not trying very hard to fall in line, behaving almost as if their call up to the army was a joke. The army had yet to show them the error of their ways.

Roll-call followed further haranguing and then we were allocated to large chicken-shed-like bungalows for processing.

The following three or four days involved some exercise, health screening, relatively gentle punishments and very brutal haircuts but mostly we spent our time queuing to fill in endless sheets of carbonated paper onto which we signed away our lives in return for a few bits of army-issue threads, boots and fine-dining equipment including water-bottle, cooking pots and the ubiquitous *pikstel* (knife, fork, spoon combo). We even signed for a large steel storage box called a 'Trommel' – not the sort of thing anyone was likely to lose!

So much of it was alien to me, meeting blokes from across the country, some with very different accents and backgrounds, people I'd never imagined existed. Some guys taught me important survival skills like how to make free calls from the public payphone outside our bungalow.

Meal times quickly became a popular interlude to our day; breakfast often included fried eggs, which was a bonus because we seldom got eggs for brekkie at home, though admittedly the eggs at home never had a blue tinge about them!

Most of the guys in the bungalow got on well, I was making new friends, and the punishments weren't as bad as people had made out, and so it seemed that perhaps this forced army-thing wasn't gonna be too bad after all.

Then, just as the tsunami of carbonated paper subsided, the entire cohort of three hundred or so new Troopers were called to attention on the parade ground in front of a cabal of big cheese officers including Colonel T. Beyleveldt, Officer Commanding School of Armour.

The Colonel told us he'd come up from Bloemfontein, bringing with him yet another tsunami of carbon paper and proceeded to deliver a rousing speech in which he described the pride of being part of the South African Armoured Corps (SAAC) and why we should strive to do our very best for God, country and self during the coming two years.

Admittedly, for me anyway, it was quite a rousing speech, and the possibility of becoming a Tank commander was mentioned, dispelling any lingering thoughts I had of forgoing the opportunity to grab the chance to achieve the best I could during service, unlike some guys in the bungalow who said stuff like: "*kuk* man, why sign up for even more of this army bullshit, that'll only give these bastards more excuse to screw us around."

The following three days involved a battery of tests, interviews and question-naires on a 'selection' course. In the end it would've been disappointing not to have been offered assignment to a different unit, surely there could be no more remote location than Zeerust, other than Siberia perhaps!

It seemed that wherever I got posted, it could only be an improvement on the status quo, and then there was the big carrot on offer – junior officer training (AKA junior leader or JL training). This was an opportunity to rise above the crowd a little bit, maybe get treated better, for example officers and NCOs ate most meals on china plates rather than stamped-steel army issue mess hall *vark-panne* (pig-plates).

So a week after leaving Durban, we were called back onto the parade ground for the umpteenth time. Names were called and 'successful' candidates told to hand back most of their recently issued kit (cue yet another paper tsunami), before being loaded onto buses and transferred to a number of onward bases for basic training.

School of Armour, Army Training Wing, Armoured Corps' primary role was to train Olifant (Elephant) Main Battle Tank (MBT) crews, armoured car commanders and Squadron junior leaders (Lieutenants and Corporals).

The January '86 intake totalled about 120 guys who were assigned by some unseen hand (probably not IBM this time) to one MBT and three armoured car Squadrons, each with its own 32-bed bungalow.

By this stage we'd been in the system a week and those first seven days at Zeerust seemed a bit like a vacation in a bad 1960's holiday camp but at least they had been relatively pain free. Instructors there were likely on a short leash and probably been ordered to be 'nice', to break us in gently, perhaps to lull us into a more complacent view of army life. That changed soon as 'selection course' was completed.

From the moment we were shipped to our respective units the mood changed. Instructors from the School escorted us the 500 kilometres to Bloemfontein.

On arrival at the Pantserskool, the guys in my group were assigned to the 2nd Armoured Car Group AKA Bravo Squadron.

We were advised that to complete the course, which with an expected 40% drop-out rate was by no means assured, we'd have to survive ten months of rigorous physical, psychological and knowledge-based examination and, in theory, be prepared for whatever challenges lay beyond.

For many successful JLs, the second year might mean 'time to take things easy, kick back and enjoy a relatively chilled year before completion of duty'.

There were potentially plum onward postings to 'cushy' training units, or in-country bases with an Armoured Corps presence, this is where I hoped and expected to end up.

For a small number of successful JLs, the second year would involve despatch for a 12-month tour to the relatively dangerous SWA/Angola border camps, 2000km to the north, to command equally young second- year troops.

And for some of those, fate would see them spend months locked in almost daily mortal combat against an overwhelmingly stronger, better equipped but less well-trained enemy.

And finally, sadly, a small number were destined to give their lives for their country.

I just happened to be one of those whose destiny it was to be on, or near, the bleeding edge of the largest mechanised warfare ever prosecuted in Southern Africa, and the largest build up of mechanised military hardware in Africa since WW2.

My involvement on the frontline was by no means assured when I signed up for JL's because there were plenty of opportunities for me to alter the course of my National Service journey and with hindsight it's quite easy to note the decisions, and mistakes I made during 1986 which ultimately influenced the decisions made by others steering my fate.

Given recent history, it was nigh on impossible for anyone to presage the magnitude of the cataclysm that was awaiting us unwitting teenagers. We had no idea what lay ahead, how could we?

I was totally oblivious, ignorant in fact, to the harsh realities of the two-decades-old Angolan War and the guiding over-watch and support provided by Communist countries.

The on-off Angolan civil war, and SADF's involvement in it, was conducted largely outside the reach of government-controlled media, consequently very little was known of South Africa's often clandestine involvement therein.

Primarily, the South African Government was more interested in crushing the terrorist organisation SWAPO to preserve the status quo with its South West African (Namibia) protectorate, rather than getting embroiled in Angola's armed power struggle.

As most kids did in the 70's, I played Cowboys and 'Injuns' with the boys who lived in my road, oblivious that some older boys were travelling deep into Angola to root out bands of terrorists in a kind of insurgency war of attrition, a bit like that faced by US and Allied forces against the Taliban in Afghanistan in the past decade.

We played 'battles and wars' in the large pine forest adjoining our house, learning to lay booby-traps and build impregnable rock forts with branches interlaced to form a roof.

The forest next to the family house was so popular that I once approached my dad with a request that he should buy it in lieu of my birthday and Christmas presents for the rest of my life! I think this was motivated by the potential loss of our playground following the construction of a nearby massive residential complex ironically named 'Paradise Valley'.

No shit! That is what they really called this sprawling monstrosity consisting about 800 apartments nestling in the forest about 2 km from our home. That name, to me, is a perfect example of irony, *it was Paradise* until they dumped a few million tons of cast concrete onto it, and yet they still had the audacity to call it Paradise Valley – more like Paradise Lost!

However, the massive construction site and lax health and safety regulations provided us kids with yet another fun playground but the truth is… I was no alpha male sports star rampaging Rambo-style through my teens seeking out fights or intentionally infringing the law, with the notable exception of the tiny matter regarding the legal age for alcohol consumption.

Gifted with absolutely no musical talent other than, allegedly, a half-decent singing voice, Mom finally gave up trying to force me to learn piano. My folks musical taste was firmly rooted in the 60's whereas my sisters and I were more inclined to listen to our few prized music cassettes of unsanctioned New Romantic music popularised by the likes of Duran Duran, Pet Shop Boys, Depeche Mode and Frankie goes to Hollywood. Paul Hardcastle surprised me when he told the world "the average age of a combat soldier in Vietnam was 19". It seemed incredible to us that boys so young were sent to war.

When the technology finally arrived in SA, we'd bootleg tunes 'illegally' from the Friday night Top 40 radio show directly onto a TDK tape-cassette using one of those hi-tech all-in-one radio-cassette players.

By the time I turned 17, meeting girls, or the pursuit of opportunities to meet girls, was second only in importance to hanging out with my 'crew' of school mates and maybe getting mildly drunk on four small bottles of beer on a Friday night and if extremely fortunate, getting a smooch and hip-grind on the dance-floor.

The Angolan war wasn't really on my radar so to speak although I was vaguely aware of occasional news reports about soldiers dying 'on operational duties on The Border', and then there were times in Church that Reverend Hays would ask us to pray for sons of the congregation either 'called-up' to the army or currently engaged in 'the Operational Area'.

The idea of real warfare in the sheltered modern world I lived in seemed surreal; a make-believe world where people faced one another with lethal weapons and without compassion squeezed the trigger that ended someone's life. Surely we'd learned our lesson from the great wars of the century; surely humankind had evolved beyond that?

School of Armour front gate 1986. (School of Armour)

1

Basic Training

Standing to attention on the parade ground for what seemed like hours, sweltering under the harsh Bloemfontein summer sun, it was hard to believe that only a week before I'd been *jolling* (partying) hard with my little 'crew', trying desperately, but unsuccessfully, to find a girl willing to have sex with me, or a facsimile thereof, before my enforced removal from Durban.

Now, Durban, family and friends were like a million miles from the dusty, sun-baked expanse of hard ground upon which the newly buzz-cut, sorry-ass pimply teenagers stood at attention awaiting the following instalment of their currently shared fate.

Most people know what 'basic training' is…these two seemingly innocuous words are quite unambiguous when strung together like this. *Army* basic training on the other hand means different things to different people; its exact nature depends on the demands of a particular unit or individual instructor.

In the South African Army, all new recruits were required to endure three months of 'Basics', with as much of the mental and physical 'break-em-down to build-em-up' shite the trainers could get away with.

Some units, like the Parabats or Infantry, may argue their own basic training was tougher than that of the Armoured Corps, or that their Corporal or Sergeant Major was the hardest motherfucker in the known universe, potty-trained by Satan himself!

Hell, who knows? They might well be right but I don't care too much for that kind of subjective comparison; what I can say with absolute confidence, given my first-hand experience, is that *Pantserskool* Basics did a fantastic job of pummelling the shite out of us boys. Basic training toughened us up and ensured a good foundation for the rigours and challenges ahead; it also pulled us together, taught us the invaluable lesson of working as a team, a unit, and ultimately imbued a sense of honour to be connected to an extremely proud Corps within one of the finest armies in the modern world.

In those days, Health and Safety consisted mainly of common sense and I don't think anyone in our unit died or got too seriously hurt during Basics.

People still ask me today if I think young men should undergo some form of 'basic training' because it teaches 'em respect. "Hell yeah", I say! "Why not include the girls too – I'm all for equality." Of course, it depends on who you ask; many older people believe that youngsters should endure a spell of basic training to "'get 'em straightened out" whilst most young people think it would be a "gross infringement of their "human rights" I lean toward the older person's perspective on this because I saw for myself that a great many of the lads got straightened out during this phase while learning key skills that stand most people in good stead for a lifetime.

Some guys got a bit fucked-up by it but, in essence, Basics provided every new armed forces recruit with the foundation for soldiering, and it didn't matter whether you sought distinction on the battlefield as a career soldier, became a highly qualified medic repairing bodies in the field or even turned up as the laziest-on-record *sleg-gat* (slack-arse). *Every* recruit had to complete 13 weeks of infantry-based induction.

G1K1 medical classification meant good health, we never really knew what the 'G' or 'K' stood for, but we knew that as the number increased towards 5 the less good your condition/health and the greater the likelihood of being issued an 'Exemption' note. For some, the classification G5K5 (full exemption on medical grounds) was highly prized; a ticket to escape the call-up. During those first weeks in the army I witnessed some very creative strategies to feign mental illness and, inevitably, there were a few wily dodgers that wriggled their way free of the clutches of an army with a voracious appetite for young men to assist the ruling National Party maintain the increasingly unpopular status-quo.

I might've considered feigning some kind of illness but recalled all too vividly the time we deliberately croaked and squeaked our way through compulsory choir auditions for Pinetown Boys' High School. The choir mistress quickly wised up and called the intimidating headmaster to come stand next to each of us in turn as we auditioned. Very bad luck indeed! I was ordered to join the choir. In the early 1980's, in a country largely defined by its phenomenal military pedigree and almost unrivalled hardness on the rugby field – it was definitely not a place for softies – and choir-singing was considered to be so soft it was almost a capital crime against manhood and manliness!

Maybe I was a bit of a softie but I certainly didn't need to advertise any potential 'weakness' to be exploited by my merciless peers. There were other 'softie' markers, for example, my sisters, aged nine, could intentionally cause distress by crushing ants underfoot. "Look at me Dave, I'm killing ants" my sister Jenny could taunt, sending me running off to mom, deeply upset at this unnecessary act of cruelty.

It's probably fair to say I wasn't of born-n-bred 'army pedigree', but by the end of Basics I, like most my contemporaries, could completely strip and reassemble all moving parts of the R-5 (short-barrel) machine gun in under 12 seconds. However, long before we were allowed to handle any live ammo at the *skietbaan* (shooting range), or get anywhere near the steering wheel of an armoured vehicle, we had to endure countless hours honing parade-ground drills…left-turn, right-turn, about-turn, mark-time, double-time, slow-time, left-wheel etc. All this conducted in Afrikaans which, by the way, is an excellent drill language because the clipped, terse commands flow more quickly off the tongue than the rounder sounds of English.

Having some understanding of the proud and tumultuous history of the Afrikaaner is essential for anyone spending time with one, let alone with hundreds of them.

Their Dutch ancestors were tough-as-nails *Voortrekkers* who discovered largely uninhabited lands. What followed were generations of armed struggle, initially against tribal Africans who were moving down from the north, but later, when gold was discovered, against Imperialist Britain, a regime that invented the very first concentration camps for the internment of intransigent Boers.

Generations living as frontiersman had inculcated a deep spiritual connection with the military and an almost inbred dislike of the English.

Their colourful language betrays their irrepressible spirit, especially when *vloeking* (swearing), they express their disgust by damning things 'in the name of God'. Insults invariably involve liberal reference to genitalia and bodily functions, sometimes using language that is hard to distinguish between terms of endearment or ire, such as *poephol* (bum-hole), *piel neuse* (dick-nose), *etter-oog* (pus-eye), *klein kak* (small shit) and my personal favourite *poes* (pussy/fanny/twat et al).

All around the country military units had just acquired a new intake of boys whose marching skills varied from 'experienced through Army Cadets at school' to 'inexperienced and severely uncoordinated', some hilariously so.

We gave our drill Sergeant ample excuse to keep the Squadron marching for hours, penalise us frequently with additional punishment push-ups, star jumps or sprints to a specified tree and back again when laggards amongst us provided justification for him to demand repeated trips to this or some other distant landmark.

Much to my chagrin, I hadn't been allowed to join Army Cadets at Pinetown boys High School, instead I'd been forced into choir practise which left me at a bit of a disadvantage on the parade ground. I did however have a sneaky ace up my sleeve because (and I wouldn't have admitted this to anyone back then), I was a former Boys Brigade member.

There, I said it!

Aged seven, Cub Scouts was a total blast; the best badges were fire-making and camp building. A few years later Ma suggested I join Boy's Brigade (BB), a more zealous version of Scouts. One of the BB instructors, Brian, a crazy Parabat Angolan War veteran with a number of 'kills' under his belt, drilled us almost as if we were in the army and about to face-off against the 'enemy'. So, for kids, we were quite good at marching. Not only that, I'd learned to march with a heavy side-drum balanced on my left leg while rat-tat-tatting in-time with the brass wind-section. Sometimes on Sundays, side-drummers, with the colours flying in the vanguard, would lead parades through town to the harmonious tune of our little brass marching band. Consequently, I knew a bit more than most of my Bravo Squad peers when it came to marching in-step and in-time which was a bonus because my coordination was not top of the class to start with!

During basic training I was often hurt, blistered and bruised. Physical exhaustion became part of daily life, so the physicality of Basics normalised but a particularly notable discomfort throughout this phase was the ill-fitting *staal-dak* (steel helmet).

The *staal-dak* was not remarkably dissimilar in appearance and design to the helmets worn by the Allies at the Somme. Their one-size-fits-all design was OK when walking about, but it had a mind all of its own when the wearer was running and diving to the ground during PT or *opfok* (punishment); it bounced independently of the head, the narrow rim on its edge bashing away at soft, fleshy parts of the neck or nose!

Obviously there was more to Basics than just unending hours of marching and opfok. Daily knowledge-based classroom and field-based training was well structured, as would be expected from an army of SADF's calibre. However, our physical fitness appeared to concern instructors more than almost anything else. They demonstrated this concern on a daily basis, sometimes interrupting structured classroom training to focus on fitness training but cleverly disguising the training in the form of punishment. Punishment tended to help both with fitness and knowledge-based development. In other words, after each punishment, we all knew not to repeat a particular misdeed (in theory) *and*, we'd all improved our fitness after, for example, a six-hour *opfok* down at Koeie Kamp (Tempe's infamously treacherous 'field of hurt'). This taught us, uh, um…I'm not sure… but it was probably something very important.

In addition to 'punishment-related' fitness development, we also enjoyed daily PT (Physical Torture) sessions.

In general, PT and *opvok* sessions were either:

- Constructive PT – intelligent science-based training designed to improve cardiovascular health and cut puppy-fat e.g. the weekly 2.4 km fitness test (with, or without, heavy backpack, always with rifle). Just shy of 18 years, late developer, one of the youngest in the Squadron, I was nowhere near the fittest or strongest, but thanks to a few half-hearted years participating in school cross-country races wasn't among the slowest either. Another particular feature of Constructive PT was the matter of teamwork. "…*Julle maatjies naai vir julle*", (your friends are fucking with you), the instructor would bellow, this was because a few guys may've been a bit slow dragging themselves out the mud or traversing an obstacle. *"Daar gaan julle weer"*, (there you go again) he'd simply point and send us off on yet another painful lap, intentionally leaving the Squad in no doubt as to who the weak link was. There were occasions where the slowest guys would be helped along by the stronger lads but if the Squad determined that someone was being *sleg gat* (lazy arse) they'd probably get targeted for late-night punishment. Admittedly there were days when the intense PT broke me down, but thankfully never got given a late-night bungalow beat-down.

- Destructive PT – surprisingly, this was the most common form of exercise we encountered. It was mostly designed to break the spirit and usually involving carrying something heavy like a person or steel object d'armour for back-numbing periods of time. Sergeant often started our morning like this…*"Julle kaserne lyk soos n hoer se handsak op n Maandag oggend na n lang naweek!"* (Your bungalow looks like a whore's handbag on a Monday morning after a long-weekend!) *"Tel op julle trommels jou sleg kak."* (Pick up your steel trunk you lazy shits!) On hearing those words I'd instinctively feel a twinge in my lower-back. We all knew this was gonna hurt again! This happened when Corporal decided some element of our 6am bungalow inspection wasn't of a high enough standard, because perhaps we hadn't polished the gleaming *pis krip* (piss trough) well enough, or a fleck of dust theatrically discovered under a bed or atop a cupboard, or maybe some slack-arse hadn't ironed the corners of his bed well enough, or the large guy in the bed opposite didn't 'pack' his exhausted, stretched bed-springs under his increasingly concave mattress! Some days we were convinced it was none of these and he just fancied fucking with us. Our opinions mattered not in this situation, his word was law, and on his command we'd pick up our neatly packed steel strongbox, which only weighed about 20kg but was, of course, an unwieldy rectangular shape, most assuredly not ergonomically designed for high-speed running around a bungalow. On a very good morning we might only have to hold the strongbox off the ground for 5 minutes (which always felt much longer); on a bad morning, we'd get chased around the perimeter of the bungalow, our running punctuated by moments of respite of the push-up, star jump or sit-up variety. Aside from the strain to the lower-back, the inevitable maelstrom occurring inside the steel box ensured that the neatly ordered contents looked more like the Sergeant's characterisation of that 'whore's handbag on a Monday morning after a long-weekend'. We never established how Sarge knew so much about whore's handbags but inspection punishment made for an invigorating start to each glorious day, but whatever happened, both punisher and the punished knew we had to finish in time for morning roll-call parade and then breakfast, on schedule, no exceptions!

Everyone knows an army marches on its stomach and when on base we always had a pretty hearty breakfast but probably only to ensure we had sufficient strength for more physical fun such as 'Pole PT' which normally worked out as six recruits per telephone pole for an hour, minimum.

Pole PT was a drill that demanded team-work, because 'a load shared is a load halved' and also, if anyone fell out-of-step while running, their shoulder would be moving upward as the pole was moving downward instantly tenderising their trapezius! *"Wissel!"* (Change!), Corporal's barked command would require the team to lift the creosote telephone pole above our heads, gently bringing it back to rest on the opposite shoulder, after hours of this, the pole tended to drop less gently, or brush the side of the head tearing at the ear.

From the start of Basics, and with the gentle persuasion of frequent *opfok*, we quickly learned how much time was needed to prepare for the following days' inspection. In the beginning it took hours but we soon discovered how we could cut corners to save precious time. Some guys got into the habit of sleeping under the bed on just a few spare blankets to avoid disturbing 'the inspection bed'. This was in contravention of army rules-n-regulations but it meant 'the inspection bed' with its almost rigid starched blanket needed only minor cosmetic touch-ups each morning. A dab of shaving foam here and a quick comb there, a flash iron of the exposed area of sheeting near the pillow and the bed was done; 15 minutes saved.

Eventually, my inspection blanket was so well formed I could carefully pack it away when off base, and then fit it like a glove back onto the mattress on our return. Ten minutes of TLC later and the bed could be returned to an appropriate state of inspection readiness.

Typically, a Sunday (day of 'rest', thank God) was a good day to catch up on outstanding studies, ironing and cleaning. All the boys would work together to deep-clean the length of the bungalow floor; all beds, cupboards and strongboxes were carried outside and floor-polish spread across the entire floor surface before we dragged each other around on blankets – some rich kids even brought electric floor polishers, what a bonus that was!

Once the floor was cleaned, all Troop movement prior to inspection would only be in socks or with towel mitts over our boots to ensure no inadvertent scuff spoiled our morning.

Individually, we were responsible for the condition of the area immediately around our own bed; the half-height steel cupboard and the strongbox. Every item of clothing on display was ironed and folded and throughout the bungalow all equipment was packed or disassembled in an identical way and was either on display in the cupboards or strongboxes, or laid in a predetermined configuration on the uniformly made 'inspection beds'.

'Standard' inspection required a limited selection of kit to be on display, while a *vol uitpak inspeksie* (fully unpacked inspection) including everything we had was almost guaranteed to catch someone out.

Communal areas were cleaned by teams on rota. This included polishing the brass latches on the windows, sweeping the concrete skirt around the bungalow and cleaning the shower floor and walls, six crappers and the three metre-long *pis-krip* – and they were not just cleaned and dried but 'fucking factory cleaned *julle lei-gatte*' (you lazy-arses).

If any bloke needed a piss after 05:45am, he'd have to wait 'til after inspection, or be prepared to re-clean the splashes from the zinc piss-trough himself! It was detrimental to your personal wellbeing to be seen as the cause of a significant oversight that would earn us extra punishment sessions later in the day, or perhaps a follow-up extra *vol uitpak inspeksie* scheduled for that same evening which really screwed up the planned evening study and R&R!

2

Phase 2, Junior Leaders' Officer Training

Basic training ensured a solid foundation to our fitness, discipline and camaraderie so by the end of the three-month induction, the remaining lads were forged into a pretty tight band of brothers. There were, as always, a few exceptions to the rule but soldiering is mostly a team activity, and a unit or battle group cannot function very well unless all participants are highly trained, understand their tasks and are extremely reliable under pressure.

Across the country, tens of thousands of boys from the January '86 intake completed their basic training and simultaneously received their first 4-day pass home. Immediately thereafter, each recruit began Phase 2, or specialist, training associated with their corps. Some lads managed to change corps, some applied for the Parachute Battalion while others, who had qualifications such as a mechanic or chef, were often transferred out to maximise use of their skill-set. I had none of the above but was chuffed to still be eligible for Junior Leaders.

Those who continued with Phase 2 were asked to nominate their preference for the upcoming six-month JL phase, either;

- NCO (non-commissioned officer) training where after initially earning 'one-stripe' or lance Corporal rank after four months, thereafter continue for a further four months to earn *'twee-streep'* (two-stripes) and become a full Corporal on successful completion of the training or,
- CO (commissioned officer) training, initially earning CO 'designate' rank after 4 months (not a formally recognised rank) but then becoming a one-star Lieutenant on successful completion of JLs or even a two-star (full) Lieutenant (only on offer to the older guys (22/23 year olds) who already had a university degree).

Military protocol places commissioned officer rank well above those of the non-commissioned officers, meaning, in theory, that a handle-bar moustache wearing, twenty-year career, battle-hardened veteran Sergeant Major had to defer to a nineteen-year-old pimply Lieutenant. That's a pretty odd status quo but had no bearing on my decision to request CO training course I had no intention of abusing that quirk of military hierarchy if I ever became a Lieutenant.

My reason for choosing the CO route was that it seemed there were more perks and fewer early morning responsibilities than for NCOs and also a lot less need to shout at troops – I wasn't so well suited to that task.

The bottom line…we had no option but to endure two years, my thinking was take advantage of it, aim high and achieve the best possible – it would make the folks proud.

My request to undertake CO training was approved. New Squadrons were formed to align with our specific area of training. Some of us were moved to a neighbouring bungalow (Alpha Squadron) to be with the other lads selected for CO's course.

Training increased in intensity but as the months passed we became ever more adept at managing the rigours of early morning inspections, sweltering/freezing (dependant on season) class-room sessions, intense physical training and regular punishment for minor misdeeds; like failing bungalow inspections, failing academic tests (score lower than 70%), or perhaps enduring the wrath of 'Sarge' (they didn't like this Americanism) the day after his girlfriend tossed all his clothes into the street or the Natal provincial rugby team won a shock victory over his beloved Blue Bulls. Whatever the cause we came to fear punishment less, because by then we were so well-conditioned (even the smokers and the chunky ones were super fit by this stage) and well on our way to achieving officer rank.

A bungalow mate and bed-neighbour, 'Oosie' Oosthuizen, was a tough, fit Afrikaaner despite being a virtual chain smoker from his youth. I was gobsmacked he could wake at 5am, or whatever time, roll over and reach for a pack of Chesterfields and light one up all before even opening his eyes.

Indoor smoking was still acceptable, so we endured it.

Back in Pinetown, my pal next door's mom was a heavy smoker, every morning she'd lean out their kitchen barn-door, suck on her first fag of the day then cough heavily, eventually shifting the phlegm from chest to throat before ejecting the oyster-like contents into her garden. That experience had been deeply off-putting and I'd vowed never to touch a cigarette. Yes, partly cos I'd heard negative stuff from mom, an intensive care nurse, about patients with lung cancer, but in truth, the greatest disincentive of all was that beautiful bark each morning from the woman next door.

Not even the 'hurry-up-and-wait' boredom common in the army could elicit the slightest spark of interest in the habit, although it seemed many boys started smoking during National Service. I started smoking after the war.

In some respects, JLs was the best part of the year despite never-ending lectures and tests.

Suddenly and without advance notice, we were given permission to stop shaving our top lip for two weeks. After two weeks Squadron Sergeant Major inspected the progress and those with insufficient fluff on their top lip, were ordered to remove it; those with a decent enough showing were allowed to continue to grow a moustache. Initially, I didn't think I cared, but on day three decided to join in. Despite the delayed start, when Sarge inspected us a fortnight later it was a source of great pride when he selected me to join the latter group.

The *snor* (moustache) was very fashionable in the army and above all it signified manliness. I needed all the manliness I could lay my hands on so the fluff clung to my lip like a leech for the remainder of my service.

By now we were all competent riflemen, having endured many arduous days at the *skietbaan* (shooting range). The shooting range was synonymous with punishment sprints to the 1000m mark and back with our ill-fitting hard canvas 'webbing', invariably full of picnic gear, jangling and banging the steel helmet smashing into the back of our necks as usual.

The only small consolation was that the R-5 weapon issued to Armoured Corps Troopers was the smallest and lightest machine gun on offer in the army and fitted comfortably inside the restricted space of a gun turret. The standard issue R-4 was a little longer but, to be fair, also much lighter than the unwieldy R-1 used by earlier generations of conscript.

So while our R-5's may've been one of the smallest weapon systems on offer, Armoured Corps boys also got to play with some of the very biggest tax-payer funded military toys.

The biggest toy of all at the School of Armour was the 55-tonne Olifant MBT, a variant of the British Centurion Tank. The Olifant was a relatively modern platform with laser sights and gun stabiliser technology which gave fire-on-the-move capability, with a 105mm main gun boasting immense firepower delivered by a veritable smorgasbord of projectile derivatives. She was at the very top of the ground-force food-chain, but perhaps a little too big for the SADF defence requirements because it had been over 40 years since a South African MBT had been deployed in battle with Allied forces during WW2, so by 1986 only one Olifant Squadron was being trained with each 6-monthly intake.

Photo 1 Olifant disembarks her low loader at De Brug training ground. Family day at the end of training year. (Jenny Mannall)

My Squadron had not been chosen to be among that elite band of tanker boys, and we never established the mechanism used to determine which guys were selected to become E-Squadron Tankers, but my friends, like Clint, in E-Squad said it had something to do with their having freakishly big heads.

Once again, an unseen hand determined our fate. One Squad inherited the Olifant while two Squadrons, including my own, inherited the antiquated Eland Armoured Car (AKA Noddy Car – so named because it looked rather like that bubble car in the children's story).

The Eland (which was Panhard derived) served its original French designers well back in the day when it looked modern during the First Indochina war!

Next to the Olifant, our Eland, a 4-ton 1950's era armoured midget, was definitely the runt of the Armoured Corps pack, though it wasn't all bad news for us. South African engineers retrofitted a more modern, 1970's-era, turret with two variants, either a 60mm mortar pipe or a 90mm cannon, which was copy-n-pasted into a fully traversable turret from an earlier naval application. Most boys preferred training on the 90mm cannon variant – a point-and-shoot weapon capable of destroying a lightly armoured vehicle at 2,000 metres with a single well-placed shot. It was far more fun to play with than the mortar which required fiddling around with clever, but time-consuming calculations: the exact amount of explosive charge required had to be calculated and combined with a math formula to ascertain the correct firing-angle to propel the small projectile on target. Proficiency in the use of both turret types was necessary to complete gunnery training. Working the flywheels and sights of the 90mm in the frigid cold that winter was, to say the very least, character building but we'd happily swap out with the driver so we could reach up out from the driver cabin and hold the heated gun barrel to thaw the fingers.

Another pre-requisite of JLs was successful completion of driver training. Mastering the Noddy Car certainly taught us to respect previous generations of Armoured Corps soldiers who'd doubtless endured significant hardship in battle using these clunky, sometimes unreliable, four-wheeled steel boxes; to us this kit seemed so pre-historic.

Noddy had no power-assisted steering, at all. It required considerable strength to turn the wheels while the vehicle was moving, and when stationary the steering was effectively locked. It sported no fancy modern gearbox – which meant we had to master the 'double de-clutch' technique while negotiating the hilliest, most uneven terrain the army could lay its hands on – imagine Land Rover Defender territory on steroids! Unfortunately this rough terrain at the driver training ground at Tempe took a handful of young lives over the years when vehicles overturned.

Crew commanders had to be proficient drivers and gunners and, to earn rank, had to demonstrate detailed understanding of the capabilities and limitations of the equipment they were responsible for. From radios to radiators, and from sharp shooting to swapping spark plugs, commanders had to know it all and know it well, so we spent months honing our gunnery, driving and technical skills before being tested in 'pressure' situations.

I did well enough at most stuff to ensure my progression through the course; in fact one of the toughest challenges of all was simply trying to stay awake in the stuffy corrugated zinc classrooms during long-winded lectures on enemy vehicles and equipment.

Dozing off during lessons would result in, at least, a 20-second dunk in a fire bucket full of cold water while reciting a nursery-rhyme. It could also result in a quick sprint round the perimeter of the lecture hall, or if a few were of us were looking a bit sleepy, we'd all get sent out for a quick run to get the juices flowing.

At the time, it didn't seem like we'd need to remember or ever apply any of information on weaponry and tactics for real, but to complete JLs we needed to score at least 70% in each subject area. Those who failed were offered an opportunity to re-take the test, but that meant late-night studying sessions and because late-night studying was entirely optional, it mattered not how late we'd gone to sleep, we still had to prepare for 06:00 inspection every morning.

The only exception to standing inspection at 06:00, other than an overnight stay in hospital, was for those troops who'd spent the previous night on guard-duty but it was only on completion of basic training that the Squadron became eligible for this time honoured, and sometimes life-saving, responsibility.

We swore a solemn oath to maintain a high state of operational alertness while on duty to ensure bad things didn't occur. To keep us alert on guard-duty, commanders reinforced the 'heightened-security risk' message and insisted that our base faced constant threat from terrorist activities! We didn't really buy it. For most of us it seemed unlikely there were seriously malicious forces at work. We stood guard every fourth or fifth night for the remainder of the training year and, as far as I know, there was never a single serious outbreak of bad things – probably because we were so diligent. The routine was:

- 1st beat: 18:00-20:00, then again from 24:00-02:00 (best beat)
- 2nd beat: 20:00-22:00, then 02:00-04:00 (worst beat)
- 3rd beat: 22:00-24:00, then 04:00-06:00 (50/50 beat)

Each beat saw two soldiers designated to one of five areas on base:

1. Main gate (almost impossible to get 40-winks, although I tried)
2. Vehicle park (plenty of opportunity for sleeping)
3. Perimeter fence (risky and very uncomfortable, yet quite feasible to find a spot for a catnap)
4. *Kaserne* (Bungalows) (definitely get to spend some time inspecting bungalow internal areas during the early shifts, especially in the freezing winter months)
5. Control room (monitoring radios indoors, very little sleeping opportunity but the best beat by far during winter).

It wasn't all bad, the 06:00 finish meant we missed bungalow inspection and got to be first in line at *menasie* (mess hall) for breakfast when the food was at its 'best' and most plentiful.

Naïve as we were, the greatest hazard with guard duty then seemed to be the risk of getting busted 'asleep on duty'. We reasoned, if there were such great terrorist threats, why were officers and NCOs living it up in their plush accommodation block just over the road outside the main gates of the base, wouldn't they need security too?

Not that I'm proud of this, but quite a few of us viewed post-midnight guard duty as an opportunity to find creative places to catch up on much needed sleep. There were a number of dark corners on base, like the vehicle park with rows of oversized vehicles perfectly suited for catching a quick 20-minute nap, perhaps on a cushioned front-seat of an unlocked Samil 100 Troop transporter, or when necessary just on the hard ground in the deep shadows underneath an Olifant MBT.

Apparently, this shameful business of skiving-off on guard-duty was not uncommon although never openly discussed because all kinds of shit would've broken loose and hit the fan if it was discovered. Such transgression and dereliction of duty would probably lead to expulsion from JLs altogether!

Guard duty was compulsory for all cannon-fodder Troopers, although as it is in life, so it was in the Army that exceptions could be made when it suited those in charge, despite the ever-present security threat of potential 'bad things' occurring. A top athlete for example, who might bring glory to the unit, would be eligible for a coveted 'sports pass' which exempted the bearer from certain activities if those activities clashed with training or competition requirements.

Co come rain or shine, every evening at 17:45 a detachment of 31 guards marched onto the dusty parade ground for inspection and roll-call by the guard commander to ensure:

1. All designated guards were present and armed with live ammo,
2. We looked smart enough and our weapons were clean enough to meet that night's potential bad thing.

If you happened to be selected for guard duty, there was one caveat, a potential reprieve from the great honour of maintaining base security. Night watch only required 30 guards, the 31st guard, the lad most neatly turned out on parade, would be given a free night off!

Winning inspection was awesome, not only because it meant a solid night's sleep on the blankets under our bed, but also because we quickly realised that due to some administrative failing, Squadron instructors didn't know who the 31st guard was. With a little ducking-and-diving, the 31st guard could exploit the loophole because, like the rest of the detachment, he wouldn't be expected for roll-call until 8am the following morning along with the remainder of the guard detachment.

In other words, winning guard inspection parade meant a free lie-in! What more incentive does an 18 year old need? The competition became fierce but with my experience of endlessly buffing the knobbles on brass-buckles and boots for Boys Brigade was often right up there in contention to win guard-parade inspection.

The evening guard detachment always looked a little odd as we gingerly marched onto the parade ground trying in vain not to disturb the finely ground powder that lay atop the rock-hard surface lest a light patina of dust formed over the toecap's deep gloss.

The gloss of our 'inspection boots' was like a window to our inspection readiness; poor preparation was easily spotted by seasoned NCOs.

With the exception of weapons cleanliness, boot shine trumped all other aspects of the inspection thus, success at inspection demanded long hours, over many weeks, painstakingly smoothing and buffing boot leather using Kiwi Military Brown Polish, cotton wool and water. Some guys even took their boots home for the family maid to buff! Others even tried ironing the toe caps, but the results were mostly unsatisfactory; elbow grease won the day.

Halfway through JLs, a new guard-duty incentive was introduced so that, in addition to scoring the free night off, anyone who 'won' three guard parades during the year would get a bonus weekend pass.

The weekend pass (WP) was an extremely rare and cherished privilege for national servicemen, we were only entitled to five of these during a training year, the first upon completion of Basics and a further four fairly evenly spaced between May and December.

We lived for these few fleeting moments of respite, so a free weekend pass was like being gifted an extra birthday and Christmas in one! I really wanted an extra WP, at least one! We all did, with the exception of the sports-pass bastards who got so much time off base, they didn't need it quite so desperately; and they seldom stood guard anyway so their chances of winning three times were quite remote.

I already had one guard-parade inspection 'victory' in the bag when they introduced the incentive, meaning I'd only need two more to score the bonus.

The new incentive had the desired effect, guys became more competitive, inspection standards went up and, conversely, opportunities to win went down.

By this stage, the Squadron had been through all kinds of punishment shit and team-building activities and we were becoming a bit like brothers, extremely comfortable talking about anything and everything. Consequently, there was incessant chatter on matters of a sexual nature; some boasted of conquests, others hinted at the fun they had with their *Cherrie* (girlfriend) on a weekend pass, and here I was, still a virgin! Fuck, if the okes discovered this unhappy state of affairs it would've done my credentials no good at all, the manliness imbued by my moustache would be swept away at a stroke.

Girls were a conundrum and a mystery. Although I got on great with my sisters, other girls, 'hotties', were a completely different proposition and I was still a bit clumsy and awkward around them.

As a boy, my first crush, and heartbreak was over a 13-year-old girl called Monique. Hanging out with her as 'friends' was manageable but I couldn't quite pluck up the courage to hold her hand or ask her out on a date. Back then it was the custom to 'formalise' a relationship by 'asking the girl out' and I definitely wasn't brave enough to lean over and take that first kiss. That would take another two years, long after my young heart had been crushed when I heard on the grapevine that my best friend, who'd met Monique through me, invited her to a *bioscope* (movie cinema), held her hand and even started kissing her, and then 'asked her out!' That was a tough lesson but it taught me to be a little more upfront in admitting my need to work on my confidence with chicks.

Despite my lack of early prowess in the girl-department, in the army it seemed better to maintain a vague pretence of 'having been there before, many, many times before' rather than let slip overt bully fodder about such sensitive matters.

All this ribald bungalow chatter begun to build a head of steam which in turn increased the sense of urgency and desire to cross the Rubicon for real, to open Pandora's Box and sample the treasures within. I needed more time off base.

I needed that extra weekend pass!

Despite the increased competition at guard parade, my second win came in July, but the all-important third win was far more elusive, so in desperation I turned to Theron.

We'd heard stories about this guy in another Squadron with incredible inspection boots, professionally buffed with a mirror-like shine, the word was that this guy was winning guard parade practically every time he turned up!

Theron's boots it seemed were the key to unlocking that free weekend pass and the pleasure potential it promised. I approached Theron, asked to look at his prize boots which he removed from the shelf above his bed like some kind of trophy. They were magnificent, without doubt the best shine I'd ever seen, so I pitched my offer; loan me the boots for my next guard inspection and in return, I'd stand his following guard duty when, and if, he failed to win inspection.

If all went to plan, I'd only need them for about 30 minutes and the boots would be returned in pristine condition. Of course, even if I failed to win, Theron's prize boots would be swapped out with mine before actually standing beat.

The plan worked and I became one of only two or three guys at School of Armour in 1986 to score a bonus weekend for winning guard duty.

As soon as the pass was authorised, I rushed off to Durban, said hello to my family and then hit the bars and clubs.

I came to learn that girls are most astute in matters of male sexuality and easily detect the stench of desperation from across the dance-floor, no matter how well camouflaged with cheap liquor and even cheaper cologne.

Unsurprisingly, I didn't get laid…again!

Not everyone spent WP in such self-centred pursuits, once off base some guys had serious girlfriends to 'visit', others went home to 'work on the farm' or spend time *kuiering* (visiting) with family, but there were plenty like me who simply saw the WP as an excuse to break from disciplined routines, party, sleep in late and/ or engage in the trivial pursuit of skirt.

Of course, some family time was factored in. I especially had time for Mom's home cooking and assistance with laundry, but like many 18-year olds, I gave family time lower priority than party time.

Normally the WP started on a Thursday evening at 18:00 and ended on a Monday evening at 20:00. If a guy lived nearby he could be home within an hour, whereas those who lived further afield such as in Cape Town (1000kms), Johannesburg (400kms), or as in my case, Durban (600-700kms dependant on route) lost significant time in-transit.

Hitchhiking was a popular mode of transport for low-paid servicemen. The white South African community mostly supported the young *dienspligtiges* (national servicemen) 'doing their bit' so thumb-out hitching, when wearing the 'chocolate browns' (uniform), wasn't too onerous and normally it wasn't long before some generous-hearted soul pulled over to offer a lift.

Those who could afford it booked a flight home while others used an overnight train service which, as it turned out, offered a massive and unexpected advantage to the Banana (Durban) boys.

The Durban to Bloemfontein train departed quite late on a Monday night (late enough to have dinner at home), and then only arrived the following morning at 06:30, gifting us a few extra precious hours off base and, to top it off, avoid the Tuesday morning 06:00 inspection! Once word got round about this windfall, the number of Banana boys catching the train swelled significantly until eventually they had to despatch the larger Samil 100 Troop transport to return the slightly hung-over 'beach-bums' from the train station on a Tuesday morning.

If the train arrived on schedule we'd be back on base before mess hall closed and in time to grab breakfast, if not, we'd have to wait for 10am tea and make up for the lost meal by grabbing a couple handfuls of Ouma rusks (large and dry, but tasty, traditional Afrikaans biscuit – great dunked in tea or coffee).

Of all the possible things that could go wrong with the weekend pass, missing breakfast on the Tuesday morning was by far the least concerning.

At the time of our 3rd weekend pass we heard of a local entrepreneur who'd begun to offer a minibus service, driving the shorter 600km route to Durban by cutting through some of the most sparsely populated parts of the country. It seemed a great idea, the cost was relatively low and the journey time promised to be circa six hours.

We reasoned that if we departed base soon after 18:00 we'd be in Durban by midnight, early enough to get a quick drink and perhaps some potential damsel action – that virginity thing was like a millstone around my neck by now!

I booked myself a seat on the minibus for the six-hour journey to Durban and sensibly secured a train ticket returning late Monday evening. Two of my Durban pals, Scott McCartney and Finn Kronholm (that's his first name) were primed for a big night at an appropriately seedy local nightclub, the Imperial Hotel.

The minibus was a bit crammed, but cosy and warm. The journey started well enough as we drove away from the well-lit city boundary into a moonless, dark and cold Orange Free State mid-winter night.

Before long I was fast asleep, the warmth of our minibus and steady thrumming of tyres on tarmac hit me like an overdose of sleeping tablets, the kind of sleep you'd have after being forced to stay awake for three days in a war zone – not that we had any idea what that could be like. Yet!

Suddenly a light came on in the cabin and I felt myself being shaken awake. As consciousness gradually dawned I became aware of Brian McGregor yanking on my arm. Brian, a friend from High School, was trying to tell me something. "Wake up Dave, there's a problem with the minibus!"

Jeez, that news woke me right up, or maybe it was the blast of icy air rushing into the open side-door like a shot of adrenaline to the heart that got me going.

As the sleep-fog cleared, my immediate concern became the finely-timed schedule for that evening's entertainment, and then the more practical considerations surfaced like, "Where the fuck are we?" and, "Can he get the damn thing fixed?" None of us was a competent mechanic; we were merely trainee officers and knew only about limited stuff such as spark plugs and oil filters; beyond that the engine was something akin to witchcraft!

There must've been some fairly heated exchanges before I'd arisen from the deep because the driver was barely communicating with the boys, and to make matters worse he offered no solution to my rapidly unravelling timetable! Brian grabbed his *balsak* (tog bag), jumped down off the bus and started walking. With a wave he beckoned me to follow.

Hopping out from the protective warmth of the minibus I gained a tiny insight into what it must've been like for Neil Armstrong and Buzz Aldrin taking those first tentative steps on the moon's surface, far from home and in an extremely hostile, alien environment.

Unlike those pioneering astronauts however, we didn't have proper protective gear for the suddenly frigid conditions, nor the support of a command centre, but thankfully, like Mr Armstrong, I wasn't completely alone in this alien environment. My Buzz was Brian McGregor, or perhaps I was Buzz because Brian stepped out first. Whatever, it mattered not, we had a mission to attend and the two of us optimistically set off in the direction of Durban. Distance to target: unknown.

Some of the other stranded spacemen began to walk up the road in the direction we'd come from because in this situation there was two distinct schools of thought. A driver travelling at 120km per hour, chancing upon a hitchhiker wearing the chocolate brown SADF uniform in the pitch-black night will either;

1. Be startled, hit the accelerator and speed past before realising it's a soldier. Very occasionally in this scenario a guy might belatedly slam on brakes, but more likely, the sudden rush of adrenaline initiated a fight-or-flight response. By the time the driver realised there was no need for flight the hitchhiker was a tiny action-man-sized speck in the rear-view mirror, or…
2. Resolve to do better and pick up hitchhiking national servicemen at the very next opportunity. So our untested theory was that the guys who walked back in the direction of Bloemfontein would've initiated that fight-or-flight response in the driver. Then, just as the driver's adrenaline abated, Brian and I would be coming into focus on the ribbon of tarmac ahead. Bingo!

As the gravity of our predicament dawned, I interrogated Brian for a sit-rep (situation report) and quickly discovered that;

a) The driver had had no back-up, nor clearly had he concerned himself with a maintenance schedule, or if he had, the schedule was shit, even by African standards.

b) The minibus had worked for three hours so he estimated we were approximately 350km from home.
c) The only living thing within 50km was untamed and wild except for in a peppering of far-off farmsteads and tribal huts in between.

We'd landed in what seemed the darkest coldest part of the country, not a single light was visible, anywhere. Even the moon was hidden from view by a thick blanket of cloud, and what quickly became apparent was that it seemed almost no-one used this road at this time of night. There was little option but for us to keep walking, to stay warm and progress toward the objective.

As the minutes dragged by I continually recalibrated my ETA, imagining the possibilities if we were offered a ride all the way home within the next five minutes. Eventually, at around midnight, even my most optimistic calculations of distance and potential speed forced me to abandon any hope of getting home in time for 'last orders', let alone getting in early enough to snare some saucy siren in the nightclub. Furthermore, there was no means of communication and therefore no way of telling the boys to wait up for me.

The barren lunar-like world we'd landed in was, fortuitously, more densely populated than the Sea of Tranquillity, but not a lot more. Fewer than a dozen cars sped past us in either direction over the next three or four hours.

Some guys, including those who chose to go back up the damn road, had scored lifts, and group by group the boys were offered lifts until eventually Brian and I were the last suckers still plodding into the cold blackness of that bitter Orange Free State winter's night.

We continued our unscheduled route march, ironically very near to Golden Gate National Park which was the stunning setting for our final challenge on JLs, the 4-day route march, though on that occasion I'd have the pleasure of a comfy ride home lying down in the rear of a Unimog military ambulance.

On the final night of the march four of us shared some 3-day-old cooked chicken and as we crossed the finish line the following day were whisked to Bloemfontein's Military hospital with a severe bout of food poisoning. Scoring two nights in hospital with clean sheets, nurses and no *opfok*. It was well worth the discomfort.

Finally, four hours and 15 clicks down the road we finally got offered a lift, but this was nothing like the trip in the Unimog ambulance.

At first it seemed an unbelievable stroke of luck, the guy was headed for Durban and would drop us off right near home, however the early enthusiasm dipped when he told us to jump in the uncovered rear of his *bakkie* (small truck).

Quite quickly we realised that the cold winter night got considerably colder once 120 kilometres per hour of wind-chill was added into the mix! This truly was like hopping from the fridge and into the freezer. Suddenly, it became very acceptable to get close and hug a bloke! Sleeping was the furthest thing from our minds. Now, just surviving the blistering cold was the only thing that mattered, not even the unforeseen loss of potential virginity vanquishing opportunities mattered now.

By the time we arrived in Pinetown, around 08:00, some 14 hours after leaving Bloemfontein, Brian and I had learned a new kind of respect for the Inuit (Eskimo), and our African brothers often forced to endure similar hardship.

The long hot bath that followed the horrendous journey was almost as satisfying as slipping under my clean duvet for a few hours of rock-solid sleep. Five hours later I was on the phone with my crew arranging Friday evening's activities.

We never received rebate, nor established if the minibus breakdown wasn't simply a clever scam designed to take us to the middle of nowhere, kill the engine, off-load us, wait until the last passenger disappeared over the horizon and then find, magically, that the engine works and pull a U-turn back to Bloemfontein. This would save a lot of time and petrol, thank you very much! But perhaps I'm being too cynical.

With such a frigid start to the weekend, it was quite unsurprising that there were zero opportunities to break the seal on my sex life. Surely it couldn't have been the stench of my stale perfume Eau de Desperado?

By August of that year most of us had successfully progressed through first phase of officer training and were presented with a small white shoulder flash – not a formal rank, it was merely to prepare the shoulders for the weight of carrying a Lieutenant's star in November.

The non-commissioned guys earned their Lance Corporal's *een-streep* (one-stripe), so unlike our commissioned officer 'rank', or *Kak-huis Offesier* (shit-house officer) as it was colloquially known, Lance Corporal is a formally recognised rank. This mean that for a few months during the training, our NCO colleagues were regarded more highly in the rigid military hierarchy than us COs.

The standing joke was that the CO award looked like bird shat on our shoulder and, by wiping it, had left a *wit streepie* (white stripe).

It's often said that someone who takes life with a pinch of salt may very well reduce the likelihood of heart problems later in life but that same laissez-faire approach can also result in life-altering consequences along the way.

Even this late into training I was still blissfully unaware that us conscripts might get involved in actual warfare, or perhaps I preferred to convince myself that the war was out there and too far removed to be a real threat to someone like me. Sure, we might have to engage in some local 'township' patrol or riot control against an opposition with little, if any, military hardware but no more than that.

My uncles were among those who said, "don't worry *boet* (brother), once you complete basic training army life gets pretty *rustig* (chilled)".

There was no talk at the family dinner table about live-fire action in a combat setting. In my ignorance, I assumed all the fuss and hype was really just the army messing with us. What's more, I reasoned that if there was any proper soldiering to be done to combat low-level, small-unit terrorist activities, which is how I imagined it, those small groups of 'terrs' would be engaged and repulsed by men who really wanted to play at war, the hardened nutcases of Reconnaissance (Recce's) and 32 Battalion (comprising South Africans and Angolans). I wasn't even aware that 32 Battalion had a Squadron of our 90mm crews embedded within their ranks!

Based on my 'sound' reasoning that real warfare would never affect me, I treated training year as a bit of a painful game in which I became comfortable handling dangerous, exploding things, got awarded my Noddy Car driver's licence for not rolling the little beast over and received the gunnery award for blowing up stuff accurately from far away.

My 1970's upbringing and '80's schooling had a hint of the Victorian era about it. Corporal punishment in high school was commonplace and Mom ensured old-school values were quite strictly enforced, so I knew all about 'strict', however the army took those rules to a whole new level, just as my adolescent self was seeking a lot more freedom. This imbalance, Army Rules vs. Adolescent Dave, led to a judicious amount of rule bending, just enough not to get into too much trouble, or so I thought.

Some guys had said that the liberal application of gearbox oil on skin gave a great tan although tanning was strictly forbidden in the army. During weekend guard duty at a remote ammo dump I decided to give my lily-white butt cheeks the oil treatment during a four-hour rest period between beats. Bloemfontein's altitude and crisp, clean air means the sun is mercilessly strong.

Unsurprisingly I fell asleep and by the time someone woke me, the sun had already begun to drop in the sky. My backside was fucking scorched! It was so blistered and sore that I literally could not sit on it for three days even the movement of fabric over my rear end as I walked caused me to break sweat.

There was no chance of requesting medical assistance because the burn would have definitely been red-flagged up the chain-of-command. I'm sure this was a minor infraction and, had my transgression been discovered, it probably wouldn't have upset my journey to Lieutenant-hood too much though it surely would have, at the very least, precipitated a decent bout of *opfok*.

When I became friendly with fellow CO Louis Van der Spud (not his real name), a guy who bent the rules on an industrial scale, my fate was set to be irrevocably altered.

Louis confided in me that he regularly drove the 50 clicks to his girlfriend's house for the odd night off base. Cue envy. It seemed fantastical to me that he had such freedom but, as a top player for the SADF Army Rugby Team, he pretty much had the run of things.

After Basics he'd brought his own car on to base (to ensure he could get to regular training sessions). Occasionally, he was flown to Pretoria or Cape Town for team training and matches. Being such a high-profile sportsman in the premier national game meant his sporting commitments pretty much trumped almost all else meaning he got precious time off, even during some of the toughest phases of JLs, and I suspected he was destined to become a window-dressing officer rather than frontline, dust-caked cannon fodder like us regular Joe's. There was little more disheartening when, during filthy field training ops involving overnight bivvy in the cold, face smeared with 'black-is-beautiful' war paint, one of your team is excused to attend sport parade thereby scoring an early shower, mattress and pillow.

Louis was therefore almost untouchable. As our friendship developed he offered me an opportunity to spend a weekend night at his girlfriend's parent's house. By now, an eight month veteran of the army, I was raring to go.

We devised a simple plan. He'd drive off base as normal, I'd apply some of my newly learned detection avoidance and camo techniques, sneak off, scale an area of the 12ft base perimeter fence hidden from most views, then meet him at a pre-arranged location under a highway access road nearby.

The heady rush of adrenaline at making good my escape, the rare pleasure of clean, freshly ironed sheets and a firm, comfortable mattress, topped off with the most perfect poached eggs on toast, sprinkled with ground *biltong* (cured meat) for an early breakfast before returning in time for church parade, was about the most exciting thing I'd done so far in the army, and definitely to be repeated, ASAP.

The ploy worked well, for a while. Each time I'd return to base, scale the perimeter fence and rejoin the Squadron with no one any the wiser. I was like the proverbial cat that'd just licked the cream, although admittedly I'd not had as much cream as my friend Louis. I justified my actions to myself like this, I'd probably get at least this much time off-base during this phase of our training if I were great at sport, and reasoned I was doing no real harm. One time I agreed to hitchhike to Odendaalsrus which was a bit risky, however I was extremely proud that it took the Oom en Tannie (older gent and lady, Afrikaans) who picked me up a full half hour to figure out I wasn't a born Afrikaans speaker, I'd become fluent!

Before long the clandestine trips off-base got a little edgier. We started visiting Thaba Nchu Sun, a Southern Sun casino about 30 clicks off-base.

Conservative laws on gambling at that time meant Thaba Nchu Sun was literally the only mainstream (legal) casino for hundreds of kilometres, in any direction.

Part of the famous Sun City group, the recently constructed Thaba Nchu was the most modern and wonderful entertainment complex I'd ever seen. And if I was impressed, so too were the locals, so we were now far more likely to be spotted playing Blackjack at the casino by off-duty personnel, than we were when 'over nighting' in the tiny *dorp* (town) of Odendaalsrus with Louis' girlfriend. And yet we took the risk.

I was oblivious to something else, Louis had developed a bit of a gambling habit and was often in debt, even resorting to borrowing money from guys in the Squad. In the end he may have stolen money from one guy which resulted in a civil lawsuit. This gave rise to a situation in which I had to choose between supporting my friend or leaving him to hang out and dry.

I chose to give evidence in his defence and in so doing probably upset my superiors and, what's more, the trial was scheduled for the same week the School of Armour made its annual pilgrimage to Lohatla (Army Battle School) to join with other mechanised units in joint exercises.

Lohatla was a place large enough for the big guns to have an unlimited play area without risk of accidentally encountering civilians; a place of vast open spaces and variable hilly terrain that was a perfect setting for different combat scenarios.

The smart thing to have done at this moment in my life would've been to turn my back on my friend Louis, go to Lohatla and gain first-hand experience of large scale integrated mechanised manoeuvres, but loyalty won the day, and oh, it also meant almost a week on base without inspection or any other military interference, so I allowed myself to get drawn into the case, and much to the Major's chagrin, was exempted from the Lohatla gig.

Cue more visits to the casino – but when the Squadron returned from Lohatla with tales of unbelievable action during night combat, and of working in concert with an array of impressive military hardware including a prototype Howitzer variant called the G-6, I wondered if my decision had been foolhardy.

Our unofficial absences from Lohatla did not go unnoticed by the big brass, but we were within touching distance of achieving 1st Lieutenant rank and were comfortably managing the final stages, so it shouldn't have mattered. Then, two weeks after the court case, our absence was noted one final time.

It was a late 3am session at Thaba Nchu and we came home richer than when we'd left, or so we thought.

On returning to base, we cleverly decided to sleep in an adjacent unoccupied bungalow – the regular residents were out on field manoeuvres. We'd had a few complimentary rum-n-cokes at the Casino but were still 'sharp' enough to work out that if we *dossed* (slept) in the vacant bungalow, we'd save ourselves a lot of time preparing for 06:00 inspection.

Photo 2 Army Battle School, Lohathla now known as Combat Training Centre. Looking over the training area towards *Koppie Alleen* (small head alone), a very prominent rocky outcrop used as a point of navigation. The open terrain is perfect for large mechanised manoeuvres but is almost irrelevant in the Angolan context. (Captain John Ecclestone, 2009)

3

Junior Leaders' NCO Training

The dreadfully cold, vice-grip of shitting myself constricted my chest the instant I woke, just after 8am! I slapped Louis awake, we dashed to our bungalow, whipped off our *civvies* (civilian clothing), jumped into our brown overalls and boots combo required at this time of day, no time for socks, and then rushed out to join the Squadron on the parade ground, attempting, but failing, to act as nonchalantly as possible.

The instant I locked eyes with some of my pals, I knew we were in extremely deep shit; their eyes said it all, some admonishing, some pitiful. We'd totally fucked up and the bombs were about to start falling on us!

Very quickly, the regimental Sergeant Major (RSM), one scary motherfucker, got involved! After a verbal roasting and a few hours of one-on-one opvok, we were cleaned up and marched at double-time in front of Major Grobbelaar.

Fuck! Was he pissed off or what?! I could scarcely keep pace with all the bureaucracy, but within the hour we were charged and found guilty of AWOL and summarily ejected from officer training. It was all over!

What a bitter disappointment that was. After having worked so hard all year, endured all those hardships only to fuck it all up for a few shots of rum, and adrenaline.

I was walking away with nothing but shame!

My folks had already booked their flights to Bloemfontein for the much anticipated pass-out parade. How would I explain this debacle?

I figured there had to be some way back and approached my training officers who agreed to put in a good word for Trinity.

Sa'Majoor marched me back in to Grobbelaar's office the following day. Still clearly pissed-off, he'd only been willing to see me again because of the positive commendations offered by some of his officers but, he said, "There is no way in hell you will become a Lieutenant!'

I got offered a transfer to the NCO course, which I snatched in a heartbeat.

Despite the disappointment I felt as the *Sa'Majoor* double-timed me out of the office, the consolation reprieve meant all the training and paining would not

Photo 3 Open day – Me demonstrating 60mm Ratel to proud families.
(Graham Mannall)

Photo 4 Eland Armoured car (Noddy) on show at Family day. (Elizabeth Mannall)

be in vain and my ambition to achieve something noteworthy in the army was resurrected.

That same day, I bade goodbye to Alpha and moved to Charlie Squad with the other NCOs and tried to put the setback behind me.

The friendly rivalry between NCO and CO groups was already apparent, so without proving myself to the non-coms, I wouldn't gain full acceptance among a band of lads that had already shared significant tough trials together as a unit.

As the furore over the AWOL incident died down, I came to terms with realities of life as a non-com, lost the little white shoulder flash ('bird-shit stain') and gained a Lance Corporal's stripe.

All this didn't make much difference in the immediate day-to-day life on base, but the full implications of my fuck-up had yet to run its course. Just a few weeks later, when selection took place to assign newly qualified officers and NCOs to onward postings, the blemish on my record, coupled with the fact I was new to the Squadron, meant I'd probably be near the back of the queue and have to settle for one of the less popular postings. The law of the jungle was that the better (nicer) postings would go to those at the top of the pile. I had no chance, although there was one last opportunity to shine.

South Africa is a stunningly beautiful country but with very diverse economic contrasts, perfectly illustrated by travelling the short distance from Thaba Nchu casino's bright lights to nearby Botshabelo 'township', a place where the only bright light on offer comes from the sun. After sunset, traditional oil-burners provided households with lighting and, thanks to a benevolent state, the town was bathed throughout the night in a hazy murky-yellow glow, a phenomenon caused by about a dozen large, ultra-high, electric street lamps and a thick blanket of smoke rising from residents' open wood fires which were still being used in timeless ways for cooking and heating. The resultant smog, trapped in an inversion layer just above the valley floor, created a somewhat surreal atmosphere in these poor 'townships'.

I would never have known of this vast disparity, nor seen at first-hand how the black people, some of whom worked at the casino, had to live their lives were it not for our two-week tour in Botshabelo Township.

Perhaps I needed some sort of cosmic reminder of my gambling folly and Charlie Squadron, like most conscript units, was required to complete a short stint of township patrols. Soon after I became a Lance Corporal, we were despatched to the settlement nearest the scene of my heinous AWOL crime, and there we established our HQ in the town hall.

I know that some SADF conscripts endured very difficult times on township patrols because some were brooding and desperately hostile places where poverty and tribal mistrust was exacerbated by living without equality under the thumb of a government who chose to subjugate rather than empower her large Third World populace (blacks outnumbered whites 6:1).

As a consequence of tribal history and more recent involvement of European governance, township dwellers sometimes endured terrible inter-racial/tribal violence, criminality and a shared discontent for the status quo. Add to this powder-keg, the grinding poverty and poor education and career opportunities it was easy to understand why the army was sometimes called in to support the police as the first line of defence in these settlements.

At times, the tension between oppressed and 'oppressor' was intense. Guys were shot at or petrol-bombed by fellow residents but my township days were, relatively speaking, quite benign. We stood guard at installations, carried out night-time patrols with our 'Buffel' (Buffalo) open-top Troop transport headlights sometimes the only illumination amongst the shacks of the poorest regions on the outskirts of town.

During the day, our primary function mainly involved escorting bus-loads of workers safely in and out of the township to protect them from political/tribal opponents.

Probably the naughtiest thing we did was to 'slightly misuse' the pair of Night Sun spotlights positioned on a nearby hill. These Night Suns were identical to the type used during WW2 to spot enemy aircraft but here, they were pointed earthwards to provide illumination for the night patrols. Bright enough to rip your retina at a range of fifty metres, the six-foot diameter lens cover was so hot during operation a full English breakfast could be fried up for the whole Troop!

If we wanted to mess about (and this is the slight misuse), the concentrated beam of light, when pointed at a shack in the distance, at say 3,000 metres, would instantly transform the shack-dweller's world from midnight to midday, invariably disturbing the inhabitants sleep. I'm not proud of this; conditions were tough enough for these people, so this wasn't just harmless fun.

What did seem like harmless fun however, was standing guard at the old town hall, partly because this was an indoor gig, out of the cold, and partly because the place came equipped with a hot water urn for tea-making. But the cherry on the cake – because this was the town's preeminent building – was that it was home to an old-fashioned telephone switchboard, and as soon as we'd figured out how to connect the operators 'cord-board' we got busy making some free calls to family and friends.

Two weeks on 'Townships' was a breeze, but also a rude awakening to the plight of those people who spend a lifetime trapped there.

In October '86 the School of Armour celebrated its 40th anniversary with a joint trooping of the colour. Head of the Army Lt-General A. J. Liebenberg was guest of honour and Colonel Beyleveldt expected the event to be marked with as much pomp and splendour as could be mustered for the visiting big-cheese and TV cameras.

Unfortunately for us, this meant performing complex large formation marching manoeuvres the type more normally seen in communist newsreels.

Despite our conditioning, we practised so long for this event our feet blistered and it seemed as if the synovial fluid in our knee joints would dry up. As the event neared, we spent entire days just marching.

Some guys fell from the exhaustion of it. *"Medic, kom, vat die eene weg,"* (Medic, come, take this one away), *"tree aan"* (fall-in) and we simply carried on marching.

Unusually, even Colonel Beyleveldt harangued us 48 hours before the event, moaning about our 'sloppy' marching…and then we were pushed even harder, marching into the night until finally the massed Squadrons from each SAAC unit flawlessly synchronised their movements around Orange Free State's Provincial stadium. The next one would be the real deal; cameras rolling, big cheese saluting and smiling.

The day went off without a hitch, and after a photocall with the big boss our feet were glad to return to normal routine!

As JLs neared its end in November, Lance Corporals were offered, yes really offered, which implies choice, an option to undertake five weeks additional training on the intensive PT Instructor (PTI) course. The purpose of the PTI course was to provide us with in-depth knowledge of methods for training troops of our own from the new intake of recruits due in January.

About half of the Corporals-to-be, 'volunteered' for the training.

Well fuck me! PTI training phase was like being returned to Basics, but this time, on Human Growth Hormone! We got hammered good and proper, enduring gruelling PT sessions designed to show us the limit of our, and by extension, our future recruits, capacity and limitations but because we were already very fit, the instructors dialled-up the level of intensity, the gloves came off and the mud at De Brug field of pain somehow got thicker!

My very last punishment *opfok* at School of Armour was the unpleasant 'drink-n-roll' routine.

Apparently I was a little *harde-gat* (hard-arse or cheeky) with one of my instructors, Corporal Shipton, a fellow Durbanite coming to the end of his National Service. I'm sure it was a minor misdemeanour, but no doubt he wanted one more opportunity to make a lasting impression on me.

It began easily enough, rolling myself along the ground for a few hundred metres, then stopping to drink half-a-litre of water, then rolling some more, drinking more water, and repeat. For 90 minutes! The one-litre bottle was refilled four or five times and the sight of Shipton standing over me must've been quite amusing for onlookers as I retched and rolled my way behind the bungalow area (he wouldn't have done it on parade ground because the 'drink-n-roll' punishment was definitely against rules).

Like a parting gift from an old friend, it certainly was memorable.

Tough as the PTI course was, it was with no small amount of pride that I completed that final challenge. Now all we had to do was look forward to Pass-out Parade and onward posting to somewhere nice and cushy. I hoped for a benign posting to a training unit, like 1 or 2 Special Services Battalion. Thanks to my very minor transgressions it was hard to imagine getting anywhere near the top posting as an instructor at School of Armour. In truth, I probably wasn't stern enough to bark at boys, some of whom would be older than me. After all, I still looked like a 16-year-old kid – with a half-decent moustache.

4

61 Mechanised Battalion Group, Omuthiya

As it transpired, none of the best units were on offer to me. When the onward postings were announced on parade it took a lot of control not to show my shock and utter disbelief when the Major called "Korporaal Mannall" and then said, "61 Mechanised Battalion Group – Omuthiya, Northern South West Africa (Namibia)." The ground beneath my feet seemed to shake.

61 Mech! This hellhole was fuckin-well right near the border of Angola, that hitherto distant communist-backed country suffering from 20 years of civil war and strife and which also harboured the terrorist group SWAPO, responsible for mounting regular cross-border terrorist excursions deep into Northern SWA with a view to liberating their country from the clutches of the South African Government!

It was difficult to digest the gravity of the posting, which seemed the absolute fucking worst possible outcome for me. I had no particular appetite for heroic frontline action. Others, like my good friend Cpl. Paul Gladwin actually requested transfer into an active combat unit he, and others like him, requested putting themselves in harm's way.

Fuck that, I didn't want to die! It seemed nuts to me but, for the war-hungry among us, there were a number of choice onward postings available and in order of likelihood of seeing actual combat, they were:

1. 32 Light Infantry Battalion – a fearsome counter-insurgency, predominantly infantry-based unit which included a Squadron of 90mm Armoured Corp led by boys from *Pantserskool*. Nickname; Buffalo.
2. 61 Mechanised Battalion Group – AKA 61 Mech – a mechanised all-in-one kick-ass conventional main battle group consisting of Artillery, Infantry, Tanks and everything else needed to stand alone as a complete rapid reaction conventional mechanised fighting unit.
3. A number of strategic frontier bases along the SWA/Angola border, like Sector 10 at Oshikati and Sector 20 at Rundu where trackers and elite infantrymen

staged small-scale counter-insurgency operations. Life in these frontier bases was harsh and edgy as a result of the numerous mortar attacks they suffered over the years, but when it came to large-scale combat units 'in the field', the Buffalo and 61 Mech were the primary go-to offensive weapons in the ongoing struggle against Communism and the increasing tide of Cuban soldiers and Russian materiel.

4. 4 SAI (4 South African Infantry Battalion) in Middelburg, at one time referred to as 62 Mech. This unit was organised along similar lines as 61 Mech but safely ensconced deep within the borders of South Africa.

Much to his chagrin, Gladwin got his fourth choice which, inconveniently meant he was a couple thousand clicks away from the danger zone. He seemed destined to spend final year of National Service engaged in training operations while living it up on Easy Street and speeding off almost every weekend to his parent's hometown, Springs, on his high-powered Honda. It was highly unlikely his Squadron would get a sniff of combat; that would require FAPLA (People's Armed Forces for the Liberation of Angola) to launch an unusually massive offensive to warrant relocating his entire unit across two countries in support of the primary border strike units, which had repeatedly proven themselves so proficient during operations including the legendary Sceptic / Smoke Shell in 1980, Protea and Daisy in 1981, and Meebos in 1982. Only a year earlier, in 1985, the two border strike units had held off a massive mechanised offensive by the communist-backed regime in Luanda.

All of this sharp-edge stuff was hitherto useless unimportant information to me because I'd only focussed on the possibility of benign onward postings and would've been quite happy to have been billeted at School of Armour, living just off-base, sharing an ultra-modern apartment with a comrade NCO, in unbelievably close proximity to young female officers, and during the week providing instruction and training to the next intake of Armoured Corps *roofs* (new recruits).

Perhaps my baby face didn't mark me out as a natural 'hard-ass motherfucker' of the type needed to intimidate and drill the crap out of new boys, or maybe my minor brush with AWOL, had left an indelible 'black mark'. Whatever the case, no explanation or rationale was offered as to the reason for posting us so far from home; some suggested it was because we were bad (naughty or second rate), perhaps this was true.

Whatever the justification, it's unlikely the Major looked at my file and said, "Ah yes, Corporal Mannall, a natural born warrior, if our country really needs defending there are few candidates better suited to this role from the 50 new Corporals we have here at our disposal." No, I'm quite sure the conversation probably went something like, *"Daai fokken Engelsman is vol kak, lat ons hom so ver as moontlik weg stuur* (That fucking Englishman is full of shit; let's send him as far away as possible).

It's amazing how everything is relative. All of a sudden a posting to Zeerust seemed far more preferable than the utter wilderness known as Omuthiya!

The area of Omuthiya is a barren swathe of semi-arid nothingness named after a nearby stream. Located just north of Etosha National Park and 150km west from the nearest 'dorp' (town) Tsumeb. Omuthiya could, not unfairly, be described as the arse-end of nowhere!

The nearest town of Tsumeb's only redeeming feature was its bar and a meagre handful of girls – all of them gorgeous! Certainly in the eye of this beholder!

Tsumeb wasn't all gloom and doom; it also boasted its very own airport, or more accurately, air-strip.

Only 60 clicks to the south-west, a drab non-descript tract of desert had been transformed into an equally drab and nondescript air-force base called *Grootfontein* (Big Fountain) – a place that would stun any new arrival.

As my vision cleared and hearing returned after the 61 Mech bombshell had been dropped on me and three other NCOs, we were ordered to travel to Zeerust, collect our Squadron Troopers who'd been training all year at 2SSB, then take a coach to Jan Smuts airport for the three-hour flight to Grootfontein. From there we'd be escorted to Omuthiya, our home for the year.

We took a final weekend pass, a last opportunity to be with family and loved ones before the start of our tour in the most heavily militarised region in Southern Africa. Unfortunately, and as usual, I was more concerned with mates, booze and sex than spending time with Mom and Dad, and as usual, the reek of virginal desperation chased even the least desirable females from my proximity. By 3am there was just me, the lone tool-box, busting-a-move on the dance floor hoping the DJ would play one more tune before closing-time and that some half-decent-looking girl would stumble up to join my uncoordinated gyrations. Naïve optimism at its best! Of course it never happened and, as usual, I was deeply hung-over when dragged to church the following morning for 09:00 service.

With pounding head I endured yet another long and tedious Anglican sermon. That was until we got to the prayer section of the service, and that's when the bomb dropped. I sobered up fast when without warning the Minister mentioned my name! He wasn't praying to help me deal with my drink-fuelled debauchery, he was asking the congregation to pray for me because I'd just become one of those guys on 'operational duties' who needed special prayers for their safekeeping! [The church included me in their prayers every Sunday for a year, Mom made sure of that. I remain deeply and eternally grateful.] It was like a sledgehammer blow, my bravado finally crumbled as I came to fully understand the gravity of my situation, but there was no way out and definitely no backing down now.

The Church and I seldom agreed on some fundamental aspects of religion so, since the age of 14, the only time I attended church willingly was during JL's and then again deep inside Angola. In Tempe, membership of the Anglican Church meant a free evening trip off-base and because there was no roll-call at this church we'd duck off and cruise the deserted Sunday streets. The Anglican set-up in Bloem was pretty decent to be fair, the Minister knew we were taking the piss, but still happily provided us with cakes and biscuits after the service we'd just missed.

After that final weekend pass of '86, eight Junior Leaders designated for 61 Mech travelled to Zeerust for a couple days to get acquainted with the boys who'd make up the three troops of 12 and an echelon. In total, we were about 45 lads drawn together to become Charlie Squadron, 61 Mechanised Battalion.

Photo 5 Steph Rossouw and myself. Newly commissioned Corporals arriving at Zeerust to collect the troops who would form Charlie Squad, 61 Mech. (Steph Rossouw)

Like me, these boys all started National Service in January; some had even been aboard that very first train from Durban. They would have been offered the chance to complete JL's but they'd either been unwilling, uninterested, or incapable. The guys we inherited from Zeerust were a healthy mix of all three.

During year one, these boys got their fair share of *opvok*, but unlike on JLs their instructors didn't have the same carrot-n-stick ours had. Ours were always threatening to expel us from JLs if we didn't get our *lei gat* (lazy arse) off the floor and carry the 'thing' [insert name of heavy inanimate object of choice], a few metres further or minutes longer. For some of the Zeerust lads, the hardest part had ended seven months before, on completion of Basics, and consequently some of them had become more accustomed to adopting a surly and abrasive attitude toward rank, especially a rank of such junior standing as brand-new Corporal.

Again, I was confused and puzzled as to why *I* was sent to handle such an unruly and uncooperative bunch of reprobates, most of them older than me, and some a lot older – one guy was 22!

I could see the scepticism in their eyes which said without words: 'who the fuck are these Corporals and Lootys anyway, they've got no more experience or credibility than us, why should we show them any respect?'

It was clear from the start that their respect was not going to be won by virtue of rank; it would have to be earned the hard way.

So we were just getting to know one another when the airplane's tailgate dropped open at Grootfontein AFB. It was imperative not to show undue concern or fear. I resolved simply to follow the orders of those who knew what we were to do next and pass them on to my small Troop of ten boys.

Only a week earlier we'd still been under the aegis of our instructors, amongst peers I knew and trusted implicitly, now I faced my first proper responsibility as Corporal to a slightly hostile Squadron who were more comfortable with each other than with an interloper JL and who preferred to take their cue from a number of shit-stirring ringleaders like Storey, Tomey, Rheeder and Robbello, a bunch of naughty fuckers that sought to test our resolve right from the start!

5

The Omuthiya Special

Flying Hercules troop-transport 'flossies' into Grootfontein AFB mid-December 1986 was as far from first class transport as is possible to get in an aircraft. There was ample leg-room for stretching out but this was only because we were sitting on the floor; there were no seats, carpets or complimentary canapés and definitely no glamorous stewardesses.

The full length of the plane's fuselage was divided in half by a webbing contraption that wouldn't have looked out of place in an S&M dungeon.

Soldaate (soldiers) carried their *balsak* (ball-bag or duffel bag), loaded with everything they owned, filed into the aluminium tube and sat shoulder to shoulder on the cold aluminium floor until the gloomy stripped-bare cabin was rammed chokka with fresh-faced boys, each on a journey into the unknown.

As the large pneumatic tailgate clunked shut ahead of take off, the four idling turbo-prop engines spooled up in a deafening crescendo. I almost imagined an attractive stewardess saying, 'Your seatbelts are fastened as follows…please strap them over your waist and clip them into the floor.' In reality, the flight engineer instructed us to clip on to floor harnesses and maintain an upright position during take off and landing, this was especially important during landing, he warned, because it involved a rapid descent in a spiralling corkscrew manoeuvre designed to reduce the risk of being shot at! What better way is there to cure a fear of flying than by replacing it with a fear of dying at the hand of terrorist gunfire during final descent?

Aside from the real and butt-clenching fear of being RPG'd out the sky, it turned out that plummeting toward earth like a corkscrew in a large jet was actually quite fun.

As soon as the tail of the Hercules dropped open things got hot, fast! The cold cabin air was quickly replaced by what seemed like a blast furnace in one of the gold mines we'd seen on our drive into Johannesburg that morning.

Disembarking from the gloomy interior into the blindingly harsh, bright sunlight and arid barrenness of the desert landscape was breathtaking. This was my first trip to a real desert, a journey into a world coloured only in shades of brown.

A house-sized air traffic control structure and adjoining 'arrivals hall' about the size of a shipping container was about all Grootfontein had to offer us intrepid teenagers.

To shield the AFB from long-range sniper and RPG attacks and protect planes from accurate mortar fire, engineers had created six-metre-high earthen embankment around the entire complex.

After disembarking we received instructions to wait.

Sheltering from the sun in shadows outside the 'arrivals hall', we encountered even more hues of brown in the form of the clothing and darkly tanned skin sported by weather-beaten *ou manne* (old men), so named because they'd started their National Service a year before us. These guys, their skin tanned darker than the most avid beach-bum, their clothing and hair bleached the lightest shade of brown, were now nearing completion of their tour on the border and their stories… their stories were designed to make us *kuk* (shit) ourselves.

As luck would have it, L/Cpl Peter Ashton a Tank Commander *Ou-man*, a friend from the School of Armour, was flying out on the same plane we'd arrived on. He was *klaaring out* (discharging) having just completed his National Service duty at 61 Mech. He sagely advised me that the year ahead would be pretty *rustig* (easy). He *tuned* (told) me that because 61 Mech was a border base so far from South Africa, rules were more relaxed and, more importantly, there'd been no major conflict during his 6-month tour despite the constant threat of small-cell, insurgent-type action that was unlikely to involve conventional armour like ours.

Ashton's Squadron of Olifant tanks had briefly crossed the border, travelling only a short distance into Angola with 61 Mech (obviously denied by authorities) as a show of force but, it seemed, no significant threat had emerged and they'd stood down. They were fortunate there'd been no repeat in '86 of the large mechanised offensive launched mid-'85 by Angola's military.

Reassuringly, he added that his boys had subsequently been tasked with 'mothballing' the entire 14-strong Squadron of Olifant MBTs based at 61 Mech before low-loading them back to South Africa. He believed the Russians could no longer afford to bankroll Fidel Castro's proxy war and that this considerably reduced the threat of heavily mechanised engagements.

Peter's information was solid gold! He went on to explain that a massive FAPLA mechanised offensive involving six hardened Brigades (approx. 12,000 soldiers and a lot of heavy weapons) had been launched in '85 in a failed attempt to oust the charismatic rebel leader, Jonas Savimbi. By now I already knew that

Photo 6 Owamboland terrain. (Barry Taylor)

the USSR had been generously equipping their Communist allies with one of the largest, and probably most modern, collection of military hardware anywhere in Africa.

In desperation, UNITA, the lightly armoured and pitifully under-resourced Angolan opposition turned to South Africa for help. although it wasn't always so – at an earlier time UNITA had been allied with SWAPO, consequently relations with SA were pretty sour.

World powers at the UN were largely impotent in their feeble attempts to disrupt the communist build-up in Southern Africa while simultaneously disapproving of South Africa's efforts to protect her borders, the argument confused with, and totally drowned out by, the rising tide of international opposition to the Apartheid injustices – a completely different conflict to the Cold War debacle that had overtaken the Angolan Civil War, although many still preferred tying the two struggles together. A third conflict, the disrupting of communist SWAPO to prevent them from gaining control of SWA/Namibia, only exacerbated the already muddy diplomatic situation.

Initially, targeted air-strikes, and then later, long-range artillery was as much as South Africa's government would commit to the conflict.

The Angolan dos Santos regime's plan to destroy the opposition in their capital at Jamba, in the south-east, initially made good progress encountering only small scale hit-n-run ambushes by UNITA. By then communist-backed dos Santos government had acquired a decent air force, and amassed the largest mechanised war-machine in Southern African history [didn't know this at the time though], with equipment boasting technologically advanced capabilities decades ahead of our own sanction-suppressed SADF/SAAF inventory and, more importantly, that of our flea-bitten friends in UNITA who had almost no mechanised forces at all. UNITA was powerless to stop the advance on their capital.

To counter this threat, two ground force units (61 Mech & 32 Batt) were ordered to join the fray. They engaged the enemy forces and provided an unbroken defensive line at the Lomba, halting the tank-led offensive 100km short of their target, Jamba. Then torrential tropical rains, typical in November and December, turned bone-dry desert terrain into muddy alluvial plain, almost overnight. Armoured vehicles and tanks got bogged down in the mud and were either abandoned or, if not recovered, destroyed.

The impassable conditions signalled an end to immediate hostilities but not before significant casualties were taken on both sides. Some reports claim a casualty rate 15 times greater on the FAPLA side, so maybe that's a victory in itself?

FAPLA limped home having failed to achieve their objective while the SADF dragged itself out of the mud, hoping they'd proved their resolve and capability to support UNITA and keep the Communist threat at bay.

Ashton said FAPLA hadn't gone on to launch any major offensive in his time at 61 Mech ('86) and there was very little reason to expect them back in '87. Obviously, this was an incorrect and ill-informed assumption, but who could have known at the time?

Olifant crewmen enjoyed reminding us 90mm crewmen that our weapon wasn't rated for MBT busting; it had neither the range nor the destructive capacity of the Olifant 105mm gun.

During previous operations in the long-running conflict against SWAPO, and typically against more lightly armoured targets, the 90mm platform had proven itself extremely effective. However, a whole new level of commitment by Soviet backers in the late seventies to mid-eighties had seen the injection into that other conflict, the Angolan Civil War, of almost one thousand Russian MBTs! This had been a massive game changer for forces on the ground. If, or when, these MBTs were deployed against UNITA, the light Infantry resistance movement would be unable to hold back the tide of tracked steel – even the mighty SADF would be hard-pressed to resist such a tsunami of Tanks.

Despite this bad news, our commanders assured us the 90mm cannon would never be deployed against Russian MBT's without the impressive Olifant at our side.

Some observers reasoned the 90mm cannon couldn't be confidently committed against Russian MBTs because the 90mm weapon was incapable of penetrating the thick steel hull of a 40-ton T54/55, whereas the SADF Olifant MBT, they said, with its stabilised laser rangefinder, 105mm cannon, exotic array of munitions, like the HESH and SCARAB rounds, was a one-hit-wonder in battle. Any weapon system that uses the term 'depleted uranium' in its arsenal should be feared, and the Olifant was no exception!

Now, our 90mm turret no longer rode atop the Eland armoured car as it had done in training, here it had been dropped into a Ratel AFV, the 6-wheel vehicle favoured by 61 Mech due to its mobility and lightning attack capabilities in the sandy, *bush veldt* entangled terrain. Weighing just shy of 20 tons, the Ratel was significantly scrawnier and less thickly plated than the 55-ton Elephant. On this basis alone, we were assured, 61 Mech's Ratel AFV's wouldn't be ordered toe to toe against Russian MBTs, and that was fine by me.

Reflecting on Ashton's insight that 61 Mech's Olifant Squadron had been mothballed and sent back to SA, I figured the hazard in Northern SWA wouldn't be as fearsome as some had warned, and this 'punishment posting', as I saw it, probably wasn't going to be as bad as I'd first thought, so I thought, *"screw you Major, or whoever it was who decided to send me here, I can learn to handle a bit of subtropical semi-desert heat, and if that's the worst you can throw at me."* Many of my favourite childhood holidays were spent on Uncle John's sheep farm in semi-desert near Graaff Reinet in Klein Karoo where the mercury regularly topped 45 Celsius in the shade – I could take the heat!

Farm life was idyllic, mostly outdoors, working herds of sheep and goats, foaling new horses, tending to extremely nervous baby ostriches, learning to ride horses, tractors and motorbikes, swimming in irrigation dams dotted around his 4000 hectare birthright, or working alongside farmhands, all of them black dudes, like the giant Hopley and 19-year-old Akadis who'd only managed to complete two years of formal schooling.

This farm had been my first opportunity to spend quality time with black Africans. The families lived in very small houses by comparison to the farmhouse but to me they seemed happy enough with their simple way of life, husbands toiling on the farm, wives often employed in tasks associated with the farmstead and the kids seemingly so carefree.

I disliked hunting Springbok (buck) on the farm but thankfully that only happened twice, and happily on both occasions I missed the target. I was never really comfortable with killing a living thing and the first time they slaughtered a sheep on 'the altar' behind the main shed I cried! Despite that, my sisters and I relished the unique taste of unlimited quantities of fynbos scrub-fed mutton, although such a heavy meal would not have been welcome on a day as hot as the one we arrived at Grootfontein AFB.

I tried to maintain a cool, hard exterior as if to proclaim 'this is no big deal' and 'I do this kind of shit all the time' all the while trying hard not to look like a deer in headlights or expose the slightest sign of weakness that would be exploited by the new Troopers of Charlie Squadron.

Perhaps, I should've been less concerned with acting cool, and more appropriately scared shitless, but how could we know that when we lined up at Grootfontein for the final time, 13 months later, our Squad would be decimated, most of the survivors deeply scarred – some for life. We were all destined to be casualties of war; we just didn't know it yet.

61 Mechanised Battalion Group's base at Omuthiya was a utilitarian, isolated border outpost mostly comprising a small tent-town, a handful of semi-permanent corrugated metal structures and a swimming pool, all built by troops in the years since Battle Group Juliet, established in the late seventies, pulled a number of corps together under a single chain of command and proven so successful in countering the burgeoning heavy metal threat from the north.

In 1979, the Chief of Defence awarded permanency to Juliet, formally rebranding her 61 Battalion – a mechanised fast-attack unit.

The most remarkable features on base at Omuthiya were; firstly, a large swimming pool (which was quite a surprise – we never saw that on the tourist brochure) dug into the sandy ground of bush-clad Owamboland by those who'd gone before (respect to them) and secondly, and equally astonishingly, an officers and NCOs' bar, an incongruous log-cabin style thing that wouldn't have looked out of place in the Swiss Alps or Aspen, Colorado. Everything else was straight out of the handbook setting out requirements for a remote border outpost.

The dust from the Troop transports had hardly settled before Major Pine Pienaar, a cuddly softly spoken man, called us to attention on the parade ground and introduced himself as Charlie Squadron Commander. Major Pienaar seemed far too nice a guy for the task of overseeing and leading the eclectic bunch of miscreants we'd collected from Zeerust. The whole base was abuzz with new arrivals to the various corps, from Armour to Artillery, Infantry to Signals and Mechanics to Medics.

Troop accommodation areas looked like something out of a Somalian refugee camp but with neater, smaller rows of tents sprouting from the dusty earth. Lines of planted trees offered precious shade while neat paths of white aggregate demarcated each battle unit or section.

Charlie Squadron was billeted in eight tents near the parade ground. Others, like Alpha and Bravo Company and Golf and Foxtrot Batteries, were similarly configured nearby.

Five sturdy metal-framed beds were provided per tent. The quartermaster issued each guy an army-issue mattress and a new strongbox for personal belongings.

After settling the troops in, lootys and NCOs were shown to their accommodations which were far better than those of the troops. Finally, it seemed, that the year of hard slog on JLs was beginning to pay dividends.

Cue disappointment.

Ours was a standard-size tent, identical to the Troopers, though on the upside, we'd only be three per tent and ours included a complimentary steel cupboard for hanging stuff in.

Army protocol dictated that NCOs and COs be separated for fear of cross-contamination, so Cpl Steph Roussouw, a pal from Bloem and Cpl. A.J Venter became my new best friends, while Lt Adrian Hind, Lt Martin Bremer and Lt Michael O'Connor shacked up together some distance away.

After a grand tour of the 50-shades-of-brown, sand-swept base, new JL's were invited to the 'traditional swearing-in ceremony' at 'The Omuthiya' – the log-cabin style *kroeg* (bar) toward the north of the camp, and thankfully, not too far from my tent.

Since our arrival at Grootfontein AFB, we'd heard rumours about this unofficial and totally awful rite of passage involving the army's preferred lubricant – alcohol.

Like most 18 year olds, I already understood the benefits and pitfalls of alcohol, had had ample experience of getting comfortably numb after three or four pints, or of over doing it like the time where my *Bunny Chow* (curry in half-loaf bread) was forcibly evacuated from my gut onto Sander Road, New Germany. Fortunately on that occasion Pete had stopped the car in time to get the door open. But the experience I'd had with alcohol up to this point was no preparation whatsoever for the Omuthiya Special, a concoction so toxic it had to be poured in a steel army-issue 'fire-bucket', a mug used on-base for all drinks, hot or cold. The 600ml steel outer cladding to the durable plastic water-bottle was most useful in the field when used for heating drinks over a fire or *esbit* (firelighter tabs carried in our in ration packs).

The Omuthiya barman filled six fire-buckets to the brim with a sickly mix of spirits. Next to each he placed a warm 340ml can of beer.

To complete the swearing-in ceremony, each initiate had ten seconds to empty the fire-bucket chased by a can of warm Castle Lager, also in ten seconds!

As we stepped up to the bar to begin our initiation, I noticed a cauldron-like bubbling on the curdling, surface scum of the Omuthiya Special.

"Ready, and go!"

There was no time to think. I grabbed my bucket, put it to my mouth and gagged at the foulness washing down my throat. Desperately keen not to be shown up in front of the senior staff who'd gathered to welcome us aboard, I tried to override my buds so as not to taste the disgusting stew; '…nine…ten' and it was gone though I still had to suppress my internal protection system's powerful urge to heave the gloopy muck back up. The beer, despite being warm as cat's piss, was like sweet nectar after the toxic toilet cleaner, alcoholic froth that had just preceded it.

I did it! I held it down and passed the 'test'. I felt OK at first but someone sensibly suggested we should surreptitiously sneak off to evacuate the poison before it had time to fully absorb, and we intended doing just that, as soon as we could make good our escape.

As we were leaving, our Squadron Sergeant pulled us three Corporals into a huddle and began delivering a drunken and rambling welcome speech about the need to: "work together as a team, be reliable, tough and…'

OH MY GOD!! THUMP THUMP THUMP!

Next thing I knew was the most painful pounding permeating my entire skull.

Totally disoriented, I forced my eyelids open in a blinding light. It took some time to establish my whereabouts. Eventually I realised I was in my own bed. It was almost 10:00. The sun had turned our tent into a sauna. My bedding and clothing were covered in spew, even my spare uniform, the one hanging INSIDE the metal cupboard was covered in sick!

The last thing I remembered was the Sergeant's rambling pep talk but knew nothing at all of what transpired in the intervening twelve hours.

Rossouw and Venter appeared to be just as sick. It seemed far worse than the food poisoning I suffered on the Golden Gate route march a couple months earlier. We needed assistance, of a medical kind.

Major Pienaar was vehemently against alcohol and took an extremely dim view of his new NCOs' condition, so after a stinging rebuke he allowed us to visit the sick bay where a greenhorn medic proceeded to continue his training by practising his needlework skills on our forearms. IV needles are not for the faint of heart and the new medic still needed a lot of practice. It came as some relief that on his fourth attempt, the medic finally secured the needle and I could lie back and allow the saline and pain-relief drip to do their thing.

The lootys had somehow managed to get away and expel the poison early on suffering few ill effects.

Rossouw later filled me in on some of the missing hours, although he admitted there were also blanks in his memory. From what he recalled, apparently we stumbled down to our Troopers tents and proceeded to give them a bit of hell but before this went on too long he said, "Mannall, we thought you were gonna drown in puke man!"

There was never an explanation as to why I opened the cupboard and puked on my spare uniform, that had served no purpose other than to add to my laundry pile.

We'd survived the Omuthiya Special, just!

Introductions over, we were in, now fully-fledged members of an elite band of officers and non-commissioned officers of 61 Mech, albeit lime green, like a month-old slice of mouldy bread.

Our cherished *Pantser* Corps black berets were replaced with the infantry green ones required at 61 Mech. That didn't go down well at all! Nor too the R4 machine guns (standard Infantry issue) which replaced our R5's.

The 40-man Squadron began to settle into something approaching a routine. Gone were early morning inspections and endless marching but in came endless fitness and combat readiness training, and despite our remote location, troops were expected to maintain a tidy environment in and around base.

The Troopers in our Squad had endured their fair share of inspection and punishment at 2SSB and it quickly became apparent to us that they weren't too keen on being messed around by us junior leaders. As far as some of them were concerned, their days of *opvok* and *rondvok* (getting fucked around) were a thing of the past.

Bravo Company on the other hand was all about 'being the best' the dictatorial commander apparently didn't get the memo about 'Border life' being chilled. A veteran of previous cross-border conflict, he expected the highest standard from his boys. Jeez, those guys were frequently punished, frequently inspected and regarded by most as the best Company on base.

Charlie Squadron was comic by comparison with its cuddly major, absent Squad *Sa'Majoor*, a relatively weak junior leader team and poorly-disciplined Troopers. Our guys were regularly caught out for lateness or some other transgression.

If a big cheese, like Regimental Sergeant Major Kemp AKA RSM '*Snor*' (moustache – he sported a fearsome handlebar 'tache), was anywhere in range, even boys with the worst 'fuck-you' attitudes gained an injection of pace and discipline about them, because *Snor* had one of those booming voices and a reputation that caused a sudden loosening sensation in the bladder. Aside from the fearsome sound and demeanour of the man, if anyone attracted his attention for the wrong reasons, he'd be quite happy to mete out a punishment that lasted all day long.

Unfortunately, Charlie Squad Corporals experienced Kemp's wrath at first hand. Apparently we'd been disrespectful or something so, to remind us of our proper non-commissioned status close to the bottom of the strict military hierarchy, he took us on a sightseeing tour of the picturesque, brown countryside.

"Bring tenminste twee waterbottles saam, elkeen van julle" (Bring at least two water bottles each).

That was all he said, so we knew it was going to be thirsty work as the three of us sat forlornly on the back of his Samil 50.

We knew he didn't need to take us far into the desolate wilderness if he intended doing unspeakable things with us but we were still kicking up dust about 20 clicks from base when RSM finally pulled the lorry to an abrupt stop.

"Spring af julle drie (you three, jump down), *aandag!"* He called us to attention in his trademark blood-curdling style then proceeded to unleash a volcanic verbal tirade at us for our minor misdeed.

When the lava flow finally abated he reached into the cab, grabbed a satchel and threw it at our feet.

"Here's a bag of 1000ft signal-flares, you've got water, now walk home."

With that, he hopped into the cab, whipped the truck through 180 degrees and sped back along his tracks, the dust plume visible for miles as he headed back to base with its deliciously cool swimming pool.

We were actually quite elated, it seemed like a free day off from dealing with *harregat* (hard-arse) troops and, for a change, the lootys could get off their arses and manage the Trooper intransigence.

Despite the searing heat that day, we were quite fit enough and had by now almost fully acclimatised to desert life so the task ahead appeared not at all daunting. We carried no heavy gear and, for entertainment, the RSM had given us a bag of goodies to play with. Perhaps the 1000ft flares were to be used in the event we got lost or injured. No matter, some bright spark came up with an idea to start shooting flares horizontally, at trees and stuff, and then we saw a few head of cattle (disclaimer: I'm sure that no cattle were injured in the making of our entertainment during that long walk through the desert.)

In the early days Charlie Squadron might've been accused of being a little lacklustre on the parade ground and with in-base discipline, but the boys heartily threw themselves into training on our fantastic new fighting platforms, the Ratel AFV. This vehicle was a godsend!

The Ratel AFV was a huge improvement on the 1950's Noddy Car (Eland) that we'd originally trained on. I'd fully expected us to have to continue enduring the clunky outdated armoured car. The turbo-charged Ratel came equipped with power-steering, assisted brakes, semi-automatic gearbox and in-vehicle surround-sound system as standard.

The six-wheel 18-tonne straight six, 12-litre turbocharged beast was designed to carry up to 12 soldiers and was designed with a number of turret/interior variants including point-five-oh command-and-control vehicles, an 81mm 'soft-top' mortar launch platform, and for direct combat, the 90mm and 20mm variants. The 20mm was a belt-fed rapid-fire weapon that easily punctured light armour.

Photo 7 Tyre exchange. The rare use of a crane removed the backache of loading the massive spare tyre onto the roof from ground level. (Len M. Robberts)

Charlie Squadron's 36 combat crew manned 12 of the 90mm variant, additional crewmen were assigned to two command-and-control units while the echelon guys handled the logistics vehicles.

Our upgraded fighting vehicles represented a staggering change of fortune for the combat crewmen who, up until now, had been shoe-horned into the cramped confines of Elands AKA 'turrets-on-wheels', as some accurately put it.

It took a little time for crews to learn to handle the larger, heavier vehicles, especially for driver and crew commander who together were responsible for navigating the behemoths through the difficult training ground.

During the first large-scale training exercise, Lt Bremer's vehicle got trapped in a deep trench just as Commandant Smit cruised by in his command vehicle. Smit stopped, hailed Bremer and dealt him a very tasty verbal roasting.

To his credit, Bremer stood his ground and told the commandant the kit was new to us all. In fact, the kit was nearly *brand new* too, probably about a year old, one previous owner, lovingly maintained!

Although the 90mm turret itself remained identical to the cramped model we'd trained on, the new Ratel offered a plethora of added extras, many of which would only become apparent later on.

Now the Armour boys had a lot of spare room in the vehicle's rear cabin, space which would otherwise be filled with a Platoon of infantrymen. These vehicles would be our 'home away from home' for almost six months and that extra space in the back was precious, particularly during the winter because there was, at a pinch, sufficient space for the three-man crew to stretch out in relative comfort while the massive engine retained enough heat to keep the cabin warm, for a few hours at least.

Training took precedence over all else, we spent weeks on manoeuvres in the harsh terrain in the Omuthiya region working alongside Infantry and Artillery units, learning to work in concert as a unified strike force.

Charlie's armour boys loved it, wherever we went, we travelled easily in the Ratel, whereas Alpha and Bravo infantry boys had to 'step out', meaning they had to leave the comfort of the AFV in order to attack 'enemy installations' on foot, integrating alongside our vehicles. They were never pleased if we fired a round off without warning them of the imminent muzzle blast.

Photo 8 Contemplating the behemoth. (Barry Taylor)

Photo 9 *Bloubaan* (Blue Range) training area north of Omuthiya, Ratel 90mm
integrated with 20mm Alpha Company during attack exercise. (Len M. Robberts)

6

Infantry Kill

In February, without prior notice, our routine was changed. Commandant Bok Smit, an infantry war veteran, decreed that non-infantry troops would undertake 2-weeks compulsory infantry training.

Much to the chagrin of the entire Squadron, not least Major Pienaar, we abandoned our luxurious ride, bundled on to Troop transports and shipped off for a fortnight on foot to help us 'appreciate and respect the hardship of an infantry soldier'.

I didn't have the marbles to say, "Let me assure you Commandant, we already respect the fellas who travel on foot, lug uncomfortably heavy loads and sleep on hard ground exposed to shit weather with nothing more to than a thin nylon tarp (bivvy) for shelter'.

Of course Smit knew we'd been through this during basic training. We'd all done the sleepless uncomfortable nights in the freezing cold, faces daubed 'black-is-beautiful', and the long route-marches to hone our navigation skills, and the combat drills; with little respite to test our resolve. Most guys thought this 2-week infantry jaunt was meant as a punishment for being *sleg*, rather than a training exercise.

The following day at the remote training area it was as if we were back on Basics again, camping under a sheet, cooking rations, faces painted like Rambo and most importantly, learning what a 'V' shape looked like.

For obvious reasons, tank and armoured car crewmen are not the biggest (heftiest) of people, so when it came to selecting the *Platoon* light machine gun (LMG) operator there was really only one guy suitable for the job. The product of an outdoor childhood, he was physically stronger than anyone in the Troop and therefore most well suited to carrying the cumbersome 7.62mm LMG.

We worked for about a week refining tactics, techniques and formations until the Squadron was finally ready for the 'live drill' phase scheduled to last three days.

At around mid-morning on the first day, 7 February 1987, as we slowly advanced to a stand of trees at about 250m, the radio crackled to life warning of incoming 'enemy activity from the area near the trees'.

The Platoon immediately dropped into the savannah-like grass which was just tall enough to hide the guy immediately ahead.

The first part of the drill had gone well, everything was in place, so we held our positions for a few minutes waiting for the command to approach or attack the incoming 'enemy'.

We knew the 'enemy' was at our 12 o'clock and moving steadily towards us, so the action called for us to wait for them to get close before launching a surprise frontal assault.

I held my position at the rear of the left flank which consisted of five soldiers with the LMG just ahead of me as we remained hunched on the ground.

And then…CRACK!

A single high-powered gunshot broke the silence and before the echo died away someone shouted, "Who the fuck was that?"

And then 'No, no, no!' – a plaintive wail from the guy just ahead of me.

Protocol dictated that before we engaged the 'enemy', safety catches were in the 'on' position. The LMG gunner had made a mistake, his safety catch was off, weapon cocked and loaded.

Due to his inexperience, or perhaps just a momentary lapse of concentration, he'd tickled the LMG trigger just hard enough to release the hammer onto the chambered round.

That was fucking unbelievably bad luck for Trooper Johann Labuschagne crouched just three metres ahead of the LMG in the formation.

The bullet could've travelled anywhere, 99.99% of available trajectories would've seen the supersonic projectile, about the size of a baby's thumb, fly harmlessly for a few kilometres before dropping to earth, hurting nobody, the whole incident worth nothing more than disciplinary hearing and a few hours opfok.

Instead, the high-powered bullet took the 0.01% trajectory toward Labuschagne's head, barely slowing as it punctured the base of his skull and exited in the area of the left eye-socket.

This was my first encounter with violent human death, but I knew instinctively that Johann died the moment that 7.62mm bullet struck and in that I took some solace. Just one look at his lifeless body, the deathly yellow pallor and ghastly exit-wound, highlighted the futility of life-support, but none of us spoke of it. We'd fight for him until ordered to stop.

In an instant we transformed ourselves from mock infantrymen to real-life medics. A team of four or five of us administered first-aid treatment, alternating between heart massage and air supply.

Realising his airways were blocked, the medic inserted a clear plastic pipe which helped to get air into the lungs far more easily but then discovered the air we were forcing into his lungs was escaping from his shattered eye socket area. We shared the grisly task of applying pressure to the thick wadding where his eye had been to prevent air escaping. To ensure whatever blood remaining in his body reached Johann's heart, we elevated his feet. But our efforts proved worthless. When the doctor's helicopter finally touched down, almost two hours later, he immediately pronounced Labuschagne deceased, at which point we had no choice but to stand-down, accept the inevitable and say *totsiens* (goodbye) to one of our own, a decent boy, a loving son and a fallen patriot. RIP.

Once the body had been taken from us we turned and went back to the business of being mock infantry, the Squad numbed and shocked by our first encounter with sudden loss through violent death.

The incident was never properly discussed, we just started packing stuff into the strongbox many soldiers keep tucked away in the dark recesses of the brain. There wasn't time for talking about it openly or allowing any emotion to bubble up.

The army moves on, soldiers must follow.

Photo 10 Puma. This is how Labuschagne departed. (Barry Taylor)

There was another less obvious casualty that day. The LMG lad was removed, never to be seen or heard of again. We thought he'd get some jail-time and if lucky, some psychological support.

Labuschagne's parents visited the base at Omuthiya and visited the site of their desperate anguish.

We didn't have words for them. We didn't know how to deal with our own feelings, let alone offering support to grieving parents. Sorry.

We were too damn young to fully comprehend the extent of their tragedy and, as ever, the world just kept on turning while the demands of the army remained unrelenting.

The infantry phase was foreshortened; it had been a bad idea anyway! Armour boys were ill-equipped for the rigours of running about with heavy LMGs, we were far more accustomed to the Browning 7.62mm turret-mounted variety.

The Commandant must've copped a Samil truck-full of shit-stew for allowing Johann's death to occur on his watch.

Within a fortnight Major Pienaar announced he was leaving 61 Mech, his replacement soon thereafter, the diminutive Captain PJ Cloete, then became the only permanent force (career) soldier in Charlie Squadron but he made up for his short-handed lack of stature with his bark. He'd just completed a rotation with 32 Battalion and those boys knew all about life on the bleeding edge of warfare.

7

Communication Operations

One of the primary defensive functions of bases dotted along the SWA/Angola Border was communications operations (Comm Ops).

The purpose of Comm Ops was to engage the indigenous (First Nation) peoples of the region. These were mostly people of the Owambo tribe (pronounced Oh-vum-boh), a semi-nomadic group of hunter-gatherers who in their recent history, like say the past thousand years or so, had begun settling in tiny clusters or homesteads.

Typically, a homestead consisted of a large *kraal,* a round dwelling made of sticks set upon a covering of hardened cow-dung floor tamped down by the movement of bare feet over many years. The main *kraal* was normally surrounded by an inner perimeter fence of sticks bound together with bark or strips of animal-hide, and an outer perimeter fence surrounding the entire homestead consisting of about half-a-dozen other smaller, less important *kraals*. This ingenious layout of the homestead offered a sort of layer-cake security arrangement – like a prehistoric Pentagon or Camp Bastion – but dating back to a time when a quarry of rocks were the only weapons of mass destruction known to man.

When we'd conducted the trooping of the colour at the School's 40-year anniversary parade the previous year, it had been a grand affair, attended by some of the biggest cheeses the army could muster. We'd practised the drills endlessly and when we marched past the TV cameras, 40 deep, in perfect alignment, it had been with a genuine sense of pride that we represented School of Armour at such an auspicious event; there was maybe even 15 nanoseconds of fame, as they filmed our march past and the 'eyes-left' salute to the big cheese.

On township patrols, I was able to see at first-hand the plight of some black South Africans – although we didn't move among them much it was a somewhat humbling experience. Comm Ops on the other hand offered the chance to engage with the Owambo tribes people individually which I found very rewarding. The three-week operation was more like a journey back in human history, back to a time when day-to-day survival really was the only way of life and people were happy with just the basic necessities such as food and shelter. I was quite unprepared for the warmth of their welcome and the simple sincerity of their outlook on life.

Charlie Squad, with Cpt. Cloete riding in Three-Zero (30) – our command vehicle – set up temporary camp in the middle of nowhere. Each of the three troops, Three One (31), Three Two (32) & Three Three (33) were designated co-ordinates specific daytime patrols. Our orders were to make contact with the tribal people, gather intelligence on potential terrorist (SWAPO) movements or activity, and spread goodwill.

This wasn't a risk free enterprise, about a month later two soldiers were ambushed by SWAPO terrorists as they entered the homestead. The soldiers died. Their comrades on overwatch delivered a similar ending to the terrorists.

Each Troop of four vehicles (e.g. 31, 31A, 31B, 31C) set off into their designated areas. There were no roads or road-signs; this was map-n-compass navigation, so we were never certain what we might find each day.

When spotting a distant homestead we'd make a steady non-threatening approach then, with help of an interpreter, request permission to meet with the head of the settlement.

These old-school Africans, who trace their heritage back 10,000 years, knew why we were there, they'd seen this all before, their barren land had been the crossing-over place for SWAPO forces during the long struggle to 'liberate' Namibia.

The Owambo people had no interest in politics or power struggles, their precarious struggle for survival was the most pressing issue in their lives. Despite this we found them very generous in their hospitality.

Our arrival usually created a bit of a stir in the timeless homesteads with children running out to greet us, a few wizened heads popping up out the shade of the *kraals,* or a cattle herder pausing in his work.

Normally, the head of homestead would invite us to the main *kraal* where we would sit in a circle to talk, share pleasantries and pass round the ubiquitous jam jar of honey-coloured home brew. It was as if we had been transported back in time, perhaps a thousand years or more, with the notable exception of the glass jam jar, and it was difficult not to admire these simple human beings. The ebb and flow of their lives was totally dominated by passage of the seasons, the health of that year's harvest and their tiny herd of malnourished cattle.

These prehistoric wanderers knew they were caught in the power struggle between people from the north and people from the south and this meant their simple existence was occasionally interrupted by men from the north carrying

AK47s moving southwards and us white boys coming from the south and asking for help to track and identify 'terrorists'.

It was impossible to be certain what those Owambo grandees thought of us, or if they took sides in the conflict, their concept of modern government and pencil politics was almost non-existent. What they hoped for was stability and lots of rain. What mattered most to us was whether they were harbouring, or could identify, anyone who posed a credible threat.

Whatever their allegiance in the cross-border conflagration, their hospitality was usually first class and sometimes extremely generous. Jam jars filled with Mohungu, a beer derived from a local fruit, were passed around the circle and readily refilled.

While we attended to bush diplomacy, other Troopers maintained watch from the vehicles, but inside the kraal politeness dictated we drink at least a little of the amber nectar.

Mohungu juice actually turned out to be some pretty good stuff, so we'd regularly find reasons in the early evening, during Comm Ops, to visit local *Kuka shops* (informal bottle store or off-licence) to 'improve' relations between SADF and the locals.

Part of that goodwill normally involved developing trade agreements to procure a few litres of the chilled sweet-tasting, mind-mellowing brew at 20 cents a jar. A litre was enough to get a man relaxed and slurring, two litres and he would struggle to walk straight.

Photo 11 Tribal homestead. (Barry Taylor)

Photo 12 Kuka shop in Owamboland. (Barry Taylor)

Photo 13 Time for fun on Comm-ops, Owamboland, an hour after this photo was captured the vehicle on the right was laying stranded on its side after rolling during handbrake-turn training (unsanctioned of course). (Martin Bremer)

On one such occasion, the naughtiest of the three loots, Bremer, decided to ask one of his crewmen to test the handbrake-turn capabilities of the 7-metre long, six-wheel Ratel on the smooth flats of a salt pan; he endured a shit-storm after Rheeder, his driver, rolled the 18-tonne APC onto its side.

Drunken exploits aside, one particular homestead visit resonated with me more than any other. It was early afternoon on a typically hot day in the desert so it was quite a relief to get out the scorching heat. Our well-practised routine saw me lead a small delegation of troops into the cool, dark *kraal.* The matriarch, clearly head of this settlement, invited us to sit with her and a few of the elders.

The matriarch confirmed they'd not seen anything untoward in recent weeks and we went on to discuss other things such as the health of their cattle and the lack of rain. Conversation had flowed for about 20 minutes, the jam jar doing the rounds, when the matriarch said something to the interpreter, looked at me and laughed. The interpreter leaned over and told me in all seriousness that the matriarch had just offered me her daughter's hand in marriage!

Her daughter was probably no more than 15 years old so it's not unfair to say the Owambo people were more relaxed on 'age of consent' than most western societies. Nonetheless it was pleasing to be considered suitable marriage material by the matriarch though considering the competition, I didn't let it go to my head.

Interestingly, tribal folk weren't concerned by the clothing conventions demanded by more 'advanced' western civilisations. Ladies covered the baby-making and toileting equipment but everything else was exposed.

I examined the two topless ladies sitting side by side a little more closely. The matriarch and her daughter were at opposite ends of the age and beauty spectrum. The matriarch was an exhausted breeding machine, her frail body wizened by many thousand scorching summer days and just as many freezing desert nights, her skin as wrinkled and tough as elephant hide. Her breasts, or what remained of them after suckling an unknowable number of children, were the thinnest longest flaps of skin tissue imaginable, so long in fact, that her well-worn, elongated nipples nestled in her lap as she sat drinking home brew and chatting to me. At the other end of the spectrum, her daughter was blessed with the firmest roundest pair of breasts an 18-year-old boy-virgin could imagine.

This was happening at a time when South Africa was still fully in the grip of a moral crusade banning almost all forms of nudity, the only girls allowed to pose topless for men's magazines were the ones born with star-shaped nipples, so the scene playing out in front of me was quite intriguing and when combined with the mellowing effects of the Mohungu beer coursing through my veins the offer of marriage seemed somewhat appealing.

Reaching for the jam jar, I slugged a mouthful, passed it back toward the matriarch before politely declining the generous breasts, uh, I mean, her generous offer.

This was a lust match made in Owamboland and there was no way that I, the great untouched white virgin boy, would get within squeezing distance of this fulsome firm female.

Growing up in SA meant that black girls were never on the menu anyway and for a time it was even illegal to marry a black person, or person from a different 'race', but the sweet beer-fuelled irony of that moment didn't escape me even then…those six weekend passes during the previous year, the hours busting moves on the dance floor, reeking of desperation, downing western lagers, struggling to muster enough courage just to get a platonic conversation going with some self-obsessed princess were, from my present viewpoint a waste of time. Here, in the middle of the desert with no music or lights, no fancy chit-chat or bullshit, just simple humanity and sincerity, life seemed more complete. This was old-school dating and it seemed a lot less complicated!

Through this, and many other experiences on Comm Ops, we gained an abiding admiration for the tribal people of Owamboland, it was impossible not to respect them for their implacable inner strength, indefatigability and a ruggedness gained by surviving a precarious life eked out in one of the harshest, most barren, inhospitable places on earth. I knew then that my admiration for these hardy people would last a lifetime.

8

Don't Fly Virgin

After almost five months on the Border I celebrated my 19th birthday. We were all getting older, toughening up and most importantly, with the combination of field training, Comm Ops and a handful of Squadron outings to Tsumeb, we'd begun to shape into a tighter unit. We wore our Charlie Squad flash, a mailed fist, with pride and swagger. However, some lads continued to be a little *harregat* (hard-arse or bad attitude), unwilling to take what they deemed to be spurious orders from the JL's. To be fair, most of this was conducted in jest with one notable exception: during a gunnery session Lance Corporal Bobby Robbello and I had a squabble that turned into a rather embarrassing wrestling match in the dirt in front of the Ratels. I resorted to biting his ear a split second after he grabbed my nut bag and squeezed! It was a desperate move but, in the circumstances, very acceptable defensive tactic because once the nut-crush action had been deployed, the gloves came off!

We both experienced excruciating pain and less than a second later the squabble was over, a draw, for which I was quietly grateful because fighting and aggression was not really my modus operandi.

We were fortunate not to be spotted by a PF (permanent force), invariably a person with rank who would be very likely to punish such transgression.

My childhood had been largely free of significant violence; sure there was the occasional bit of playful wrestling with pals in the neighbourhood and even my membership at the local Karate school was going well 'til they introduced 'full contact' sparring which normally involved me getting punched in the face by my 'mate' Sean. I quit Karate soon thereafter and the only other 'fight' I'd had since was in first year high school (Standard 6), age 13.

These dickheads at school, who later became some of my very best friends, decided they didn't like me, for no good reason. Scotty, a frustrated Glasgow Rangers fan, had been niggling at me for weeks, and then one day he pushed his pal Pete directly into my path as I walked past them down the corridor during lunch break. This farcically choreographed stunt was designed to deliver the catalyst for a *rawl* (fight). Pete, who packed a mean right hook, immediately stuttered a 'challenge' to meet him behind the Fairydene Hotel after school that same day!

There was no alternative but to accept the challenge, otherwise the abuse would've escalated from there.

If Mom had known about this she would've stepped in, like she did the time some twat bullied me a bit in junior school.

This time I had to stand on my own and face the music.

The Fairydene Hotel was only two clicks from home so I jogged the short distance barefoot and shirtless, nerves rattling, palms clammy as I steeled myself to face the bully-boys.

Pete turned up with his older *boet* (brother) David who was much stronger than me, so I feared the worst but thankfully he didn't intervene until the end, and in truth the hotel's name, the venue for our rumble, was quite apt.

We were like a pair of fucking fairies dancing around each other, me trying to avoid Pete's club-fist until finally I got in close, grappled him and managed to wrestle him to the ground immediately deploying my fearsome 'scissor grip'.

With my legs locked tightly around his skinny mid-section, the 'scissors' seemed to be having a dramatic effect although he still managed to deliver a painful right hook to my skull which only seemed to increase the power in my legs.

Pete was squealing so loudly I thought there was a Black Mamba in the grass or something… turned out he was calling his brother over for an assist. When David ambled over, unlaced my legs to free his bro, I thought we'd have to continue the fight but happily Pete conceded.

I'd won the first, and only, proper street fight of my childhood. There's no doubt the fight could've gone badly for me if Pete had made facial contact with his bony fist, so the win didn't presage any more fighting. Fighting, I realised, wasn't for me. From then on I studiously avoided town bullies and was far happier 'playing the lover' than 'being the fighter'.

Unsurprisingly, the National Service call up system was inherently sexist, racist and disabled-ist. You wouldn't be called up if you were disabled, you definitely wouldn't get called up if you were black and there was no way to get a call up if you had a fanny, and that was probably a good thing because most of us were desperate for any sort of female attention.

If they did allow chicks in the army, all sorts of draconian rules and regulations would be needed to control access to sexual intercourse and the showers.

The lucky few would inevitably get discovered shagging somewhere on base, leading to demotion or expulsion.

Invariably, scuffles would ensue with brothers-in-arms reduced to scrapping over the affections of sisters-in-arms, or worse, get slapped down by a lesbian Lieutenant who fancied the same girl!

As it was, some guys went to the extent of feigning illness in a bid to get close to the 61 Mech doctor who, at times, seemed like the only female in the world!

The base literally was in the middle of nowhere so if we wanted to see girls we had to get to Tsumeb but these scheduled monthly trips were far too infrequent, and the female population far to sparse/conservative for the demands of our young loins.

Once again, the key to freedom was the celebrated sports pass. Unable to make the 61 rugby team, I found the perfect sport for me, *Tou-Trek* (Tug o' war!).

Joining the tug o'war team meant we scored a few more Tsumeb trips for local tournaments, which really meant additional opportunities to hang off the back of a truck desperately trying to see some frocks as we drove through the tiny town.

Team coach Major Danie Laas, second-in-command 61 Mech and an avid enthusiast of the sport, drilled us hard. Months into the 'season' our calloused hands had become almost as tough as the unshod feet of the Owambo goat herders we met on Comm Ops.

Tug o' war competitions were based on strict team-weight criteria meaning light-middleweights like me didn't get ripped off the rope by a team of 120kg heavyweight oxen. Eight guys to a team, the anchor and front man controlling the pull, we trained together for hours with some fitness work and forearm strengthening, but mainly we spent our time trying, in vain to rip a large tree from the ground using only a regulation-sized rope and seven spindly pairs of legs, plus the anchor.

Despite our best efforts, the tree remained rooted to the light brown earth and our 560kg team reached its competitive zenith during the annual SWA National *Tou-Trek* Championships held in the tiny city of Swakopmund on the south-west coast.

Getting to the championships at Swakopmund meant a 1,000 mile round trip on the hard, metal benches of a Samil 50 transport truck, but the opportunity to get an overnighter in a small city within sniffing distance of attractive 'wench' more than made up for the discomfort, however, in truth, as we contemplated our tug-o' war defeat on the 10-hour drive back to the border, there was no ignoring the fact I wasn't making much progress in the girl department either. Shyness, desperation, pressure, insecurity…whatever the reason it was becoming too much to bare.

Admittedly, in the last year of high school there been a few missed opportunities to 'break the seal', but back then it just didn't seem to matter quite as much, or perhaps it was fear, or maybe the 'no sex before marriage' mantra inculcated at a young age was still influencing me at a subconscious level.

Whatever the reason, during high school years, I was happy to draw the line before the big bang occurred. For example, one weekend, at two different parties, I kissed a handful of different girls. Some lucky ladies even got 'treated' to a little hip-grind action while others were the 'grateful recipients' of a wandering hand!

Mysteriously it seemed everyone was satisfied with this arrangement at the time, but in retrospect, I knew that had I been braver and pushed a little harder, doors may've opened and the virginity issue could've been put to bed once and for all.

There had been an on again/off again relationship with a girl who had the voice of an angel and at times I had been tempted to cross the line with her but wasn't sure she was 'the right one'. She and I happened to be 'off again' when 61 Mech was sent on the first of two scheduled passes in April '87.

The logistics of getting more than 400 guys back to South Africa meant the usual weekend pass arrangement in year one wasn't at all feasible. Instead the entire unit was scheduled to shut down for two 3-week passes during the year, temporary base security provided by soldiers shipped in from SA.

The boys were dispersing across South Africa and the logistics guys did a good job organising flights to get each of us to our nearest large airport, thereafter guys had to make their own arrangements.

Toughened by five months in searing subtropical heat, intensive mechanised bush warfare training, Comm Ops and the Labuschagne debacle, our crew cuts and slightly arrogant demeanour marked us out as Squaddies.

Being one of the Durban boys, I was flown (Troop transport class) to Louis Botha International Airport. Walking through the terminal I felt extremely proud to be representing 61 Mech while sporting the orange, white and blue armoured corps dress belt (same as the national flag). Faded Corporal stripes embellished with three orange *streepies* (small stripes) projected my *ou-man* status to all who cared.

The three small orange stripes were a semi-formal method adopted by mechanised infantry units to denote seniority between Platoon Corporals and crew commanders who were also full Corporals. The most senior, Platoon Sergeant (acting), wore three small stripes. The Armoured Corps crew commanders needed only to be Lance Corporals so didn't really have this hierarchy problem but had nonetheless adopted the practise at 61 Mech. The fact is we were required to adopt a Sergeant's role from time to time as we had no 'Sa'Majoor' and only occasionally a single PF Sergeant which meant that everyone shuffled up a bit to fill the gaps in Charlie's ranks so our working title was 'Troop Sergeant'.

On the 20-minute drive home from the airport with my folks, I shared some of the fantastic stories of things we'd experienced on the border before the discussion turned to planning the remaining twenty days.

It's fair to say there was some tension relating to my proposed schedule of events which mostly revolved around my mates, alcohol and [unspoken] The Unbroken Virginity!

To me, there was only one other important thing to do – to take and successfully complete, the civilian driving exam. Failure was not an option!

Failure would've precipitated a shower of abuse back on base because, like me, most guys held a number of army driving licences for a range of heavy vehicles and what's more, anyone who'd mastered the ancient Noddy Car should find a civilian car child's play!

Ironically, I took the test in a VW Beetle, not dissimilar in look or vintage to the Noddy, but when the examiner turned up I started to wonder if I'd brought the wrong size car. The guy was a freaking monster, he must've weighed at least 130kg, most of it fat. As he shoehorned himself into the creaking passenger seat the shock absorbers settled deeper than they had at any time previously in the car's 20 years on the road, I imagined little scabs of rust popping off the coil springs and gave the battered VW engine a bit more juice than usual on the hill start, and when it came to manoeuvring I had to lean forward a bit to peer past his beer-built bulk to see the side mirror. He truly was impressively well fed but still it was easier than driving Noddy!

The driving test seemed to be going well until he instructed me to detour down the steepest road I'd been on since *Debrug* driver training ground at Tempe.

The deviation from planned route was perplexing until he instructed me to pull the car to a stop in front of a small house under construction. Unsure how this could be part of the test I got out the car with him, and then he told me the house we'd stopped at was his! He'd just wanted to swing by and inspect the progress of the workers. In the middle of my driving test he'd got me to run an errand… only in South Africa.

I figured if he intended failing me he wouldn't have bothered to show me his house and sure enough, as the rickety Beetle pulled off back up that steepest hill, under perfect control, he announced I'd passed!

The following two weeks were awesome, almost. Something was still missing.... but in the final week Dad ambushed me! "Son, we've arranged a three-night family break, a caravan and camping holiday to Midmar Dam so we can have some time together as a family before you go back to the border."

Immediately I kicked back, "Midmar Dam!? I didn't swear, but wanted to. I never cussed in front of the folks. We [the crew] are going *jolling* (partying) Friday and Saturday night, I can't be going on some boring camping trip!"

"David!" Mom always called me David, "We've had precious little family time together, you're leaving again soon, it'll be great to spend some quality time together camping".

Mom understood the value of spending time with loved ones. I didn't, and countered, "Please don't use 'fun' and 'camping' in the same sentence... seriously Ma, all I do is camp. My life is like one continuous camping trip at the moment!"

But I had to admit to myself that it wasn't really the camping I was rebelling against – camping was normal for us guys on the border. Nor was it the time with my family that bothered me, rather it was my need to party and find a way to pop my damn cherry.

It really didn't matter what excuses I wheeled out, Mom had made up her mind and the rest us fell in line. She was RSM 'Snor' of camp Mannall.

Trinity, the cool 90mm gunslinger from up north, recently driver's licensed, Comm Ops veteran and leader-of-men had had his wings clipped and was pissed off at the prospect of heading back to the Operational area none the wiser with women and probably beginning to wonder if he could find the route back to the daughter of the Ovambo matriarch with those breasts that looked like a Cocker Spaniel's ears.

Monosyllabic grunts were the extent of my surly exchanges during the two-hour journey to the dam; long faced, I helped set up the caravan and tent while reflecting on a disappointingly unproductive three-week pass crowned by the ignominy of spending a few nights caravanning with the folks and my sisters.

However, as they often do, things took an unexpected twist on the second day when a couple of female university students, one of them very tasty looking, erected a small tent at the twelve-o'clock position less than 40 metres from our base of operations.

Girls that do camping! This was a fantastic coup; all I needed was some way to break the ice without my wingmen and bottled Dutch courage!

Photo 14 Midmar dam, the night Queen V called. (David Mannall)

I ambled by, noticed they were struggling without a mallet, offered ours and was in!

After a good few hours chatting we agreed to hang out later that evening.

That night I wolfed down the *braai* (BBQ) food, eager to get back to my new friends, hoping my 'smooth' credentials weren't too badly dented by the hideously uncool act of eating with my parents.

After helping to wash and pack away the dishes (or not), I excused myself, spruced myself up a bit, making it more likely, hopefully, that I'd impress my new friends.

The ladies, at 21 years old, were much older than I but, surprisingly, were still keen to hang out.

A bit like going into battle, the events of that momentous evening were a blur punctuated by climactic moments of clarity.

It appears, from the moments I can recall, that the pretty one and I took a walk, a long walk. There was flirting and by 22:00, there was kissing. Soon thereafter we were seeking privacy. I knew a lot about camouflage techniques so it was no problem finding a suitably secluded spot near the dam to cosy up.

For the sake of propriety I shan't recount everything I remember about this friendly-fire contact, but before I knew it, the sun was licking at the horizon and this woman, let's call her Queen V, had taken me to places I'd never known. It had been without doubt the most exciting night of my young life, even shooting High Explosiv e rounds at soft targets from the 90mm cannon didn't come close!

Finally, the cursed virginity business was unequivocally and most assuredly a thing of the past, which at some basic level also made my return to the Border more palatable, safe in the knowledge that I too was a complete man and could finally join in the telling of war stories all of my own – including the one where I spent over an hour in the ablution block with a girl, showering until the water tanks ran cold.

After sneaking back into my folks caravan to grab a fresh set of clothing, slightly ashamed by my 'misdeed', I returned to her tent for some post-coital sleeping-bag spooning.

Laying there, pressed up against her firm butt, it dawned on me how precious time was – we delayed no more and tried not to wake her girlfriend in the process.

For the rest of that day I was like the cat that licked the cream out the bowl and could hardly thank the folks enough for taking me on such great camping trip.

Sadly, that was the last time I saw Queen V but she'd given me a fantastical thing and, what's more ensured I'd never fly Virgin again.

9

Bittersweet

Two days after my first real girl encounter, just before our flight was due to depart Durban for Omuthiya, my on again/off again girlfriend approached me about rekindling our relationship. I jumped at the opportunity, even though we knew it would be another three months until the next pass, before we got together.

Returning to the border from that three-week pass seemed like just another farewell and 'see ya soon', but for some families this was their final goodbye. They didn't know it then but this final goodbye would soon become a bittersweet moment they would cling to for the rest of their days.

As we corkscrewed back into Grootfontein AFB, the chatter on board was remarkably different from our first landing back in November. The boys, unaware of our shared imminent fate, were far more confident this time when the tail-gate opened onto the barren, inhospitable terrain.

I wasted little time in taking the chance to tell my fellow Corporals about hitting the jackpot a few days earlier. Venter admonished me saying, "Listen Trinity, you don't want to marry such a good looking girl, because every other oke is going to try *neek* (shag) her!"

His logic was undeniably compelling, for about one second, it seemed a bit of a defeatist approach to me!

Our stories of youthful adventure and derring-do on that three-week pass were shared and retold as we resumed the by now familiar routines of border life while focussing on the countdown to our next big mission, the next, and final, three-week pass in August.

At some stage we organised some homemade entertainment in the mess hall for the lads of 61 which involved joke telling a few comedy skits and, dare I say it, some cross-dressing. For some reason that always elicits a good laugh.

Around this time my folks announced that they'd long wanted to see the raw beauty of SWA/Namibia for themselves so they planned a monumental 4,000 click road trip which included a visit to our base at Omuthiya, That night they came for dinner at the popular Omuthiya Steakhouse and Grill which Charlie Squad 'inherited' from previous generations of Armoured Corps men.

Photo 15 From R-L O'Connor, Frenchie, Taylor and myself, providing troops of 61 Mech with some cross-dressing entertainment. The Omuthiya mess hall was converted for the stage show. Duncan Taylor excellently played the part of husband to a dress-wearing wife (me) who was over-excited to be among so many fit young men. Duncan can be seen struggling to contain my 'provocative' exuberance. (David Mannall)

Photo 16 Charlie Squad boys work the grill at the Omuthiya Steakhouse. (Len M. Robberts)

Photo 17 Some of Charlie's boys enjoying a few beers listening to U2. Just a typical
night circa June 1987 at 61 Mech. (Photo Warren Adams). Standing from left to right:
Kurt (Stompie) Oelofse (gunner 33, injured 3 Oct), Warren Adams (gunner 33A),
Dave Chester (echelon driver), Gary Pearman-White (gunner 33C, injured during MiG
attack on 8 October), Glen Woodhouse (driver 33, injured on 3 October), Wayne Fraser
(echelon Sergeant and former crew commander of the ill fated 33C. Seated: Frikkie
(Bees) De Jäger (driver 33C, killed 8 October 1987), Raymond Clark (driver 33B)

The purpose-built steakhouse opened Friday nights with guys from the Squad
working either front-house or back in the small, hot kitchen. The most popular
dish was 'Monkey Gland' Rump steak.

Food on base was relatively good but the Omuthiya Steakhouse was a roaring
success. The change in diet and flavours was welcome, as was the opportunity for
infantrymen to treat an Armoured Corps lad like a waitress.

The restaurant also gave lads the chance to be a bit 'normal', to make some
choices for themselves for a change. For the Charlie boys it meant a fun change
of routine.

Then, in July, without warning a large contingent of SADF infantrymen arrived
from a South Africa and set up temporary camp near the perimeter fence of our
base. Like so often in the army, we didn't know what the deal was a good friend
from Pinetown, Cpl. Kevin Reid turned up with the contingent giving me a
chance to hang out and catch up on news from home.

I couldn't help laughing when Kevin told me the story of our good friend Pete
Baker, who in truth was a bit hapless when it came to soldiering a bit like the
comic strip character Sad Sack.

Patriotic Pete was the kind of guy who had South Africa in his veins and really wanted to do his bit for the country. So for his second year actually requested a posting to the Operational Area. As a consequence he found himself up on the Caprivi Strip, the narrowest part of the country on the map, an area on the far Eastern border, working as a truck driver.

A few weeks into his tour on the Caprivi his truck ran out of fuel just a few clicks from base. This was a significant no-no in the army and it meant 'Driver inspection' had not been completed before his departure that day. On the border such an oversight could have pretty drastic consequences.

Guys had paid the ultimate price on the border simply cos they ran out of fuel and then got tangled with a band of insurgents on the long walk back to base.

Pete abandoned the vehicle, intending to come back later with a can of diesel, but before he could cover his tracks the unit Commander came upon the abandoned vehicle and, in a fit of Commandanting, immediately revoked Pete's licenses and demoted him to co-driver, of a water bunker. Then, just a week or two later, some miscommunication between Pete and the water-bunker's driver resulted in him getting his leg crushed at the ankle, by a friggin water pipe!

Although Pete was gutted to be removed from the border, the upside was that he'd get to spend months in rehab on 'light duties' back in SA which meant the likelihood of him sustaining further injury during National Service was significantly reduced. It also left him with significant scars to show everyone he met (and I mean EVERYONE), evidence of his contribution to making our country safe from the Rooi Gevaar (Red Danger as the Communist threat over the border came to be known).

I also learned from Kevin's CO that his regiment made this annual pilgrimage for a two-week taste of border action, and this year they'd been instructed to visit Omuthiya, which seemed plausible enough to me at the time, but it wasn't long before we discovered the real reason for their encampment on 61 Mech's doorstep.

A couple days after those Infantry boys turned up on our doorstep, the full Battalion was ordered to 'fall-in' on parade for an important announcement. There was a sense that something unusual was going on and this was confirmed the moment Commandant Smit stepped up to address his battle group: "It has become clear to the South African Government that the FAPLA are preparing for a major offensive…"

What he didn't tell us was that FAPLA were already doing a lot more than fucking preparing an offensive. By July, four Brigades and two tactical groups were already on the move. Six more Brigades were in final stages of battle readiness and preparing to move with a further two Brigades held in reserve! In manpower terms, the force despatched to route UNITA totalled at least 25,000 soldiers of mixed ability with some of the best trained and most heavily equipped in the vanguard.

As it turned out, and despite my naïve predictions when we first landed at *Grootfontein*, the Angolan Government had done anything but capitulate after their '85 setback. With the help of Fidel Castro and a superpower in supernova, FAPLA quickly acquired unprecedented stockpiles of ultra modern and some of 'last season's' Soviet hardware.

Cuban and Russian specialists provided intensive training for around 60,000 Angolan combat troops and significantly augmented the Angolan Air Force and their intelligence gathering capabilities.

Russian Generals assumed responsibility for command and control. Without a shadow of doubt this was a Communist led and Communist sponsored conflict.

This was the *Rooi Gevaar* (Red Danger) we'd been warned about, and I'd thought that was just propaganda.

Smit continued, "The Battalion will immediately prepare for full combat readiness. We move out at 02:00 tomorrow travelling 350km to our border crossing near Rundu where we will await further orders."

Photo 18
The 61 Mech column
en route Bittersoet. (Len
M. Robberts)

Photo 19 Desert convoy. View over the spare tyre on Ratel roof. (Barry Taylor)

I felt the blood drain from my face as the implications of those few words sunk in, but he wasn't finished, "This means your three-week pass has been cancelled, please write a letter home to your family which the Commanding Officers will hold until you return."

My mind was racing – fear displaced by the massive disappointment from the sudden forfeit of a few weeks of freedom. "Fucking hell no, not the three-week pass! What the fuck? That's surely not legal," the guys muttered as they gawped at each other in disbelief. We were dismissed from the parade ground with no time to properly digest the news before the Captain and Quartermaster (the only two career staff in Charlie Squad at that time) began issuing orders to the JL's which we in turn relayed to our troops.

We knew what we needed to do but we'd never done it on this scale or at such short notice. *Balsaks* (kitbags) were stuffed with meagre belongings, Troop transport trucks loaded with tons of ammunition, we pretty much emptied everything from the armoury. We loaded a truck full of spare tyres and another with food rations. Water and fuel bunkers were replenished, using safe hose-handling techniques. A few of us tapped our chef friends up for some priceless wet rations.

Before our departure, gathered near the Squadron tents to evaluate the dire situation.

Photo 20 Camping in the relatively civilised Rundu-Bittersoet area awaiting the "Go" command. (Len M. Robberts)

Photo 21 Permanent border base like Eenhana and Rundu. (Barry Taylor)

Photo 22 61 Mech – Charlie Squad (3- series) vehicles can be seen among the massed mechanised force preparing for final inspection parade while awaiting final orders. (Len M. Robberts)

Some said it wasn't legal to remove the three-week pass, countered by others saying, "Anything is legal if the government says it is, right?"

To a man we were pissed-off at the loss of freedom but there was an electric sense of anticipation about the lads. After eight long months on the border, it now seemed we might get a sniff of action.

Despite the grumbling, we had no alternative. The die, it seemed, had been cast so we wrote our 'last' letters home, closed up the side flaps on our tents and mounted up.

At 02:00, the first of 150 fully laden vehicles, carrying or crewed by a little over 400 young men, began their mass exodus from 61 Mech.

Years later, Kevin Reid recounted their astonishment when his contingent woke the following morning to learn that our entire unit had decamped. The arrival of Kevin's unit at Omuthiya had been no coincidence, their mission: securing the base in our absence.

As the sun rose over the vanguard of our convoy, it seemed as if we were untouchable, an integral part of an impressive rubber and steel armoured snake stretching almost as far as the eye could see.

Our lumbering behemoths totally dominated the deserted narrow tarmac life-line that served remote border outposts along the north-eastern SWA/Angola border. All these places I'd never paid much attention to before, Rundu, Oshakati, Ondangwa, Ruacana, Sectors 'One Zero' and 'Two Zero', places of strategic military importance in a war that was increasingly becoming our problem.

The usual on-air banter between crew commanders was replaced with debate about the likelihood of breaking international treaties by crossing into Angola when we reached *Bittersoet* (Bittersweet), the insertion point. The other big talking point was the contentious issue of Ratel 90's leading an offensive against Russian MBT's. Once again we tended to agree that without the Olifant MBT in-theatre, there was no way the 90mm would be expected to go into Tank battles so we came to the conclusion that the FAPLA threat probably wasn't all that significant.

Arriving at Rundu was something of an eye-opener. The remote border outpost was a remarkable place, like a small town but under sandbags where civilians lived alongside career military officers in residential areas while National Servicemen maintained base security and provided outreach work into the local area – mostly in response to SWAPO insurgent activities.

Bunkers reinforced with sandbags, watchtowers on high alert, this was the sort of place where sleeping on guard duty was a seriously unhealthy proposition.

This was the nearest we'd been to the line in the sand that demarcated Angola's actual border and this particular far-flung outpost had been the subject of more than its fair share of terrorist activity over the years.

61 Mech set up temporary camp on the town's dusty rugby field where within days our initial excitement gave way to boredom as we waited for the unwelcome order to enter Angola.

After a week we decided that the government had changed its mind and was no longer prepared to risk international condemnation by inserting such a high-profile unit into Angola.

Two days later our 'expert' predictions appeared to be borne out when we received orders to return at best speed to Omuthiya. It seemed we were standing down.

The relief among the Squadron was palpable; smoke from celebratory Chesterfields clogged the air, all of us were pretty chuffed at our last minute reprieve.

Unknown to us, not all boys in the Battalion had been given the same order.

Sierra Battery (Artillery), commanded by Major Theo Wilken, was ordered to depart last and instead of heading home, headed north, into Angola, but not

Photo 23 Tony Joubert messing about with 81mm HE bomb in Ratel smoke launcher. (Anthony de Robillard)

Photo 24 Golf Battery's awesome G5 cannons and trucks ready for departure into Angola – very conspicuous even before they began belching 155mm projectiles at marathon distances. (Len M. Robberts)

with their conspicuous long-range G5 155mm towed Howitzers, rather with the much smaller 120mm M5 mortars to minimise SADF profile in Angola (for diplomatic reasons). Perhaps, quite legitimately, SADF military planners thought they might be able to help UNITA stop the FAPLA advance with some mobile artillery action.

Protected by our cousins from 32 Battalion, Sierra Battery began a long slow trek towards an area near a river called Lomba, about 350 clicks NNW of *Bittersoet*, the crossing-over point where the Engineer Corps had built a temporary bridge.

Charlie Squad was given only need-to-know intel (intelligence), and at this stage we didn't need to know that the big cheese had been aware for some months of reports relating to a "surge of military activity" near the country's capital Luanda, and of the "massive mobilisation" of enemy forces and, more recently, that the light Infantry UNITA operatives were being swamped by a tsunami of heavily armoured FAPLA Brigades moving southward.

At about the same time 61 Mech's 'nearly war veterans' departed *Bittersoet* and headed for Omuthiya in celebratory mood. We thought we'd been let off the hook, believing our war was over, before it had even begun.

Speculation mounted about the likely reinstatement of that imminent and treasured three-week pass which had been so unceremoniously ripped from our grasp ten days earlier.

Unsurprisingly the 350 click journey back to base was a good opportunity for a little light relief and tomfoolery. The snaking convoy became quite stretched out on the return leg so we interpreted the order to 'make best speed back to Omuthiya' quite literally. I jumped into the driver's cabin to see what the beast was capable of on the open road, eventually topping out just shy of 130km/h in a breathtakingly foolish display of 'heroics'. The Ratel stands tall and has a relatively high centre of gravity due to the weight of the turret – the slightest over-correction on the steering wheel at that speed would have had catastrophic consequences.

The celebratory mood dissipated quickly on our arrival to Omuthiya when the full truth of 61's potential involvement in the war was finally made clear to us. The day after we arrived back from Bittersoet, we were marched just north of the base, lined up – as if facing a firing Squad – then given five seconds to take cover in the shallow trench behind us. Seconds later three appointed officers opened fire at us with automatic weapons.

It seemed quite a surreal scenario, but as we were peppered with dust and a little shrapnel pinging off the adjacent trench wall, there was absolutely no doubt that they were firing directly at the trench and not above our heads.

When it ended, less than a minute later, we were surprised to find there'd only been a small number of very minor shrapnel wounds among the Squad and one infantry guy took a bullet in the arse. We assumed this was a warm-up for the fireworks to come.

By now, whispers were rife about Sierra Battery's mysterious vanishing act; some speculated that they had indeed crossed the border into Angola.

Once again we were called onto parade where RSM brought us to attention before handing over to a serious-looking Commandant Smit who announced, "There will be no demobilisation. Sierra Battery entered Angola today and the full weight of 61 Battle Group will be joining them within two weeks. Until then we will undertake full-scale Battalion training ops in preparation for expected contact with enemy forces."

Fuck it! Right there, that was the death knell of our three-week pass but that loss was nothing in comparison to what lay ahead, we now knew absolutely that we were heading into a war zone.

During the next ten days we lived in the bush off-base, as we'd done many times before, participating in the largest, most complex battle drills we'd experienced to date. The Lohatla (Army Battle School) trip I missed in '86 would've probably been on a similar scale, but unlike Lohatla there were no limits on munitions use here.

The "gloves came off", artillery fire was brought in at close quarters and infantry boys walked their skinny asses off. More than ever, coordinated map work was essential to ensure every unit worked in concert, especially during 'fire and move' exercises with the big guns dropping their load nearby.

There was a ripple of excitement when we learned of the inclusion of the extremely accurate G6 cannon as stand-in replacement for Sierra Battery. The futuristic looking G6 was a fully integrated mobile 155mm howitzer developed by SA engineers at ARMSCOR – fresh off the test ground with flying colours, they were the stars of the show at Omuthiya but were as yet unproven in the unrelentingly harsh Angolan conditions.

These 40-tonne artillery giants, with their unprecedented speed, range and accuracy, boasted a two-minute launch window from the moment it arrived on location to firing their first shot. In artillery terms this was light speed, so to me, with these futuristic beasts on watch it seemed we'd have a massive advantage over an enemy that couldn't get anywhere near us. And that felt good.

The weapon boasted impressive features including:

- 40km effective range of fire
- Autoloader, which dramatically improved the rate of fire, and most notably
- Transition from moving to stop-and-fire in under two minutes

We detected the mounting pressure on senior officers; their battle orders crackled through the headset in terse clipped commands.

Charlie Squad gunners were having the best of times. A new collection of car wrecks and tractor tyre emplacements had been installed to replicate enemy positions or stationery targets, all of them placed in clearings and quite visible from a distance.

One afternoon we were in the thick of 'contact' when my Troop of four vehicles (Troop 2) was ordered to break off and take up new positions on a hillock overlooking the 'enemy' installations with the aim of opening a new front.

We broke ranks, retreated a short distance from the fray, then made our way over the back of the hillock. From our cover positions within the vegetation we had a perfect line of sight to the targets; we weren't taking any incoming fire having snuck up on the enemy's flank. Then we unleashed a barrage of concentrated 90mm fire unlike anything we had practised before. Unconcerned by the normal tactic of fire-and-move, we maintained position for almost an hour and completely emptied the remaining 60 rounds of the total 71 bomb payload (29 in turret, 42 located in retro-fitted bomb racks in vehicle). Herb Zeelie, my gunner, was having a blast, merrily overkilling the shit out of targets.

At that rate of fire, turret ordinance ran low quickly so I agreed to jump down off the vehicle and pass bombs into the turret from the bomb racks inside the left-hand side door. The gunner and I replenished our turret while driver David Corey did his best to clear 7.62mm and 90mm spent shell casings that had fallen to the floor of the turret during rapid fire.

Within four minutes we were fully cleared and reloaded, ready to return to the fray with the pneumatic side door of the vehicle hissing shut.

Corey moved our vehicle to a new position on the line. I called up the next target and from then on he and I simply tried to fire as many rounds as we could before ceasefire was ordered.

Although unsanctioned, our rapid load-and-fire drill provided invaluable training. Prior to this we'd never fired more than 30 or 40 bombs in a single mock battle or day at the shooting range. We learned how important it was to ensure the correct combinations of payload to ensure we weren't left with a turret-load of *Skroot* (anti-personnel buckshot) or HE (High Explosive) when what was required on the target area might be HEAT (High Explosive Anti-Tank) ammo. We also discovered repeated 90mm recoil blasts left us feeling like we'd been slapped repeatedly with a wet towel on our sunburned faces. But ironically, the most important lesson we learned was to not waste munitions because we exhausted our supply before ceasefire was called. Our last two bombs were *Skroot* and finally we ended up unable to defend ourselves with anything more than our two 1948 model 7.62mm Brownings.

Nonetheless we were quite chuffed with our high-speed antics, the only way to have exceeded the 71 bomb payload would've been to rearm the Ratel during a day's combat and that had never been necessary. Restock was always scheduled to occur at the end of each day's training action.

Gunner Herb Zeelie claimed something of a record for himself that day because no one we knew of in the Squad had ever fired more than the full 90mm Ratel payload in a single day.

Other than honing our gunnery skills there was a more visible side effect to the high-speed gunnery that afternoon. The extreme heat generated by 71 rounds altered the molecular structure of the army-issue brown paint on the three-metre-long barrel changing it to light brownish/pink.

The vehicle was my responsibility, Lt Bremer had been made to pay 10% of the costs to repair his rolled Ratel during hand-brake turn training on the Shona so I fervently hoped the barrel would return to brown when it cooled down a few hours later, but that never happened. Screwing around on the shooting range was obviously discouraged, so when it came time to rearm the vehicles later that evening, it had to be done somewhat surreptitiously to avoid alerting the Captain we used up our entire payload. It would've been hard to explain to him how we legitimately fired so many rounds during a single afternoon's contact. Harder still would be explaining away the heat-bleached pink paintwork. None of us had seen this happen to any other weapon and it was a little disconcerting.

A crew commander was ultimately responsible for whatever happened on, or to, his vehicle but, as it turned out, the big cheese had far fatter fish to fry than to concern himself with our pink-barrelled excesses, or perhaps they knew this experience would soon pay lifesaving dividends after the fun of mock battles had long been forgotten.

10

Operation *Moduler* (Modular)

Meals Ready to Eat (MRE), or Ration Packs – 'rat-packs' as they're known colloquially – are one of the most successful military innovations, ever.

The rat-pack provides the human body with 24hrs of nutritional requirements neatly packaged in a small plastic-wrapped cardboard box not much bigger or heavier than a thick, hardcover book. Just add water.

The adage that 'an army marches on its stomach' is accurate and as a general rule of thumb, the quality of an army's Rat-pack provides good intelligence for how highly the army, and by extension the nation, regards its soldiers.

Access to sufficient nourishment is at times more important than the quality and suitability of equipment, just two or three days without food and most soldiers would be incapable of functioning effectively. The compact Rat-pack allows soldiers to go well beyond supply lines for days or even weeks at a time without need of resupply.

A successful army is well trained, well equipped, well fed, well replenished, and sometimes, very damn lucky.

We'd been living on rat-packs continuously since departing for *Bittersoet* a few weeks earlier, and over the course of the year had become quite accustomed to the limited diet they offered.

From the rear of logistics vehicle 39 Foxtrot, Charlie Squad's Quartermaster Sergeant Olaf Schidlowski (ex 202 Battalion) issued out ten-pack boxes to Troop Sergeants. We, in turn, issued the individual rats to each of the 12 Troop members, including the Looty.

Each ten-pack box contained two of the five different 'meals' on the menu. Identified 1 to 5, each of the rat-pack boxes contained contents that came as standard across the full range like: powdered tea (which tasted as bad as it sounds), coffee, sugar and three *esbit* (fire tablets). These tablets, as the name suggests, could be used to start a fire but were mostly applied directly under a 'fire bucket' of water, or used to heat the contents of one or more of the three small food tins which always included a meat/pickled fish and vegetable option plus a mystery guest tin. Energy bars, fruit bars, biscuits and cheese were ideal long-life products and perfect for inclusion in the cardboard boxes.

Guys learned which number of box or items they preferred so there was always a little trading and exchange activity at the weekly resupply.

Battle preparations ended 26 August. The following day we drove once more to Bittersoet, this time in no doubt whatsoever that we were headed into Angola, into the unknown. My usual jovial, light-hearted banter was rapidly being replaced by deepening concern and a growing sense of dread.

Four days later, on 1 September 1987, we crossed the border into Angola at around 4am. Operation Modular was underway.

Officially, we became an invading army the moment our tyres breeched Angolan soil although we were still relatively safe inside Allied (UNITA) controlled territory.

Just hours after crossing the border we got our first views of the cost of war when our convoy moved past a UNITA rehabilitation camp. Emaciated, limbless or otherwise wounded men warmed themselves in small groups huddled around morning fires. I could scarcely imagine a group of sorrier-looking souls. It was a shocking sight, like an unexpected and frightening special effect on a House-of-Horrors fairground ride – except that in this case there were no mechanisms

Photo 25 61 Mech heading northwards to the frontline. (Len M. Robberts)

to power the macabre figures. This was the real thing, a sinister scene that was reminiscent of a 1940's newsreel showing a squalid Second World War prisoner camp. Everywhere we looked there were scores of injured young black men, the damaged detritus of Angola's long and bloody Civil War.

This was the closest we'd been to actual UNITA cadre and it only took this brief encounter with their Third World set-up to see why they needed our help. They clearly had very limited resources at their disposal and appeared the archetypal underdog upon whom terrible hardship had been wrought. And the number of wounded at this camp was startling, leaving no doubt in our minds that the conflict we were joining involved close contact with a very real, and exceedingly dangerous, enemy.

As those of the broken UNITA boys that could stood up, stood proud and tall and reverently saluted us as we trundled through their guerrilla outpost, I was suffused by an electric crackle of deep pride and a healthy dose of awe and admiration for these men. I stood taller than ever on the crew commander's seat and returned their sincere and respectful greeting. This was, for me, the moment that their struggle became our struggle, brothers-in-arms against a common enemy until the bitter end, or until my completion of National Service in three and a half months time.

In the absence of successful diplomacy, UNITA's two-decades-long struggle to defend their peoples' blood-soaked territory seemed absolutely justified, and in that moment I exonerated myself of any guilt for preparing to prosecute war in a foreign country – but this was no grand heroic choice, the train was thundering down the tracks, there was no getting off now so I'll interrupt my account to offer a little insight and background on the conflict as seen from a Western perspective. No doubt Cubans, Russians and others, for example SWAPO and the ANC, harbour a differing view.

My teenage view at that time went something like this…South African politics was pretty fucked up by the time the '80's rolled round. The apartheid policy of excluding people based on skin colour was wrong, plain and simple. Increasingly, Communist-leaning liberal opposition pushed for rapid democratisation buoyed by the reasonably held view by most neutral parties that colour subjugation was abhorrent and apartheid should be repealed. SA had become a pariah internationally.

As a teenager the boycotts on sport and music were the ones most noticeable to me. Like most people, I don't like to think of myself as racist but I was acutely aware that the black population outnumbered the white by about 6-to-1 so a truly democratic solution at that time would simply have handed power to a Communist-backed black party which, I feared, would turn SA into an economic basket-case unable to support the masses. Such a government might also have had a massive axe to grind with us white folks as happened in other former African colonial outposts, including the one 61 Mech had just violated. It's true that black Africans did not have a great track record when it came to the ruling of modern nation states which often encompassed different tribal groups within borders delineated in many instances by pre-Victorian, culturally ignorant Westerners. Humans are tribal by nature and few places on earth are as culturally defined by tribalism as is Africa. And then there was the contemporary issue of Zimbabwe and that racist fool Mugabe whose installation as President greatly assuaged guilt-ridden liberal Europeans who fell mysteriously silent when Mugabe set about slaughtering white farmers and political opponents while simultaneously reversing the country's fiscal well-being. In Zimbabwe, the price of bread went up daily and you literally needed a shopping trolley full of cash to exchange for a shopping trolley of groceries. It was the poorest (read black) people who suffered most, that is unless they belonged to Mugabe's inner-circle or political party. I had little expectation that the lot of the tribal black South African would be much different if we ever had a full 'democracy'.

My naïve hope back then was for an 'integrationist agenda' by a white-governed state that would see black Africans fully empowered to work shoulder to shoulder with white Africans, in just the same way we were about to fight for the common good alongside our black African brothers – we were empowering them, not robbing them of anything. In the fullness of time, when parity was achieved then we might have an electorate that made democratic choices based on leadership rather than skin colour or tribal gene pool.

South Africa's support for UNITA divided international opinion and prompted the United Nations to pass a loosely worded resolution preventing the SA Government from 'committing acts of aggression'. The irony of this resolution was that in the hurly-burly bullshit masquerading as international diplomacy, it seemed OK for Fidel and the Soviets –because they couldn't control 'em anyway – to funnel billions of dollars of military hardware into Northern Angola to fuck with the Southern Angolans, but it was not OK for SA to maintain her border's integrity.

It almost seemed as if USA was willing to accept that the USSR had stockpiled a massive arsenal in Southern Africa. Was this some part of a much grander plan in the Cold War? It didn't make a lot of sense to me but without insight into myriad hidden geopolitical agendas – mostly relating to self-interest, oil, minerals and greed – it was difficult to be certain about the Cold War link. Anyway, this was my take on the status-quo:

1. On the surface, the Angolan conflict was in essence a black-on-black conflict and therefore raised no 'racist' overtones because, in a world full of nuance and contradiction where 'tribal' warfare is not seen as 'racism' in quite the same way as white-on-black 'racism', there was apparently no real moral dilemma for the liberals to contend with. The fact that Portugal had rapidly exited its former colony leaving in its wake a tinder-dry powder keg and political power vacuum – a perfect storm for sparking conflict – had nothing at all to do with South Africa's apartheid policies but was attributable to the gradual decline of influence from Europe after World War Two coupled with a dawning realisation that 18th and 19th Century style colonisation and exploitation belonged to a previous era. In the case of Portugal, the Carnation Revolution in '72 was the nail in the coffin for the 'Overseas Province of Angola'. They evacuated the country with the speed of a cheating husband running out the back door, his trousers somewhere around his knees. Unfortunately, African forces rapidly shifted their attention from fighting their recently departed Colonial overlords to fighting among themselves in the desperate scramble for ultimate power. The boys with the biggest guns (MPLA) snatched that power, frustrating and sidelining Savimbi and his followers, UNITA.

2. Interestingly, the fracas in Angola apparently provided a helpful blueprint for Mr. Mugabe whose unique style of democracy was ushered in when Ian Smith was ousted from Rhodesia. My childhood was peppered with dreadful accounts from Zimbabweans who had escaped the ever-worsening security situation and the rapidly falling standards of living in their country.

   Again, it was apparently more palatable to European/American policy makers to turn their backs on the white folks – mostly installed by the western expansionist agenda of the 18th and 19th Century – and allow an oxygen-thieving tyrannical black man to visit death and destruction on his populace, rather than seeking a less politically correct, but more inclusive, power-sharing deal that would ensured the enrichment of all the people of South Africa equally.

   Some Europeans, seemingly ashamed of their forefathers' misdeeds, crusaded to erase the 'blemish' of their colonial past from their collective conscience which meant, perversely, installing the lesser of two evils – a dictatorial self-interested xenophobic black president who violently subjugated black opposition while his supporters inherited valuable farmland by killing or intimidating white farmers within a legal framework that reflected Mugabe's own twisted dogma. In the main, those farms were run into the ground by the hapless cadre who cared less about the intricacies of farming and more about taking back what they believed to be rightfully theirs.

I never bought into all that shite; to me, skin colour was irrelevant. It was the individual personality and qualities of the person under the skin that matters most. This idea that one tribe could be better than another (albeit colour, creed, religious etc.) was the kind of separationist thinking that caused most wars in human history. Nevertheless, I was aware that large swathes of Africa's inhabitants still lived in the dark ages, geographically close to, but light years away from the First World cities and infrastructure developed by European settlers during the previous two centuries. Sure, some people were exploited along the way, but then I don't know of a time in history when one group of powerful people hasn't exploited another, less powerful group to advance its aims. I suppose it helps assuage the sensitivities of some liberals if the oppressed and oppressor look the same on the outside at least.

3. In Angola, a significant swathe of its citizenry didn't buy into the communist-backed 'democracy' being forced upon them and during the '70's and 80's the price of this opposition brought them squarely into the cross-hairs of Castro's Cuba and the number two world Superpower, Gorbachev's USSR. The Communists had big plans for Southern Africa. Some said that South Africa itself was the USSR's ultimate prize which, if true, would give them control of most of Southern Africa, secure valuable trade routes and give them domination of almost 90% of world gold production, when combined with their own output – but this, as they say, is speculation.

What is certain in July 1987, when that three-week pass was summarily snatched from the boys of 61 Mech, more than a billion US dollars – at a time when a billion dollars was a remarkable large sum of cash – Cold War military hardware was en-route Jamba to overwhelm and destroy their charity-shop-equipped opposition, UNITA.

These vast stockpiles of military hardware, partly funded by Cuba in its unwavering support of the ruling MPLA party (FAPLA), were last matched in quantity when Rommel and Monty slugged it out in North Africa.

The upshot of Castro's desire to be a player on the world stage was the economic crippling of Cuba; they could no longer afford to bankroll the

Angola project alone and called for the assistance of the USSR which for this and other geopolitical considerations, became more deeply embroiled in the quagmire. They must've had their eyes on some big pay-off at the end so to protect her investment in military hardware, the USSR also supplied a number high-ranking generals and specialists to oversee tactical planning, training and intelligence gathering while thousands of FAPLA personnel were secretly shipped back to Mother Russia for more in-depth training.

By the mid-eighties, the USSR had committed such vast quantities of cash and kudos on the Angolan project that she absolutely needed the right result to ensure a decent return on her investment which doubtless included the continued advancement of Soviet Russia's communist ideals. Although in 1987, the USSR itself was barely holding together. Perhaps the right result in southern Africa – from a Soviet standpoint – could have reversed her fortunes. This was a heady gamble because failure in Southern Africa could conceivably have been one of the final nails in the coffin of Communism's rapidly imploding Union.

In addition to all the Russian big cheese and hardware in theatre, over a hundred thousand Cuban troops had been shipped to Angola over the years – often unwillingly – ostensibly to win the civil war against UNITA but in reality , it seems, to further the aims of a communist agenda.

4. UNITA and its charismatic leader Jonas Savimbi, on the other hand, relied only on a handful of clandestine CIA operatives who, with the tacit but unacknowledged support of the American government, supplied a few crates of ultra-modern Stinger anti-aircraft missiles. Reagan was on-board with Savimbi but a belligerent US Congress stymied his efforts to roll back Communism in Africa thus 'the most powerful man on earth' relied mainly on a miniscule 'black-ops' budget of a measly few million dollars. CIA Operatives also provided training and intelligence support to UNITA rebels but the cold, hard truth was that White House intransigence and lack of overt support to UNITA was far short of President Reagan's commitment to the struggle against communism.

South Africa had very different strategic objectives. As I understood things, she preferred to help maintain her new ally UNITA as landlord of Southern Angola because it meant that maintaining SWA's border integrity was easier *and* she was in no mood to hand over her WW1 conquest to SWAPO, a communist-backed group of 'terrorists'. South West Africa/Namibia had been liberated by the League of Nations and handed to SA for safe-keeping, until a suitable (capitalist-leaning) political party could be trusted to assume control. The ensuing power struggles became entwined over the years ultimately muddying the diplomatic waters to the advantage of the liberal left.

It was hard to imagine anyone wilfully welcoming Communism into the neighbourhood but certain groups successfully jumped onto the anti-racist bandwagon to cover their own motives of self-enrichment.

Over the preceding decade-and-a-half thousands of soldiers, mostly Angolan and Cuban, paid the ultimate price during this sorry chapter in Angola's tumultuous history.

The only other supporters of UNITA were the disenfranchised Angolans who had been former supporters of the vanquished third party on the scene, the FNLA, who'd drowned in the wake of the power struggle that erupted when the Portuguese jumped ship. Soon thereafter FNLA withdrew from the three-way gang-bang unable to recover their combat losses without meaningful international support. Many remaining FNLA fighters fled south, either joining UNITA or happily accepting the opportunity of paid employment and training within the ranks of the SADF like those who joined 31 and 32 Battalion. Forged in the white-heat of a battle for their stolen homeland, these fighters flourished under SADF command and training protocols to become an integral part of what was probably the most feared strike force in the SADF arsenal.

South Africa was involved in the squabble right from the start, preferring to see a sympathetic pro-western Jonas Savimbi installed in Luanda rather than the pro-communist incumbent government led initially by Antonio Neto and then by Jose Dos Santos in '79 [interestingly, still in power 35 years later; and his daughter is the wealthiest woman in Africa, a multi-billionaire – yet another shining example of African democracy.]

Now, perhaps the USSR was grasping at straws in an effort to save their union. Maybe Fidel was in too deep and needed something to 'sell' to the people of Cuba to justify their sacrifice, or maybe he really did see himself as the liberator of the black peoples – at least those of them who shared his Communist ideology. Whatever their motivation, after the setback of '85 the Communists returned to the drawing board and for two years developed their forces so that by July 1987 they had at least 12 well-trained, well-equipped operational Brigades.

Russian Generals and Specialists devised extensive battle plans involving two waves of attack, each of four Brigades. The vanguard, consisting two tactical groups – four hardened mechanised Brigades (about 10,000 men) – were tasked with establishing a buffer zone around the strategic Lomba River crossing, about 60 clicks east of the river's source. This was probably to prevent a repeat of their '85 failure which had, in part, been the consequence of the FAPLA's inability to secure a bridgehead on the Lomba because SADF engineers and bomb-droppers had managed to destroy key bridges which in turn prevented FAPLA's armoured forces from dominating the action.

The terrain and climate of the area had always played a significant part in battle strategy and was often as influential in the outcome of a battle as the combatants themselves. In the local topography, three rivers were strategically important during Operation Modular; the large, but lazy, west to east flowing Lomba with her wide marshy banks, and two tributaries flowing down from the north, the Cuzizi which joined the Lomba close to its source, and the Cunzumbia some 10 clicks farther downstream.

The advancing force moved south-east some 900km from Luanda, mostly unfettered, to a town called Cuito Cuanavale about 400 clicks from the border and then onward toward Mavinga. Then, as UNITA began small-scale hit-and-run operations against their enemy, FAPLA commanders deployed their 47th and 59th Brigades along the western banks of the 30km long Cuzizi a smaller with Tactical Group (TG1), a reconnaissance and pathfinder group of Battalion strength (like 61 Mech), in the vanguard. Simultaneously, the 21st and 16th Brigades, led by Tactical Group 2(TG2), made their way along the Eastern banks of the 50km Cunzumbia.

47th Brigade and TG1's orders were to crest the source of the Lomba to the west, then head east along the Southern bank until close enough to provide lateral support to 21st and 59th Brigades who were tasked with establishing safe crossing, before joining them in the push toward Mavinga and then onwards to UNITA's unofficial capital, Jamba in the south eastern corner of the country.

16th Brigade were instructed to maintain a position 25-30 clicks NE of the crossing, offering only artillery support until the bulk of the primary strike force had cleared the choke point at which time they would join the fray.

Years of conflict and under-investment meant few suitable river-crossings remained undamaged. Many surviving bridges were handmade log and rope structures suitable for horses and carts, or perhaps small trucks used by locals, but certainly not for the full weight of a mechanised Brigade.

SADF engineers successfully destroyed many usable bridges along the Lomba but were thwarted on their final mission, losing the race against time to reach the last remaining crossing before the FAPLA's 21st Brigade. Critically, the surviving bridge was only wide enough for vehicles to cross in single file severely restricting the flow of materiel. However, this sturdy link between the north and south banks was so narrow that our artillery gunners were unable to shut it down despite weeks of almost continual shelling. This little bridge became the epicentre for most of Operation Modular.

As September approached, and despite increasing UNITA resistance, the 21st Brigade and TG2 made their move to secure the area on the south side of the bridge. At the same time, 32 Battalion, which had been called to action first, were beginning to make contact with enemy pathfinder units as Sierra Battery completed their trek into theatre and join Quebec Battery to form what would eventually become 20 Brigade made up of 32 Battalion, 61 Battalion and two light Infantry Platoons from 101 Battalion.

Sierra Battery were now only days away from setting up fire-control with Recce OP's and introducing their 120mm mortars to 21st Brigade massing just north of the river.

Despite this, FAPLA continued to enjoy a modicum of success, initially securing the bridge with light Infantry, then pushing forward until TG2 and a Squadron of T55 tanks established a decent toehold on the south bank.

If war were a game of chess, FAPLA had gained a distinct advantage by getting a decent-sized force onto our side of the board. In terms of men and materiel, TG2 and the one Squad of T55s together represented a larger force than 61 Mech.

As 61 Mech were crossing the border at *Bittersoet* into Angola, four more FAPLA Brigades (another 100,000 men) were moving into position north of Cuito Cuanavale. These were designated to form the second wave of attack once the frontline had moved through the Lomba river area and on towards Mavinga. The second wave forces came to a halt near Cuito pending the expected imminent success of the first wave at Lomba, some 100km to the south.

In previous years, carefully crafted combat plans had come up short, in part because of the subtropical rainfall season. Having learned the lessons from this experience, Russian commanders developed a strategy that involved sending a number of hardened Brigades with enough force to overpower UNITA's defence, punch holes through the SADF lines and then quickly introduce a fresh second wave to move through Mavinga and onwards to Jamba, all before rain stopped play in December.

On 1 September '87, as we were getting our first taste of UNITA hardship, the enemy's first wave was still on schedule.

During briefings it was made abundantly clear to us that if a sizeable contingent of enemy forces were to dominate, and then spread out from the Lomba River crossing, it would be extremely difficult for our much smaller force to contain and defend the territory. It was, we were told: "Imperative they are not allowed to get across the Lomba."

Our orders were: "Make best speed to Lomba River region, engage and stop the enemy."

Jelly-bowel time!

The enemy had quite a head start on the greenhorn warriors of 61 Mech, by now the 16th, 21st, 59th, and 47th Brigades had been on the move for almost a month and already within striking distance of the Lomba. 66th Brigade was also lurking with ominous intent in the near background, adding another 2,000 soldiers to the equation.

We were still 300 clicks to the south of the Lomba, which equated to almost five days solid travelling across untamed Angolan terrain.

For clarification, a Brigade is equivalent to three Battalions like 61 Mech. We estimated that FAPLA's first wave of four hardened Brigades was more than five times the size of the total SADF force in theatre *before* accounting for the disparity of MBTs in theatre: SADF – nil, FAPLA – over 100.

Fortunately 61 Mech wouldn't be confronting this huge force alone, 32 Battalion punched well above her weight, always in the thick of action while the lightly armed UNITA units defended their territory manfully with RPG's and a motley collection of inherited weaponry.

Unfortunately for us, the Angolan Air Force was the dominant player in the sky further increasing the overwhelming advantage enjoyed by the enemy forces. Surrendering air superiority is the chess equivalent of losing the queen before the match is started. The consequence of this disparity would be evidenced later but wasn't a problem at all as our convoy rumbled through the UNITA rehab base with its wounded soldiers saluting our sacrifice.

We drove all day, pausing only for scheduled refuelling of the 480-litre tanks from diesel bunkers in our convoy. Progress was grindingly slow. The 'road' surface was poor almost immediately after we crossed the border at *Bittersoet* and it became progressively worse the deeper we ventured into the dark, untamed inner reaches of Angola.

A rare combination of a subtropical climate and the close proximity of two ancient deserts, the Kalahari to the south-east, and Namib to the south, gave

Photo 26 Charlie Squad crews take a quick break from the northward trek toward the Lomba. (Len M. Robberts)

the terrain a unique quality. It could be described as 'fertile desert', which is an oxymoron I know, but the deep, soft beach or desert sand somehow supported vast, dense forests punctuated by flat grassy alluvial *Shona* (bush country). These extensive forested areas would provide good cover from airborne attack but would also come to severely encumber the heaviest mechanised beasts on both sides of the conflict.

Most Ratel drivers were caught out by the tricky conditions at some point or other. Many of the 300BHP six-wheel-drive 18-ton behemoths simply dug themselves ever deeper into the soft soil until their full weight was resting on their mine-hardened undercarriages like a beached whale. Fortunately, after being 'beached' once or twice, the Ratel drivers soon developed techniques to deal with the treacherous terrain.

En-route the frontline, our *Tiffies* (mechanics) were in constant demand, their large tow trucks cutting fresh tracks to get past the single-file convoy to reach a stranded Ratel but if the *Tiffies* were busy elsewhere, we created a 60-ton daisy chain by using the three-metre, hollow steel tow-bars to connect two Ratels to the stricken beast and tear it from the clutches of the hot desert sand. Once his vehicle had been yanked clear, the driver had to ensure he eased off the power quickly to

Photo 27 The terrain and visibility begin to worsen the deeper we move into Angola.
(Barry Taylor)

the wheels to avoid the Ratel lurching forward and buckling the tow bar attached to the vehicle ahead. If a tow-bar buckle occurred in training, some significant and memorable punishment would invariably follow but in these circumstances, punishment was a lot less likely, but not unheard of.

Tricky terrain and regular refuelling stops meant the Battalion's average speed was never more than 5km per hour and we easily lost 20 minutes every time a Whale needed rescuing from the beach.

We came upon a number of tiny hamlets that day, normally no more than a half dozen hand-made dwellings inhabited by very dark-skinned locals. The inhabitants always interrupted whatever they were doing and stepped out of their five-man, tent-sized stick huts to offer sincere gap-toothed smiles and a grateful wave.

Like most rural Africans I'd encountered, they seemed about the friendliest people on earth. Indirectly, we were defending these people and their Stone-age simplicity from the Communist-backed marauders from the north so it was hard not to find a sense of purpose in this conflict. If FAPLA rolled this far south, the outlook for these people would be dire.

On one occasion, the convoy happened to pit-stop near one of these tiny hamlets affording us the opportunity to 'press the flesh'. We gave away some dry rations and

Some of Charlie's boys enjoying a few beers listening to U2. Just a typical night circa June 1987 at 61 Mech. (Photo Warren Adams). Standing from left to right: Kurt (Stompie) Oelofse (gunner 33, injured 3 Oct), Warren Adams (gunner 33A), Dave Chester (echelon driver), Gary Pearman-White (gunner 33C, injured during MiG attack on 8 October), Glen Woodhouse (driver 33, injured on 3 October), Wayne Fraser (echelon Sergeant and former crew commander of the ill fated 33C. Seated: Frikkie (Bees) De Jäger (driver 33C, killed 8 October 1987), Raymond Clark (driver 33B)

Gunnery training at School of Armour. The 90mm turret atop the 'Noddy' car. (School of Armour)

1st pass out after Basic Training. (Elizabeth Mannall)

Part way through Officer training.
(Elizabeth Mannall)

Back home – Alive!
(Graham Mannall)

LT Hind (KIA) (call-sign 33) in command of King Tiger as our convoy hogs the highway. (Len M. Robberts)

Owamboland desert convoy from the Sergeant Major's perspective. (Barry Taylor)

View from the 90mm turret as 53 Battalion Assault Pioneers (Storm Pioneer) mine one of the richest seams of subterranean explosive material in the world. (Barry Taylor)

Innocent victim of Angola's long civil war. Ratels; 101 Battalion. (Barry Taylor)

UNITA fighters take up the lead in preparation for Battle Group Alpha's very first attack on FAPLA. (Len M. Robberts)

UNITA 106mm recoilless anti-tank unit moving past us during a stop. (Len M. Robberts)

Battle planning and operational update deep in Angola. (Len M. Robberts)

Charlie Squadron on the move. (Len M. Robberts)

An enemy logistics vehicle feels HEAT as Charlie Squad move into the Chambinga Highlands near Cuito Cuanavale. (Martin Bremer)

View through the commanders' cupola during an attack on 49th Brigade, the thick glass made target finding extremely challenging in the dense forest. (Len M. Robberts)

Tired after a long day in the saddle. (Anthony de Robillard)

L/Cpls Donald Brown, James Sharp with Trooper vd Merwe. (Martin Bremer)

Treacherous travelling through wet season conditions, note the vehicle column has cut deep furrows in the mud. (Len M. Robberts)

The Brigade bell liberated from the 47th following their capitulation on 3rd Oct 1987. Fittingly, it now forms a centrepiece to the Hind Memorial at the Johannesburg Museum of War. (Martin Bremer)

31 Charlie destroyed and burned out following 8 October MiG strike.
(Len M. Robberts)

Charlie Squadron and the Assault Pioneer Platoon. This photo was hastily taken circa
10 October 'before we lost more guys'. (Len M. Robberts)

Olifant tank joins the party in November. (Martin Bremer)

Gunner holds two 90mm rounds while being reminded of the price of poor gunnery. (Barry Taylor)

This may be after drinking the Omuthiya Special. Cpl Venter and I getting chummy with Assault Pioneer LT Len Robberts standing on right. (Len M. Robberts)

Survivor. Angolan grime scrubbed away on our final day at Omuthiya. Posing at the NCOs' tent, our bedroom on base. (Dave Mannall)

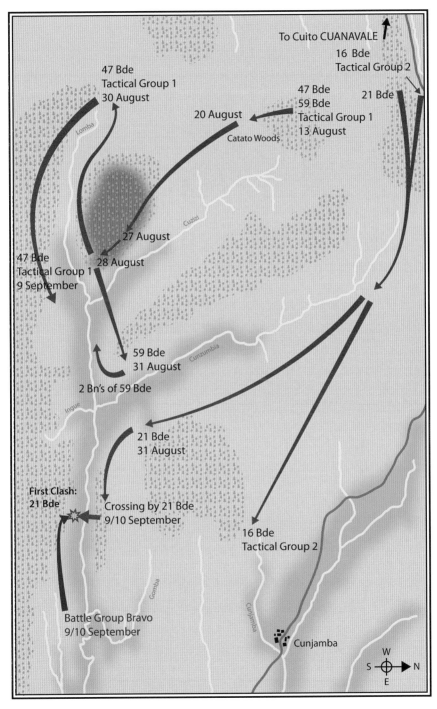

Map 1 First clash against 21st Brigade at the Lomba crossing: 9/10 September 1987. (George Anderson, adapted with permission from Johan Schoeman at www.warinangola.com)

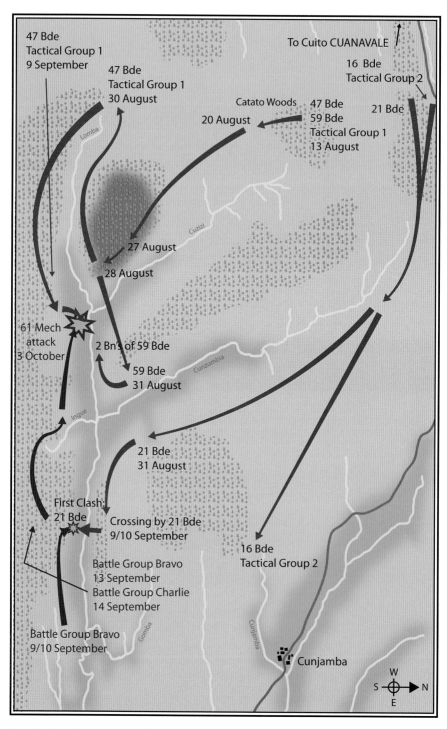

47 Bde
Tactical Group 1
9 September

47 Bde
Tactical Group 1
30 August

Catato Woods

20 August

47 Bde
59 Bde
Tactical Group 1
13 August

To Cuito CUANAVALE

16 Bde
Tactical Group 2

21 Bde

Lomba

Cuzizi

27 August

28 August

61 Mech
attack
3 October

2 Bn's of 59 Bde

59 Bde
31 August

Cunzumbia

Ingue

21 Bde
31 August

First Clash:
21 Bde

Crossing by 21 Bde
9/10 September

16 Bde
Tactical Group 2

Battle Group Bravo
13 September
Battle Group Charlie
14 September

Battle Group Bravo
9/10 September

Gomba

Cunjamba

Cunjamba

W
S — ⊕ → N
E

Map 2 The destruction of 47 Brigade: 3 October 1987. (George Anderson, adapted
with permission from Johan Schoeman at www.warinangola.com)

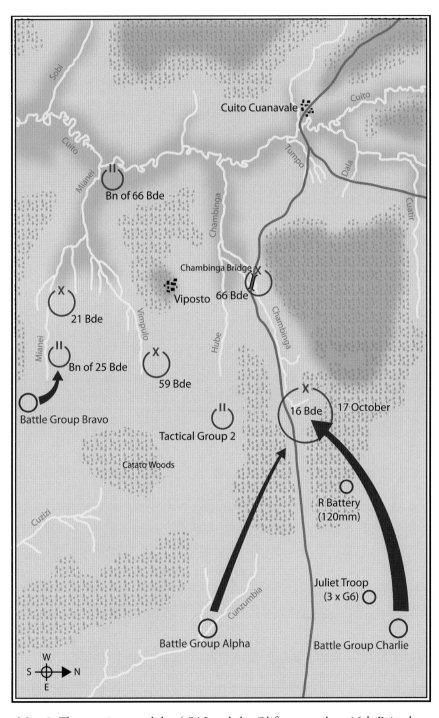

Map 3 The massive attack by 4 SAI and the Olifant squad on 16th Brigade –
9 November 1987. (George Anderson, adapted with permission from
Johan Schoeman at www.warinangola.com)

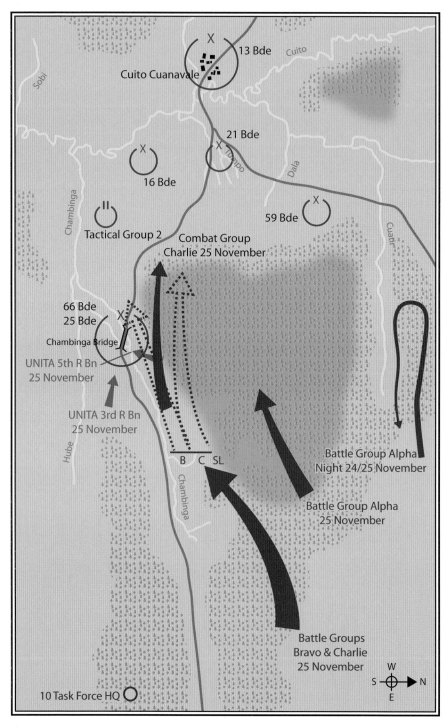

Map 4 Final attacks of Operation Modular 25/26 November 1987. (George Anderson, adapted with permission from Johan Schoeman at www.warinangola.com)

OPERATION *MODULER* (MODULAR)   129

in return enjoyed gracious hospitality from the dirt-poor, spiritually rich, Angolans who kindly shared their hot sickly 'broth' – no of us had a second helping that day.

An understanding of their Portuguese dialect would've been a distinct advantage but in the event, international sign language was sufficient to make for enjoyable communion with these simple folk because, after all we were Comm Ops veterans and Bobby Rebello did okay with his regular Portuguese.

As day turned to night, the convoy snaked steadily northwards, headlights blazing without fear of observation by enemy spotters, toward Lomba and the approaching first wave of enemy armour. In addition to the complexities of the alien terrain, crews had to contend with limited visibility – a consequence of thick plumes of dust kicked up by vehicles ahead. Often, visibility was reduced to just a few hazy metres – it was like being in a 'pea-soup' fog.

We'd had no sleep at all on the night of our border incursion so as we entered a second night without sleep, drivers rotated with another two crewmen in four-hour relays. Radio chatter was reduced to essential information which left a lot of time for quiet contemplation and focussing on keeping the vehicle moving steadily forward. With every slowly passing hour, we were inching inexorably closer to a very well-equipped and deadly foe, into to dangers as yet unknowable.

As the sun rose on our right flank, signalling our second day in Angola, Cloete's shrill voice erupted simultaneously in 12 sets of crew commander helmet headphones startling me back to full alertness, "…*visgraat nou* (adopt 'fish-rib' defensive formation now). You have one hour for breakfast and vehicle maintenance."

As we boiled water over an *Esbit* and contemplated the past 30 hours in Angola, the drivers calculated we'd covered about 120 clicks. We spoke about the wounded and impoverished locals we'd seen earlier and how none of us had expected Angola to be covered by such dense forest and apparently unending tracts of light-brown/yellow sand, surely sufficient to make 10,000 beaches.

The dust and sand was inescapable, our exposed skin was coated with it and unexposed nooks and crannies were beginning to rub like course-grain sandpaper but there wasn't time to deal with this discomfort. After a quick face wash, toothbrush and refuel we were underway for yet another long day in the saddle.

Just before sundown, the convoy was finally called to a halt 40 hours and 200 clicks since the crossing at Bittersweet. Dog-tired, parched and with dust lining our lungs we stripped and cleaned, or replaced, the Ratel's clogged air-filters. For the smokers among us, the halt offered the chance to add more shit to their already suffering lungs.

Photo 28 Cpl Venter tucks into a hearty rat pack meal while jealously guarding his prized jar of Mrs Ball's chutney. (Len M. Robberts)

We are fighting . . .

To protect Southern Africa against Russian colonialism and oppression

To protect freedom of worship and speech

To protect our families and friends

For peace

Ons veg vir . . .

Die verdediging van Suider-Afrika teen Russiese kolonialisme en onderdrukking

Vryheid van spraak en aanbidding

Ons gesinne en vriende

Vrede

No's combatemos pela . . .

Defesa. Da África austral contra o colonialismo e opressão Russa.

Liberdade de expressão e liberdade de culto

Nossa familia e amigos

Paz

Photo 29
Capture card, issued to crewmen in the event of capture by enemy forces.
(Martin Bremer)

Crews stripped off to wash at chest-high drinking taps located along each side of the water bunkers, our inaugural 'Angolan shower'.

After a hearty Rat-pack feast it wasn't long before the crews were sound asleep, either outside on the soft, cool beach sand or inside on the hard, rubber benches in the Ratel's rear cabin.

I had survived two days in Angola unscathed, 88 more days lay ahead. Others would not be so lucky. A SAAF *Bosbok* (Bushbuck) spotter plane was downed by enemy fire the very next day. The death of the pilots marked the first South African losses of the operation, but it also left commanders in no doubt as to the efficacy of the SAM 8 missile system we'd heard so much about. This, in turn, led to increased caution in relation to South African aircraft deployment.

So it was first blood to the 21st Brigade, they'd demonstrated their anti-aircraft capabilities convincingly but their sternest tests still lay ahead of them, on the ground, and we were coming.

11

Midnight in Mavinga

As we lazily stretched ourselves from our first full night's sleep on the cool crisp spring morning of 3 September we had no idea that SADF artillery boys were just completing their very first night of fire plans, that the opening salvos of Operation Modular had been exchanged while we'd been sleeping peacefully.

After a box breakfast and some last minute vehicle servicing, we rejoined the northerly trek. It was another ten hours on the 'road' before we got our first proper spike of adrenaline. Thick plumes of dark, oily smoke rose ominously into the sky ahead of us. We wondered if this was to be our first enemy contact. Ninety millimetre rounds were quickly chambered, 7.62s cocked, everyone steeling themselves for action or an order to respond.

Unsure as to the origins, or cause, of the oily smudge in the baby-blue sky, we fanned out from the track assuming defensive positions until the situation was clarified by UNITA half an hour later.

Orders to 'proceed with caution' were issued. There was no immediate danger as it transpired; the rising smoke came from a UNITA logistics (log) base which had sustained an arson attack the night before that completely destroyed the 44,000 litre diesel storage bunker from which our fuel trucks were scheduled to replenish. This was hard-core shit. It seemed someone was trying to slow our progress. The battle group needed to refuel at the strategic jungle gas station in order to reach the rebel stronghold at Mavinga. All available diesel bunkers were despatched to the next nearest jungle fuel station causing the battle group to be delayed by 24 hours.

The Ratel was equipped with two 50-litre water tanks, one either side of the vehicle, tucked behind thick steel armour plate located just above and between the massive double rear axle.

If used sparingly, 100 litres was quite a good ration for three crewmen so we seldom ran out of water. The mechanised Infantry lads had the same water ration but it had to be shared among eleven of them. We often 'loaned' them the odd bottle, never fully appreciating how much we depended on regular water replenishment until much later in the operation when supply lines were more stretched or the time when one of our water bunker took friendly fire from a Mirage jet meaning we were forced to endure a week in the heat without resupply.

The unexpected hold up at log base was like a mini spa vacation for the exhausted crewmen of Charlie Squad with the nearby river providing a fantastic setting for a luxurious 'bath' in its waters which, it was said, was infested with crocodiles. The opportunity to cool off was too tempting so some guys stood guard to ensure good health and safety practice.

Call-sign 33Bravo, commanded by Lance Corporal Fouche, developed a major engine problem not repairable in the field and was forced to stop near the log base and await the arrival of a replacement engine. Ill-fated 33Charlie, commanded by Lance Corporal Wayne Mills, was ordered to buddy up and stay behind with 33B for protection. It would be days before repairs were made and more than two weeks before the two vehicles finally rejoined the Squadron by which time we would've greeted the enemy.

Once we had finally refuelled, it took two further days of unbroken, jarring, dusty driving to travel the remaining 120 clicks to the rebel stronghold of Mavinga which, in the darkness, resembled a land-locked version of the floating outpost (atoll) in Kevin Costner's massively over-budget movie Waterworld – except that there were no cameras here, nor was anything over budget about this place. The heroes here were the cash strapped UNITA rebels who'd been using the outpost to launch counter-offensive action for almost ten years. The rebel base comprised of a few small buildings, houses and mostly medium-sized tents, similar to our base at Omuthiya but without the same sense of order. Long strings of electric bulbs, powered by a cacophony of noisy diesel generators, cast low arcs of artificial light and inky black shadows deep into the pitch-dark jungle.

Amidst the blackness of the surrounding jungle, Mavinga's yellow, electric aura gave it the appearance of a remote Las Vegas. Battle-hardened soldiers, AK47s slung over their shoulders, moved purposefully about their business; informal traders and small shops plied their brisk trade despite the late hour.

On 6 September, expeditionary SADF ground forces from 32 Battalion made first contact with FAPLA advance units of TG2 and a Squadron of 21st Brigade MBTs.

Word filtering down from the cheese was that 61 Mech was urgently needed in theatre and, as we'd lost a day at the log base, there was to be no respite on offer as we rolled slowly through the grimy settlement towards an enemy less than a day's drive away. We were about 50 clicks from the frontline!

As we moved past the brooding Angolan frontier town at midnight, almost a week after entering the country, we crossed an invisible line into the hot zone where everything became a potential target, including us!

Everyone was a little edgy; there was still so much unknown about the enemy positions and then there was the constant threat of Artillery bombardment or aerial attack. When we were clear of Mavinga, the convoy finally rested. Drivers moved their vehicles into defensive formations beneath the dense forest canopy and covered them with stretched-out camo (camouflage) nets.

A foxhole is a pit dug large enough to offer shelter during an artillery bombardment, or air-strike. The last thing anyone wanted was to be running round like a blue-arsed fly seeking cover when the bombs were landing – that would probably be too late *boetie* (little brother)! On this occasion we dug our foxholes willingly.

We came to discover that UNITA and FAPLA fighters with years of hard-won combat experience had taken foxhole design to a whole new level, sometimes spending months developing elaborate subterranean complexes for defence, protection and accommodation.

Photo 30 30 Alpha crewman du Toit takes shelter in his foxhole while MiGs circle overhead. (Len M. Robberts)

Unfortunately these complex, camouflaged trench systems had a sinister sting in the tail for mechanised forces. Aside from the obvious difficulty dislodging defenders during ground attack, moving through enemy emplacements criss-crossed with deep trenches raised the risk of beaching a wheeled vehicle if one or more tyres dropped axle-deep into a trench. These protective trenches probably cost us more lives during Operation Modular than any other type of enemy action. Those who undertook the immensely dangerous task of rescuing beached vehicles would earn more Honoris Crux (top bravery award) than during any other type of action by SADF forces.

Digging foxholes became a part of 61 Mech's daily routine, whenever we moved, we dug. Even the laziest Troopers dug 'foxies' without being told.

Despite our preparations, there were times when we'd hear the whistle of incoming enemy fire but were unable to reach a foxhole in the seconds before the Artillery shells detonated. If caught out in the open, we'd simply dive into the deep tyre ruts carved into soft sand and hope they weren't 'air-burst' bombs. Following one such incident, we couldn't help laughing at the sight of Steph Rossouw speed digging himself into a rut with his bare hands like a turtle digging a nest on the beach to lay her eggs. Steph probably laid something a little smellier than turtle eggs that time, but the attack was harmless, about 100 metres off target. Trooper Warren Adams aptly characterised his experiences of being bombed while out of reach of a foxhole as 'digging-in by using his eyelashes'. On another occasion Dries Rheeder gashed his head open with a shovel in his haste to dig a foxhole during an enemy bombardment. Unfortunately, his would be one of the least serious injuries sustained on that particular day.

We knew that when bombs started landing, the smallest sliver of razor-sharp, hideously jagged, shrapnel whizzing though the air at nearly supersonic speed, could easily tear off a limb. Anyone running around looking for a ditch to hide in when the music stopped playing was certainly dicing with death.

Since leaving Mavinga the risk of shit hitting the fan had increased exponentially and no one enjoyed playing 'musical chairs' with foxholes. Soon, every guy dug and 'owned' his own pit!

12

Battle Group Alpha

Eight days after entering Angola we arrived in theatre, comfortably within enemy Artillery range and only a few clicks from the contested Lomba river crossing held by 21st Brigade.

Collectively, the combined force of 61 Mechanised Battalion Group and 32 Light Infantry Battalion, bolstered with infantry from 101 Battalion and two Battalions of UNITA guerrillas, were now known as 20th Brigade. In total, SADF forces in theatre were equivalent in strength and size to about half of one FAPLA Brigade, though with UNITA support we were arguably the equivalent strength of a full Brigade. The five FAPLA Brigades ensconced on or near the Cuito River therefore posed a significant threat to our defence To put it mildly, SADF's 20 Brigade was seriously outnumbered and outgunned in almost every possible way.

Operating under the command of Colonel Deon Ferreira (AKA Falcon), 20 Brigade was split into three distinct battle groups (BG) – Alpha, Bravo and Charlie, each designed to offer similar tactical mechanised capacities with infantry, mortar, antitank and anti-aircraft capabilities. Mysteriously, our echelon boys, Colin Van Aswegen, Dave Chester, Gouws, Marais, Botha and Koekemoer, were despatched to support the Artillery arm of the Brigade.

Charlie Squad's 90 and Alpha Company's 20 and 81mm Ratel crews were assigned to spearhead Battle Group Alpha. In addition, Charlie Squad had inherited a Platoon of *Storm Pioneers* led by Lt Len Robberts earlier in the year. I never knew quite why they were attached with us but their primary role, as I understood things, was to blow stuff up, a bit like engineers with a combat role, and for this purpose these guys carried a large amount of TNT in their two Ratels.

A similar force was drawn from 32 Battalion to lead Battle Group Bravo, and Bravo Company, with its eight Anti-Tank Ratel 90s and two Platoons of Infantry riding in four Ratel 20s, formed up with 32 Battalion contemporaries to become BG Charlie. Each of the battle groups was assigned a Company of 101 and UNITA light infantry soldiers for close protection and pathfinding. We'd spend the next month as three distinct, quick reaction strike forces better able to attack the enemy on multiple fronts when needed.

13

Skeletons in the Closet

On 8 September, 21st Brigade was still making steady progress with their imme-diate objective to secure the Lomba River beachhead despite what had become by now an almost relentless bombardment from SADF artillery who finally had taken possession of the fearsome G5 cannons that had completed the week-long overland trek to the frontline with us thereby removing any pretence of the SADF's non-involvement in the conflict.

Recces, who by now had been in place for weeks and living mainly on a diet of bugs and leaves, reported FAPLA's gradually increased foothold on the Lomba's Southern banks while other reports gleaned from translated radio intercepts, *Bosbok* (bush buck) spotter planes and UNITA spies was that 66th and 16th Brigades remained dug in north of the Lomba, about 60 and 30 clicks away respectively. The 59th were holding a position some 15 clicks west of the river crossing offering Artillery support to the 21st.

It was assumed the 59th would quickly follow the 21st as soon as the bridge-head was cleared.

47th Brigade, the biggest badass mechanised force on either side of the conflict at that stage, came equipped with two Squadrons of T55 MBTs and a fearsome arsenal of ultramodern rocket systems, anti-aircraft installations, armoured vehi-cles and a compliment of almost 2,000 men.

Due to FAPLA's difficulty finding suitable and unhindered crossing points during the preceding ten days, 47th Brigade, led by TG1 was ordered to head westward, up-river and outside the range of SADF Artillery, to explore alternate crossing points or, failing that, to continue around the source of the Lomba River some 60 clicks west of 21st Brigade's bridgehead.

47th Brigade discovered that it was unable to deploy bridge-laying vehicles on the marshy river banks and opted instead to make best speed around the river by which time it was becaming clear that 21st Brigade would need some assistance to advance through the bridgehead. FAPLA strategists needed 47th Brigade to open a second front near the 21st Brigade river crossing to expedite their opera-tion known as *Operação Saludando Octubre* (Operation Greeting October), a title that suggests they were eager to achieve their objective before greeting November, now less than two months hence.

Opposition Generals remained upbeat that the week and the delay at the Lomba crossing had not upset their carefully planned schedule for October; this was exactly the sort of contingency they'd allowed for. A fortnight's delay clearing the Lomba should have no bearing on the eventual outcome of the battle once remaining forces cleared the final geological hurdle en route Jamba and the full weight of their massive force could be brought to bear. All they need to do was clear the Lomba choke point in the coming week or so.

If Fidel's intelligence on enemy build up had been accurate, he must've thought he'd finally backed a winner because the SADF still had no Main Battle Tanks within 2,000km of theatre. Even on its own, the FAPLA's 47th outnumbered and outmuscled 20 Brigade on almost every measure; their imminent arrival into the vicinity of the bridgehead would inevitably wreak havoc on the defending SADF/UNITA forces. When combined, the 21st and 47th should easily be capable of pushing the more lightly armoured SADF/UNITA opposition back from the river allowing 16th, 66th and 59th Brigades to flood across unfettered while the reserve forces at Cuito moved south to cover their rear.

By now, any pretence or notion that the war wouldn't affect us had faded at around the same time as the lights of Mavinga on the previous night had disappeared in the dust behind our convoy. The nearby crump of Artillery bombardment and the presence of over-flying jets were, at first, unnerving but soon became a regular feature of life on the frontline.

The day after our arrival in theatre, Battle Groups Bravo and Charlie were immediately tasked to confront forward units of 21st Brigade. Early on the morning of 9 September, BG Bravo led the first full-scale attack of Operation Modular and encountered heavy resistance from an enemy that had by now captured a UNITA logistics base south of the river crossing. The base had boasted extensive defensive fortifications and its rapid loss was an ominous portent of the enemy's strength.

BG Bravo inflicted many casualties and were making good progress but, as the mechanised group moved across the terrain, a number of 101 Battalion vehicles got trapped in trenches and were abandoned under a barrage of large-calibre fire. Some soldiers never made it out of their Troop carriers.

Later that night, members of BG Charlie distinguished themselves during a hastily planned, high-risk mission to recover under the cover of darkness four stricken vehicles in the face of incoming enemy fire. On such a night mission there was a every chance that they too could drop an axle into a trench.

Eventually, as they exhausted their supply of illumination flares, Lotter ordered his troops to set a row of wooden huts ablaze in order to illuminate the target area and then guide his troops to safety.

After that opening battle, our commanders were forced to recognise that prosecuting what seemed like trench warfare at such close quarters, without 'boots on the ground', meant oversized mechanised vehicles were sitting ducks to something as small as a shoulder mounted RPG hidden in a nearby trench. They agreed that what was needed in future was the insertion of ground troops and accurate Artillery or mortar fire in an attempt to clear the trenches. In addition to this challenge, the sheer density of some forested areas meant emplacements were sometimes impossible to see until the enemy started shooting. Engagements with the enemy were prosecuted up close, sometimes at less than 50 metres – *very* close-quarters combat for the Ratel's 90mm projectile that didn't even arm itself until it had travelled 30m.

And then, the scenario we'd been assured would never happen happened!

The day after the attack on the log base BG's Bravo and Charlie, still in the vicinity of elements of 21st Brigade, encountered two troops of T55 MBTs at some distance in an open Shona area. Working in concert, the 90mm gunners and a prototype SA-designed rocket system, known as ZT3, engaged the enemy forces.

Photo 31 Lomba River Shona (flood plain), deceptively deadly, a vehicle could drop into soft/soggy terrain and be stranded and fully exposed to enemy positions.
(Len M. Robberts)

The ZT3s destroyed three Russian tanks – quite a coup for the designers of the rocket – while the 90mm gunners apparently struggled at that range to destroy the 40-ton unit. In the end they did manage to silence some of the tanks, but at a heavy price, with the loss of a Ratel 90 crew from 32 Battalion commanded by 2nd Lt. Alves who'd trained with us at the School of Armour. During the conflagration his vehicle beached in deep sand on open Shona, a sitting target for the nearest T55 which got to within 100 metres before taking the kill shot. RIP.

A day or two later, Captain Cloete was instructed to escort a number of big cheese observers to the review the heavily scarred 9 September battlefield around the log base. FAPLA, it was understood, had withdrawn from the immediate area but Charlie Squad was nonetheless tasked with the delegation's security.

Prior to departure we were read the riot act about potential dangers: "Don't get too close to damaged vehicles, some of them might still have unexploded and unstable ordinance on board…oh and don't forget the ongoing threat of land-mines." Mines were a clear and present danger and a most deadly proposition the moment boots hit the ground.

After an hour of stealthy, slightly nervous approach we arrived at a place totally devoid of living flora. Every tree still standing had been stripped clean of foliage during what had clearly been a massive firefight. The scorched and blackened terrain was cluttered with the detritus of war. Burned-out and shattered vehicles lay untidily like some giant kid's playroom scattered over thousands of square metres.

Some lads stayed on the Ratels to provide over-watch security while a number of us took the tour as if visiting a macabre tourist attraction, a human House of Horrors.

We'd already encountered a number of burned-out vehicles during our first days on the frontline and seen numerous rusting hulks, the result of earlier offensives, during our northward trek from the border. This tour, however, included new horrors.

Scattered around and about were the shallow graves of fallen soldiers. From one of them a hand and wrist protruded from the earth, frozen by death in a gesture that seemed to beckon me closer. I didn't really think too much about the body attached to the hand but I was struck by its very unusual pallor. Oddly these macabre sights and smells of death didn't seem to affect me very much outwardly; it was all so surreal, so impersonal. More fascinated than fearful, I couldn't resist bending the rules a little to inspect a burned-out tangle of metal that had once been an Allied *Kwevoel* (Grey Lourie or 'Go-away-bird'), a light

APC from 101 Light Infantry Battalion. Aside from the fire and bomb damage, the vehicle looked ungainly with its left front wheel dropped into a trench. This was probably one of the vehicles BG Charlie had intended to recover during the night after the battle but being this deep inside the area of contact with no available cover, the *Kwevoel* had been a sitting duck for the 21st Brigade gunners. The burned remains of the vehicle driver remained on post

As I peered into the gloomy rear cabin, I saw the bodies of his mates; they too had been trapped in the vehicle as enemy fire sealed their fate. They had been roasted, quite literally to the bone, in a super-heated inferno. Whatever

Photo 32 Cpl Rossouw scouting a structure which remained intact at the UNITA logistics base initially captured by forward elements of 21st Brigade before getting knocked back by Battle groups Bravo and Charlie in various actions between 8 and 13 September. It was structures like these that were set alight to assist the attempted night rescue. (Len M. Robberts)

had transpired, it seemed the end had come quickly. The doomed soldiers were still sitting almost perfectly upright, leaning against each other like dominoes prevented from falling over by some unseen hand, almost as if they were anticipating the order to disembark. Unfortunately, neither that order nor opportunity to flee had presented itself. RIP.

Despite these horrors we were also amazed by futuristic-looking Russian tank helmets which made ours look like a relic from the Korean War. Their 7.62mm machine guns were date-stamped 1985 by the gun maker, meaning they were only two years old. We, on the other hand, were blessed with a vintage brace of 1948 Brownings on my vehicle, 32 Alpha.

A number of Charlie Squad lads posed triumphantly atop a burned out T55, like mountaineers on the summit of a 'big one'. I don't recall this particular event but photographic evidence places me at the scene. Perhaps subconsciously I was already blanking out memories. Over the coming months we encountered many destroyed vehicles belonging to both sides, few however left an impression as horrifyingly vivid as that *Kwevoel* packed with incinerated soldiers like skeletons in the closet.

Photo 33 Charlie Squad boys getting up close and personal with a Russian tank recently retired. (Len M. Robberts)

14

Battle Group Alpha and the 47th Brigade

While BGs Bravo and Charlie were tasked with containing the 21st Brigade at the Lomba crossing, BG Alpha was despatched Westward, up-river, to disrupt and slow the progress of the 47th Brigade.

After four or five days of probing and intelligence gathering, we finally squared up to the advance units of 47th Brigade. On 16 September, our 40-vehicle convoy moved under cover of darkness to within two clicks of the enemy positions. Soon after sunrise we received the order to move forward in an integrated battle formation meaning Alpha Company Ratel 20s were alongside Charlie's 90s, and just as in training the infantrymen would *stap uit* (step out) their vehicles on final approach. 33B and 33C had still not rejoined the Squad following the critical engine failure two weeks before, but although we were reduced to a ten-vehicle attack those 20mm crews alongside us added devastating firepower against the predicted light Armour and Infantry targets.

Our coordinated and controlled forward approach was going as planned although visibility across the frontline was restricted to about three vehicles either side of us because of the density of the forest. The attack called on a pair of fighter jets to synchronise with BG Alpha's advance and they delivered a well-timed bombing run to set the opposition on the back foot mere moments before we came within range.

We heard the jets screaming in steep and fast from high altitude before releasing their ordinance from a height of just 500 metres but very close to our line. Incandescent airburst explosions followed a few seconds later; these were so close it seemed as if our air force was bombing us! [We later discovered there had been a little mix up, the pilots mistaking our vehicles for enemy targets under the canopy of trees]. The ordinance was white phosphorous – ugly stuff. Just the smallest pellet of this chemical sizzles as it continues to burrow its way deep into the flesh causing dreadful injuries. This weapon was ideal for raining a blanket of pain onto troops in trenches. We counted ourselves fortunate they missed, but the surprise attack disrupted forward movement across our partially blind front-line. [I'm led to believe that our line never fully recovered its shape throughout the duration of contact].

Once deployed on the ground, Infantrymen were tasked with trench clearance, their 20mm APCs following in their wake and dealing with bigger targets. Inside their sun-roof Ratels, the 81mm Mortar boys trailed the formation, ready to unleash a barrage of HE bombs on command.

As we apprehensively moved through the dense jungle on our final approach to the target area, my senses straining to detect any movement in the deep-green bushes and undergrowth ahead, I was keenly aware of the infantry soldiers on either side of our vehicle and secretly grateful not to be quite as exposed as those brave lads.

Before too long we received our first direct, albeit inaccurate, enemy fire from positions still invisible among the greenery. The crackle and chatter of rapid AK47 fire, the 'phwip' of a near-by bullet tearing through the air or scything through the leaves of nearby foliage sent shivers of fear coursing through me. We'd been dreading, but expecting this moment since entering Angola over two weeks before. Now the crew seemed to engage autopilot, all drills, all the training, all the *opfok* had prepared us well for this moment. Not a word was uttered on the internal vehicle comm channel other than those essential for combat.

We returned fire into the general area ahead, continuing to push forward until the muzzle flashes from the enemy's weapons were close enough to be visible. Bullets ricocheted off our vehicle, a sound we had never heard before but recognised instinctively. Across our frontline, crews immediately responded to the threat by launching into fire-and-move mode, picking out possible targets for attention.

Battle orders required us to hold a straight line, to move forward in concert at a pace manageable by foot soldiers to ensure none of them were crushed by the wheels of the vehicles during tactical fire-and-move combat.

The 81mm mortar group began directing fire onto enemy positions less than 100 metres ahead of us.

32 Alpha was close enough to the adjacent vehicles to allow my driver to manage the forward movement in tandem with our neighbours 32Bravo and 32Charlie while I tried to identify the opposition's well camo'd whereabouts.

We moved forward, into a small clearing at which point incoming enemy gunfire around us increased dramatically. A barrage of small arms and occasional RPG fire erupted from a nest 40-60 metres ahead of my vehicle.

We quickly countered with HE and anti-personnel bombs while our brace of venerable Browning LMGs sprayed bullets in support of the infantry alongside us. The enemy nest was quickly subdued although further down the line on the left, our brothers in Troops One and Three still seemed heavily involved in action.

Even from a height of two-and-a-half metres above the ground, head poking out the turret, it was very difficult to see through the foliage into well-camouflaged enemy positions and difficult to get an accurate picture of damage we'd inflicted on the nest. Minutes later, muzzle flashes lit up the enemy trench again, and once more we joined with the infantrymen alongside to neutralise the threat.

Radio chatter on the Squad channel started increasing from the guys on the left front. Poor visibility in the densely wooded contact area was causing crews considerable difficulty.

Troop 3 commander, 2nd Lt Adrian Hind, lost contact with the main body of Charlie Squad, another vehicle, a Ratel 20, got beached in a trench while exposed to enemy fire. Second Lt Martin Bremer and his crew in 31 bravely conducted a recovery operation which required Bremer to exit his vehicle and connect the heavy tow bar to the stricken Ratel before his driver could extricate it from the deathtrap. Bremer was later awarded the Honoris Crux for his bravery that day.

We were still coming under attack but my adrenaline spiked as I made out the flank of a Soviet APC moving into position through the bush some 60 metres ahead. Visibility was poor and in those conditions the camo-green Russian vehicle was hard to distinguish so I was unable to identify exactly which variant of armour we were facing. Nevertheless, I could tell that the vehicle carried at least one mounted gun capable of cutting open a Ratel and was probably disgorging a fresh cohort of FAPLA foot soldiers into our immediate area.

I instinctively called up a HEAT round and specified the close-range target to my gunner. He could hardly miss from such close proximity.

Seconds later, a flash lit the vehicle's dark green flank – Zeelie had found his target! We delivered a second package to the target for good measure. Soldiers still inside the vehicle did not all get the opportunity to disembark, more skeletons.

Taking that first armoured target so easily buoyed my confidence. We'd faced a hard target, our weapon system and gunner had done exactly what they were supposed to. No triumphalism, just a target. There was much still to do.

Intel specialist Brad Saunders, riding on command Ratel Three Zero (30) just behind us at the centre of our formation, watched as an RPG floated inches above their turret between his vehicle and 30 Alpha, the 2IC command vehicle. A short while later Captain Cloete took RPG shrapnel to the elbow from a more accurate shot but he bravely maintained his post in command of the action.

We continued working the lively trenches ahead, jockeying positions as per training but by then forward movement had ceased as the enemy held sturdy in defence.

The Ratel remained impervious to the continually chattering small-arms fire, unfortunately this wasn't true for exposed Infantrymen alongside who were bravely going through their drills.

Although Infantrymen could drop prone to escape an incoming barrage of automatic fire from the trenches they had nowhere to hide or take cover, no foxhole protection from mortar attack; and that was to be the cause BG Alpha's first fatality of the operation, Rifleman P.A. Visagie of Alpha Company was critically wounded, his comrades rallied round, lay down suppressing fire and returned him to the relative safety of his vehicle.

Considering the volume of continuous incoming enemy fire across our 3-400 metre frontline it was quite surprising that his was the only fatality on the 16 September encounter with elements of 47th Brigade.

Not long after Visagie got hit, about an hour after battle started, we were ordered to deploy smoke grenades from our turret launchers and withdraw from the contact area.

Guys estimated that in addition to significant incoming mortar and small-arms fire, as many as 100 RPG rounds had been loosed at our frontline. Some crews reported surviving glancing hits at a strike angle too shallow for the RPG to penetrate. Some even survived direct hits where the closeness of contact meant the grenade hadn't yet armed itself and so failed to detonate on impact! Fuck, what luck!

An RPG travels slowly enough to be observed as it sails through the air. Ratel drivers, with their ringside seats, were understandably quite shaken from helplessly watching these rockets as they were fired at them from short range. They could do nothing but await the bang that ends it all – or the harmless 'pop' as the RPG pinged harmlessly off the vehicle.

For the crew of 33Alpha, a direct hit almost spelled the end. Driver Andre Herselman watched from inches away as an RPG shot its molten metal core through his reinforced driver's window. Two things saved his, and possibly the three-man crews', life. Firstly, the RPG struck at quite a shallow angle, meaning it had slightly further to travel through the hardened glass and this reduced its kinetic energy, and secondly, the crew later ascertained that the two-inch-thick protective pane had been installed inside out changing the aspect of the glass – something, I believe, to do with the way the glass is designed.

Whatever the cause, it was a close call for them, something they were reminded of every time we mounted up because mechanics had no spare driver-windows, so 33 Alpha spent the remainder of Operation Modular driving with partial visibility through the RPG'd pane.

Later that night, after setting up temporary base, we recounted some of our experiences. 2nd Lt. Hind copped a bit of stick for dragging the left flank off course but overall the consensus was that Charlie Squad had done OK despite not gaining territory or inflicting significant damage on 47th Brigade. The FAPLA muzzle flashes seemed almost to be coming right out of the earth because they were so well entrenched. Despite this there were far more casualties inflicted on the enemy than received by us and this statistic included quite a number of armoured vehicles. If I had paid more attention during JL's, I might've stood a better chance of identifying the type of AFV Zeelie destroyed but, it is fair to add, it was difficult to detect as it was well hidden by the dense bush. We'd never even trained for such close-quarter, low-visibility action, that is, after all, not really the Armoured Corps natural habitat.

Photo 34 Squad leader 2nd Lt O'Connor offers me a fly swatter the day after our first attack on 47th Brigade. (Len M. Robberts)

Captain Cloete was cassevac'd to Rundu for surgery to repair his arm, Troop Sergeant Venter relinquished command of 31 Alpha and was replaced by Corporal Siewert Wiid, while Adrian Hind went on to earn himself a bit of a reputation for getting lost in the jungle. A softly spoken, son of a vicar, he was apparently not best suited to the rigours of warfare. But then who of us was?

Fuck only knows what the fools at School of Armour were thinking when they sent a guy like him to the border, and what's more the bugger was still a virgin! In my opinion, he definitely needed a fun weekend at Midmar Dam with my friend-girl, Queen V, before any more killing occurred in our battle group.

Visagie's unfortunate death (RIP) did bring about another review of our modus operandi when planning future contacts. Infantrymen would not be required to *stap-uit* in such unfavourable conditions in future and this decision invariably saved lives during Ops Modular.

While the Captain was away getting patched up, 61 Mech's second-in-command, Major Danie Laas, assumed responsibility for Charlie Squad which was not only an honour for us but it also afforded the Major an opportunity to lead us in on our next skirmish a few days later. The brief contact resulted in another hit-n-run attack on TG1 and forward elements of 47th Brigade. Again the enemy adopted well-entrenched defensive positions which were difficult to clear. Stalemate.

Cloete returned to lead the fully reformed Squadron (33B & C having finally caught up with us) about a week later having partly recuperated from his wounds and surgery. His arrival back on the frontline was an important symbolic and psychological touchstone for the lads. Two weeks on the front, a number of skirmishes and near misses behind us and Charlie Squad remained very much intact. This was great for self-confidence. The longer we went without serious losses, the more we started to believe we could survive the maelstrom unscathed.

Before issuing that evening's orders, Cpt. PJ 'one-arm-bandit' Cloete called the Squad together and delivered a stirring speech during which he informed us that hospital medics had offered him exemption from frontline duties due to his injury and added, "Can you believe I chose to come back to be with you *manne* (men) instead of returning to recuperate in RSA with my girl? It seems that you boys of Charlie Squad have got to me, and the fact is there is no way I could've abandoned you, certainly not with just a gammy elbow."

Cloete's arm remained half cocked and bandaged for the remainder of Modular and, to the chagrin of his crew on Three Zero (30), this little disability meant he relied more heavily on them to attend his needs, sometimes, I'm told, with amusing consequences.

For the remainder of September there were few days of downtime. We were constantly on the move shuttling between contact points, pocking and probing at enemy positions while our commanders gathered intelligence on the enemy's progress along and over the Lomba.

Enemy aircraft conducted regular daily sorties over our positions, normally at altitude – usually they'd hang about for an hour or so, seeking out their prey. Less frequently, SAAF jets flew in from the south but these were normally quick-strike bombing runs.

Accounts began filtering down to us of fighter jet bombing strikes but thankfully none of it was near us, except on one occasion when they dropped cluster bombs in very close proximity to our temporary camp. We visited our foxholes.

Artillery bombardment was an almost constant feature of this period with both sides seeking to frustrate their enemy and score a few easy wins from distance.

On the ground, despite our diminutive size and inadequate air cover, we were holding our own. Although we hadn't achieved any significant victories – often

Photo 35 There were often calls for some minor injury or another. L/Cpl Cragg the Medic attending to James Sharp, at gunpoint. Bombardier Mc Cormack looks on while cheeky Rueben Linde gets close to camera. (Martin Bremer)

as a consequence of the terrain, trenches and an enemy extremely well practised at the art of withdrawal – between us, SADF's 20 Brigade in three Battle Groups had held up the 21st at their crossing point and slowed the 47th in their immediate objective of reaching the Lomba bridgehead. Enemy losses were mounting on the opposition team but both 21st and 47th Brigades had plenty in reserve.

Living in a war-zone is a unique experience; there were days of indolent inactivity and preparation, punctuated by scheduled, and unscheduled, moments of intensity the likes of which are almost impossible to describe or compare to anything in a normal experience. For example, one morning over rat-pack coffee, my mate Corporal Anthony De Robillard described to me how he and a few of his crewmates from our 81mm mortar fire-group, dismounted their Ratel to have a Sunday morning chin-wag with the UNITA lads assigned to their detachment. They were only separated from the forward positions of 21st Brigade by almost three clicks of open *Shona* but the battle-hardened soldiers felt fairly relaxed as they were hidden from view within the treeline.

Moments later they were confronted with the truth of how precarious their position really was when enemy 82mm mortars started whistling and landing just 100 metres short of their position. They knew the following volley would be closer still.

The normally laid-back, flip-flop wearing gunners, more used to hurling bombs from behind the frontline than being in it, sprinted, nay bolted, with rude haste, back to the protection of their Ratels. They took up new positions deeper in the treeline while the adrenaline-fuelled gunners prepared to launch a return volley.

Soon thereafter the UNITA boys urged them to withdraw before more enemy gunners got ranged in.

Wisely, De Robillard ordered a tactical withdrawal from the area, all of them a little wiser and, fortunately, none the worse for their Sunday morning bolt.

Photo 36 61 Charlie launches an 81mm mortar through the sunroof Ratel.
(Anthony de Robillard)

15

Bootlaces

By the end of September, after almost a month on the front the three battle groups of 20 Brigade had clocked up some serious mileage shuttling around Lomba's Southern bank and had lived under almost constant aerial threat from the ever-present MiG and Sukhoi jets, whose uncontested presence this far in-country made daytime travel arrangements a very risky proposition.

When required to relocate or get nearer to a staging point for our next contact, BG Alpha travelled in convoy only fanning out into battle formation when enemy contact was imminent.

Upon arrival at a temporary base, in yet another nondescript swatch of jungle, we'd laager the vehicles in relatively tight clusters and made sure that at all times we stayed within close proximity of the laager for personal safety reasons.

On days when no action was planned, we'd *hang-bal* (laze about), sometimes tanning ourselves, sometimes lying around in the shade, but always keeping a watchful eye on the MiGs and an ear on the comms while enjoying the close camaraderie of guys who by now were bonded together by shared, intense experiences. We'd all seen our share of enemy action, so the 'fuck-em-all' *hare-gat* (hard arse) attitude from our early days together as a Squadron was now firmly a thing of the past. We were comrades-in-arms.

We needed one another to ensure our survival in combat and we only had each other for company – 24 hours, seven days per week. There was really only one good way to get out of Angola, and that was all of us, together. The alternative didn't bare thinking about, but as we'd taken no serious casualties in the Squad we didn't *have* to think about it…much.

Every 7-10 days, the postal service got through to us on the frontline, and usually the Samil 50 transport truck also brought with it a small consignment of 'wet rations', fresh food that was however, usually well past its sell-by date.

Guys now cherished *pos paraade* (post parade) more than they did during basic training when still acclimatising to life in the army. Letters from home were opened at a quiet moment so that the words therein could be savoured and reread – especially if they were love letters from a girl.

One guy got the dreaded 'Dear Johnny' breakup letter! His girlfriend sent it to him knowing he was in the middle of a war-zone. Very nice!

Tight-knit though the boys became, they rarely had to suffer the ignominy of having to take a *turd* (shit/crap/poo/dump) inside the laager. Normally the furthest we'd have to venture for the daily *bos-kuk* (bush-shit) was 30-100 metres depending on forest density and the size of the layer-cake laager.

Of course, given the nature of our diet, there were days we *bos-kukked* more than once, for example, if the fresh, blue meat delivered on the back of the postal truck really was too *frot* (rotten) to have eaten, or the bush alcohol we were distilling had a slightly unsettling effect on the bowels. Needless to say the rat-pack diet played its part in this aspect of life at war.

Naturally, the *bos-kuk* wasn't the 'civilised', seated affair most people in the West are accustomed to resting ourselves on a pristine porcelain bowl with a heated soft-close seat and Sunday paper for company. No, the Angolan *bos-kuk* was like a journey back to a time when life was still harsh and barbaric so it seemed quite apt that we should defecate like this while prosecuting the oldest and most barbaric of human rituals – warfare.

It came as no surprise to discover that human beings are still very well adapted for *bos-kuk,* and, for that matter, war.

When taking a shit in Angolan bush, there was always significant threat of 'incoming' so there were few reasons to dilly-dally. Thus, the *bos-kuk* was usually completed with the minimum of fuss and in pretty short order.

Other than the use of the highly prized, limited stock and relatively modern invention of loo paper, *bos-kuk* protocol differed from that of our forefathers in another way – we always took a shovel and dug a tiny foxhole into which we buried the remnants of yesterday's rat-pack.

When it was time to find a bush, I'd pull on my overalls, slip bare foot into my well-worn army-issue leather boots, sling my R4, grab a bog roll and spade then slope off to find a suitable environment with my long, untied bootlaces dragging behind to form snake trails in the soft sand.

Happily there were no major incidents associated with this ritual, however, on more than one occasion, I'd return to a standing position to find one of my bootlaces had got itself into a little trouble by somehow slithering into the mini-foxie. When this happened there really was only one sensible course of action; to decapitate the boot-lace with the shovel as swiftly and humanely as possible, ensuring all soiled sections remained behind forever entombed with the remains of yesterday's rat pack no.5. I tried to remember to tuck the bootlaces into my boots but forgot enough times that eventually the laces were too short to touch the ground.

Days of indolence were spent hanging around being scruffy but the buzz around camp was very different on days before possible contact with the enemy. Most guys developed pre-battle routines, or rituals, as part of their mental preparation for impending conflict. Lance Corporal Donald Brown always kept a packet of expensive Camel cigarettes stashed next to his radio for that first post-battle cigarette while smoking cheaper cigs on downtime.

The ritual I developed was to ensure I always went into battle as clean as possible, maybe as a good luck omen, or maybe just in case the next person to see me unclothed was to be a mortician. I tried to ensure that clean underwear, socks and tank suit were available for battle days. During downtime, like most lads in the unit I lolled about in whatever army-issue gear I felt most comfortable wearing as little as possible due to oppressive jungle heat.

We were dirty a lot of the time with hair unkempt and scruffy after regular the disciplines of shaving and haircuts had been suspended. Patchy outcrops of facial hair on dirty skin left some of us resembling the unkempt homeless character in a Jackie Chan movie.

Our slothful appearance and attire would never have passed muster back on base but up there on the front we were more likely to meet our Maker, than find a Sergeant Major concerned by our state of dress. Of cardinal importance however was the health and readiness of our vehicles and weapon systems, but there again the brass didn't need to be too concerned because they knew little inspires a gunner to ensure his weapon's readiness, or a driver to maintain his vehicle, more than the real threat of enemy contact.

Like brothers-in-arms the world over, the boys of Charlie Squadron developed an intense closeness during the year and this camaraderie became especially strong during Operation Modular. If a bloke had a pimple on his back that needed squeezing, who better than the guy he would risk his life for to deal with it? Or if someone wanted to discuss intimate issues like sex, that too was cool and I, now armed with my vast back-catalogue of sexual experience and conquest, could discuss at length this most sensitive topic.

16

The Battle on the Lomba

Russian, Cuban and East German battle strategists despatched one third of the mechanised forces at their disposal to punch through UNITA and SADF defences and destroy Savimbi's main base at Mavinga and capital Jamba, essentially taking control of a large swathe of south eastern Angola. In order to achieve this objective the four hardened Brigades, consisting of 100 tanks and hundreds of other armoured vehicles, needed to cross the strategic Lomba River, less than 100km from their objective. Early SADF artillery involvement in August '87 caused FAPLA's advance to stall and they succeeded only in getting one Brigade of the 21st Battalion across to the southern bank. To counter this the enemy sent their hardest Battalion, the 47th, around the source of the Lomba in order to get access to the southern banks, which if they cleared, would allow the Angolan forces massing at the Lomba bridgehead free passage towards their principle objective – Mavinga. When the SADF ground in forces in the form of 61 Mechanised and 32 Light Infantry Battalions became involved, a month of skirmishes and battles on the Lomba against an enemy force made up of a Brigade of 21st Battalion, Tactical Group 1 and elements of the 47th Brigade evolved. Although SADF forces demonstrated their tactical nous and superior training, 21st Brigade forces were holding well-entrenched emplacements on the southern banks of the Lomba and were hard to shift whilst the dense bush and difficult terrain played a part in early contacts with Tactical Group 1 and the 47th Brigade. All of this changed in dramatic fashion on 3 October. That fateful single day earned its place as a great and memorable battle in the history of the proud SADF, it also marked the last day FAPLA commanders considered Mavinga a potential target heralding the beginning of a hasty and embarrassing withdrawal of all Angolan forces northwards, to the town of Cuito Cuanavale. It is therefore not unreasonable to award the battle fought on 3 October 1987 the honour of The Battle on the Lomba. (Al J. Venter, *African stories by Al Venter and friends*, 2013).

Almost 500 clicks in-country, Angola's vast subtropical forests sometimes reduced visibility too much for the successful prosecution of mechanised warfare. Conversely, the large trees and dense, jungle bush provided our vehicles with pretty good shelter from the ever present threat posed by Angolan and Cuban fighter pilots.

The reason we didn't have superiority in the air wasn't because of the quality of SAAF and its pilots, it was a matter of logistics, we were a long distance from our air bases and had neither sufficient aircraft nor suitable anti-aircraft materiel to match the MiGs and FAPLA ground-to-air missile systems.

The MiG is a classy fighter jet, unless you're on the wrong side of it, and was more than a match in a dogfight against our ageing French-made Mirage which was better suited to a ground-attack role. Further, FAPLA anti-aircraft capabilities were almost as good as those of any army in the world – the Russians had provided them with some of the very latest technology hot off the Cold War press.

SAAF pilots ran a risky gauntlet of hi-tech AA weaponry every time they screamed in from their bases in northern SWA. What's more, diplomatic considerations also affected the use of aircraft in theatre. So aside from preserving their sanctions-limited ageing fighter-jet inventory, the SA Government really didn't want to drop a plane over enemy-held territory.

As a consequence of the status quo, we lacked meaningful air support and endured almost constant buzzing from FAPLA fighters, while SAAF offered mainly surgical drop-and-run bombing raids.

It's not unfair to say Russian planes owned the sky this deep in Angola which for us meant we lived under the constant threat of aerial attack.

In the early stages of Operation Modular, the added constraint of South African diplomatic denials regarding our participation in military operations in Angola curtailed the extent to which our army chiefs might otherwise have escalated actions, including of course the deployment of our Olifant tanks. We believed this was because the Olifant was easily visible to satellite reconnaissance but moving any armoured unit during daylight hours was avoided wherever possible because, aside from their elephantine lack of stealth, the dust plumes and tracks the Olifant left in her wake would have been easily spotted by enemy observers.

As September drew to a close and the distance between 47th Brigade and the 21st bridgehead narrowed, we became more frequently embroiled in skirmish-type actions, particularly against the 47th; they seemed less well entrenched and would often melt away into the forest on contact.

Direct and indirect contact against 21st had been building in intensity as they gradually extended their foothold on the southern banks of the Lomba River. Inexorably, the FAPLA was building the strength of its forces in the immediate area of operations and by the end of September approximately 10,000 soldiers of various nationalities were in place. These soldiers were primarily young Angolan men whose ranks were augmented by a significant contingent of well-trained Cubans, a scattering of East Germans and some Russian big cheese.

The bottleneck on the Lomba's north bank was beginning to impinge on the FAPLA's plan to 'Greet October'. By now almost a month had been lost trying to move through the area and this really pissed Castro off. In the meantime, Castro's Russian and East German (communist) backers demanded a decisive settlement. The top Cuban general in Angola was increasingly beleaguered by criticism from back home and the Russian Generals despaired at their lack of success and consequently resolved to drive their forces harder and capitalise on their air superiority.

At the same time Modular participants were becoming more adept at bush warfare. Commanders ensured their intelligence gathering and battle planning was designed to give us whatever tactical advantage they could muster against the larger, better equipped force.

Intelligence gathered from POWs indicated that 47th Brigade and Tactical Group 1 were massing near the confluence of the Lomba and Cuzizi Rivers. It was believed the 47th and TG1 had given up trying to find a way past us to reach the bridgehead and, in a change of tactic, were attempting to find suitable river crossing to get back over to the north. It also seemed that their bridge-laying capabilities were not quite equal to the task of crossing the Lomba's marshy banks. Nearby, on the northern side of the river, 59th Brigade was requested to despatch more suitable bridging vehicles to the Lomba crossing. Setting them up and safely moving more than two hundred very heavy vehicles, men and materiel across to the north bank would take another couple of days. For SADF battle tacticians, this intel was solid gold but they had to act promptly. Plans were developed to exploit the concentration of materiel and apparent lack of ex-filtration route.

TG1, a Battalion strength unit, had a Squadron of Tanks, Battery of MRL systems and 30-40 Armoured Troop carriers in its arsenal although this had been somewhat depleted when engaging SADF and UNITA forces during September.

47th Mechanised Brigade was at least three times the size of TG1 and boasted a further two Squadrons of tanks, multiple Squadrons of armoured Troop carriers, rocket launchers and, it was believed, the legendary SAM-8 missile system.

At a briefing from a senior General prior to entering Angola we were told: "No one in the west has ever seen the SAM-8 (SA-8) weapon system. If we capture one of these systems and sell it on to the USA they would pick up the tab for the whole war, in fact they'd pay us a million dollars just for the operators manual!"

As it was with all previous contacts we wouldn't know the full extent of the opponent's size, strength or capabilities until we got stuck in.

We didn't have long to wait.

On 1 October we began preparing for imminent contact with the enemy. We knew it was likely to be significant because, for the first time during Operation Modular, a fully reconstituted 61 Mechanised Battalion Group would go into battle as a single unit.

After a fitful few hours of sleep we woke early on the morning of 2 October, adopted our formations and moved out toward the enemy positions.

Some time after sunrise we were stood down because the area of intended contact was too densely wooded for mechanised action. Once we'd returned to our laager we were given the remainder of the day off but advised to be prepared for a rerun the next day.

Our commanders planned a series of combined air force and artillery strikes to try to skirt and concentrate the enemy force toward what they deemed to be more favourable terrain.

We had time to relax, most preparatory work was done on 1 October when we'd bombed-up for battle but hadn't fired a single shot. Diesel needed topping off and weapons were cleaned again; otherwise we just relaxed among friends for the remainder of the day.

As a re-formed 61 Mech, we had a much larger laager than usual and when the officers were called to briefings (battle orders) with Major Laas, 2nd Lt. Hind got a little lost, turned up late and consequently got punished by the major who dealt out a rare wartime *opfok*.

October 3rd started unremarkably; we woke at 03:00 and quietly began stowing all superfluous gear such as camo nets and sleeping bags. I pulled on clean clothing and everyone psyched themselves up for what was likely to be a significant contact. Gunners across 61 Battalion carried out final weapons checks in the eerie red glow of internal cabin and turret lighting while drivers completed their vehicle checks.

As we finalised our pre-battle rituals, we were unaware that this would be the last time Charlie's close-knit cohort of combat troops would be together. For at least five of the guys this was to be their final day at war; and for one of them the final hours of life.

On the FAPLA side, many more boys were about to make the ultimate sacrifice for their country. 61 Mechanised Battalion, led by Charlie Squadron, supported by the combined Artillery of 20 Brigade were about to wreak military havoc of a kind not seen on the Mother Continent for over 40 years. The Ratel 90 was finally given the opportunity to prove herself as a Tank killer, and would do so in such emphatic style that their contribution changed the course of the entire conflict.

It is no understatement to say 3 October was to be a day unlike any other for the Squadron, our unit and the history of the SADF.

As per my usual ritual, socks, underwear, tank suit and body parts were clean, just in case. I should stress though that none of us had any intention of 'pegging-off' (dying) and going home in a bag, but this *was* proper war and people *were* dying. The stakes were high and no one took shortcuts when preparing for battle. Crew commanders knew that lives depended on decisions they took, that their gunners' accuracy might mean the difference between life and death, and that their drivers needed nerves of steel to follow orders and drive their vehicles into the thick of battle.

I couldn't contemplate living with the guilt of knowing that if I fucked up, or failed to fully prepare, it might very easily cost my comrades their lives.

When a soldier died in battle, the SA government was not entirely candid with its populace although they did inform his family, sometimes masking the true nature of the tragedy.

The Dos Santos government, accused of snatching young conscripts from remote villages, typically shielded Angolans from the true cost of their war and therefore it is widely acknowledged that estimates of their war dead are inaccurate.

On the opposite side of the Atlantic, the fate of their loved ones was seldom revealed to Cuba's long-suffering citizens – they were merely pawns in Castro's proxy war.

[Despite Angolan dominance of the sky and the advantage of a heavy-weight Russian military inventory, conservative estimates put the enemy's KIA (killed in action) during Operation Modular at over 2,000 men, some 20 times greater than the losses suffered by the UNITA cadre and vastly more than the 31 SADF personnel who also made the ultimate sacrifice during the operation. None of these soldiers should be forgotten.]

From the day we arrived at the Lomba River forward positions, we lived inside an artillery and air-raid bubble and no matter how good, or lucky, we were, it was only a matter of time before a bomb, some chunk of shrapnel, or bullet got in the way of a body part. As it was, this kind of indirect action accounted for a large share of KIA on both sides.

Four weeks since entering the 'bubble' most crews had survived 'miraculous' close shaves with shrapnel of some sort. Not even Logistics and support troops had been spared close brushes with death.

As a unified force, 61 Mech was still untested together in combat but it represented the most powerful armoured Allied force of the operation. Despite this, we were warned to expect fierce resistance from the far larger enemy which would probably include Russian MBTs.

At pre-battle briefing on 2 October, we were informed that Charlie would lead 61 Mech which the boys in the Squad believed was exactly the right call. We were rightfully confident that if anyone was going to have to square up to Russian tanks it had to be Charlie Squadron.

We still didn't have our own Olifants – they were just starting to mobilize back in South Africa – so it really was up to the 90s to face this one head on, thankfully this time with the full support of 61 Mech, which included eight 90mm 'anti-tank' Ratels from Bravo Coy.

So the plan was for the 12 Charlie Squad Ratels to lead the frontline, while Alpha Company formed up between us some 40–50 metres behind, offering additional firepower from their belt-fed 20mm buzz-saw-like armour piercing rounds. If the enemy was well dug-in, the Alpha's infantrymen were prepared to *stap-uit* (step-out) and drop into line with Charlie Squad once more.

Protection of our exposed left flank fell to the boys of Bravo Company, themselves battle hardened from having spearheaded BG Charlie in the preceding weeks. It was reassuring that such a strong unit was tasked with holding our left flank, confident they could protect us from predicted enemy encirclement. No additional flanking force was needed on our right near the Lomba because her wide marshy banks offered sufficient disincentive to any offensive flanking.

As usual, our battery of 81mm mortars, the *Ystervark* (iron pig) anti-aircraft battery and the command-and-control vehicles would trail us inside the Armoured pocket while the heavy artillery was installed much further back.

At 4am, exactly on schedule, vehicle commanders checked comms, confirmed battle readiness and pensively awaited further orders.

A short time later, the order came: "All vehicles start".

Adrenaline coursed through my veins, preparing me for the action that lay ahead.

I immediately relayed the 'engine start' order to Corrie, who punched the starter switch. The powerful 12-litre, twin-turbo diesel engine kicked into life.

The familiar roar and vibration of the two-ton engine housed in its protective steel cocoon four metres behind me was a comforting and familiar sound.

The deep cacophony of rumbling Ratel engines and the whine of hydraulic systems spooling-up erupted in the forest on all sides of us.

The radio crackled again, "Charlie Squadron, move out".

Turning the toggle on my chest-mounted radio channel selector, which controlled access to the three channels used by a crew commander, I instinctively selected the vehicle channel and relayed the order to my crewmates, "Okay, lads we're underway, let's move. David, follow call-sign 33 Charlie".

After long months of exhaustive training and five weeks in Angola, it's not too arrogant to say that my crew and I had become a well-oiled team.

Ratel drivers needed to be a particularly brave cohort. They had their front-row seats to the action but little control over targeting and shooting, occasionally alerting the crew commander to a target not spotted from the turret.

The driver who started the year on 32A had been replaced by David Corrie, I don't remember why the first guy left Omuthiya, I don't think it was a physical injury. David Corrie was an extremely capable driver but resented being pulled from his previous role where he'd been driving a support vehicle with the echelon – this would have been pretty chilled in comparison to driving a combat vehicle. David also detested being in the army and all forms of authority. As second-in-command of our Troop of four vehicles it often fell to me to attend to the dirty work when it came to issuing orders or punishment so, for a guy like David Corrie, I was simply part of the problem.

Although Herb, my gunner, didn't arrive with top-gun credentials – he tried very hard in training because things didn't come as naturally to him as they did for some of the more naturally gifted gunners – I liked him right from the start and chose him for my crew, in part because he was the runt of the Squad, the sort of guy that screws up more often than most, and the guy also endured regular mocking and abuse about his prominent buck teeth, which he normally took with very good humour, but I felt a bit sorry for the guy. Nevertheless, despite being one of the weaker gunners at the start of our 13 month border tour, repeated training exercises had elevated Herb to the top of his game. Herb Zeelie was capable of being as good as the best, and during the coming twelve hours would prove just how good he was. Repeatedly.

Herb had already proven more than capable in Angola, responding unquestioningly to each targeting command and was more accurate than opposing gunners which, without a doubt, is why I'm fortunate enough to be here to write this account.

In previous skirmishes and battles Herb had made every target, never needing more than a two shots to complete a kill, never once flinching under fire.

As the reunited 61 Mech moved out under cover of darkness on that cool morning, ghostly, green shadows in the high-tech night-vision goggles offered sketchy speckled images of the forest around us. I could easily make out the small, red light in its protective steel casing on the rear of the vehicle ahead and could quite readily distinguish trees and other potential hazards like trenches or ditches.

When we were first issued with this state-of-the-art equipment, we were impressed by the level of detail it showed even in very low-light conditions. This was our first indication that the army was taking the threat of war very seriously because these expensive items were not offered up willingly. We were sternly reminded about the truckloads of shit that would befall us if the kit got busted.

Night sights magnified ambient light so much that if someone sucked on a cigarette at 20 paces it was as though they'd switched on a torch – and if a guy used a cigarette lighter or struck a match while wearing the cumbersome headgear it was if the sun had switched on, temporarily blinding the wearer. It was quite inconceivable that we'd prosecute battle wearing night-sights because the two-metre-wide muzzle flash from our cannon would undoubtedly cause the wearer temporary blindness. Also, this gear was far too bulky to wear during the sort of high-speed activity inside the turret during battle. All the same, cumbersome as they were when attached to the face and helmet, night-vision goggles offered the safest way of navigating the pitch-black, heavily forested areas of south-eastern Angola when near to enemy positions where headlights would betray our position.

In terms of stealth, little could be done to mask the deep rumble and whine of our turbo-charged engines audible for a considerable distance, but the forest dispersed the sound making it difficult to pinpoint our exact location. We had ourselves encountered exactly the same difficulty when trying to locate moving enemy vehicles during the hours of darkness. However the same dispersal effect did not hold true for light. Without the use of night sights, beams from the headlights of 60 or more vehicles would have shot out from the darkness of the forest as they pitched and yawed over undulating terrain, making it easy for an enemy to target them.

As if in a choreographed ballet, the massed fighting force of 61 Mech, with Charlie Squadron at its head, emerged from the protection of the Ficus trees.

As we fell into a single file, the distinctive high-pitched whine of turbochargers kicked in hard to power the Ratel's 6x6 run-flat tyres through the soft soil.

With the exception of *Ystervark* (iron pig), 61 Mech fighting units were all Ratels. The SADF had invested heavily in these six-wheeled vehicles in preference to the tracked APCs or IFVs (infantry fighting vehicles) used by our FAPLA counterparts, for example the BMP2.

Our convoy maintained its steady pace through the early hours of 3 October, the inky sky gradually turning a lighter shade of blue.

David Corrie, by now an expert at manoeuvring our seven-metre behemoth through powder-soft sand, responded quietly and efficiently to my instructions through the helmet headset, though his task was simplified because we needed only to follow the deep furrows carved in the soil by the four vehicles ahead of us in the convoy.

Unless it was raining, or the air heavy with dust, most crew commanders preferred to travel standing on the adjustable height chair, waist and upper body clear of the turret, only using the seat inside the turret when necessary. My hips were constantly bruised from jarring against the narrow, turret opening when travelling over uneven terrain.

Obviously, in the thick of battle we adopted a much lower profile, sometimes battening shut the commander's cupola, particularly during an artillery bombardment.

During an earlier contact, totally focussed on the target area, I'd misjudged the height of a low-hanging branch which snagged the barrel of my 7.62mm turret-mounted Browning. As we travelled beneath the branch, it tore at the weapon swinging its barrel into my face with such force I was briefly stunned.

Herb, whose gunner's hatch was shut per protocol in preparation for contact, didn't have much to do in the three hours it took us to drive onto the staging area except chain-smoke nervously and fiddle with his Zippo lighter. On other days when he'd fallen asleep on the gunner's chair, it made for good sport watching his head loll drunkenly about inside the confines of the turret. When driving over rough terrain, it was only ever a matter of time before flesh and nearby steel connected.

Pre-contact staging went very smoothly. Despite the overwhelming size of the opposition, things felt just right that morning, as if our earlier battles and setbacks had been merely dress rehearsals for the main event, like a World Cup Final, when a smaller nation takes on a sporting superpower – or perhaps our quiet confidence stemmed from being back together with the full 61 Mech brotherhood.

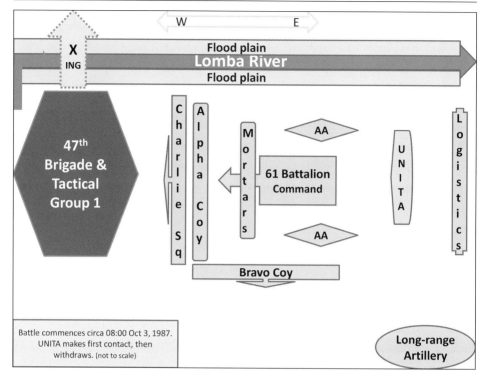

Photo 37 3 October 1987 tac map at battle start.

Just after sunrise, we arrived at our staging point where we disengaged from our support vehicles then fanned out into our prearranged, Westward-facing formation running parallel to the Lomba. As Charlie Squadron vehicles moved into line, we lost visual contact with everything except the two vehicles on either side of us. Increasingly, we were forced to rely on radio contact to ascertain our positions relevant to the rest of the formation.

From this moment on, I was only really aware of the world that was the bubble around 32 Alpha and trusted that those behind Charlie Squadron would do exactly as planned.

The sharp edge of the 61 Mech's 'dagger' formation relied absolutely on the proper functioning of all of its integrated parts: intel, artillery, infantry, mortars, medics, mechanics and anti-aircraft defence.

Little cheers a combat soldier's heart more than the call for long-range artillery and mortar boys to lob a few tons of high-explosive projectiles directly onto the target area to loosen things up before the party gets underway or, when equipment needs repair, to get mechanical support rapidly. And oh how grateful we were to the lads who drove the long convoys of supplies and food; sometimes they even managed to save us a few choice bits of blue meat from the vultures along the supply chain. Once cooked the meat tasted better than a tin of Vienna sausage-n-beans or that semen-like potato mayo we got in rat-pack #2 & 4. Even the convoys were not immune from attack and we valued highly their brave contribution to the war effort.

"Charlie Squadron, we're moving." Cloete's order delivered yet another surge of adrenaline.

At once we began rolling forward at walking speed. I, along with the other commanders of 61 Mech, dropped lower into the turret, now with only my chest and head exposed. Crews primed for imminent contact although intelligence indicated the main body of the 47th Brigade was still two clicks ahead.

After an hour of deep concentration and almost glacial forward movement, the formation was called to a halt, now only about 5-600 metres from enemy positions but still invisible through spring's fresh forest foliage.

Battle orders the night before had identified the need to accurately mark the location of enemy forces prior to launching a massive wave of MRL and artillery shells to 'clear the trees'. To do this a Company of UNITA comrades were tasked to move forward on foot, engage the enemy briefly and then quickly withdraw.

Minutes later scrawny UNITA troops with AK 47s and RPGs at the ready strode purposefully past our vehicles and disappeared into the bush ahead.

Tension continued to rise along with the arrival of dawn. The sun would rise behind our vehicles affording us a slight advantage over an enemy who would be partially blinded by the glare of the rising sun.

Less than ten minutes after the UNITA cadre stalked past our positions, sharp reports and crackles of gunfire signalled the opening salvos of battle. I instinctively dropped down into the turret as the rapid, automatic fire crackled and rose in intensity just ahead of us.

There was no turning back now, the game was on, our foe was at home, had answered the front door and, it seems, was expecting us. This realisation sparked a massive adrenaline surge, but this was no time for sweaty palms or shaky hands.

Within a couple of minutes the automatic fire subsided as the UNITA soldiers pulled back from the contact area. Five agonising minutes later and the guerrillas suddenly reappeared from the bushes ahead, ambling nonchalantly back to their vehicles as if they had just been for a relaxing stroll along the beach!

I offered the black-skinned warriors a nervous grin and a 'thumbs-up'. Although we shared no common language everyone understood the international sign language for 'everything's OK'.

"Charlie Squadron, we're holding for artillery 'ripple' bombardment. Close all hatches, now!" Captain Cloete's clipped command crackled simultaneously in each headset of the 12 crew commanders on the frontline.

I dropped down into the turret pulling the dome-shaped cupola shut. There was nothing more to do than wait at the ready and hope the artillery ordinance was on target. We'd only once before used artillery at such close quarters and it could get a bit hairy with bombs landing so close by we couldn't be certain if it was enemy or friendly fire!

We waited in heavy silence for what seemed ages but within two minutes came that familiar whistling and then crump…crump…crump as an unbroken barrage of heavy ordinance erupted in flashes in the forest no more than 200-500 metres ahead.

This was good! Dead-eye mortar men, in concert with their long-range artillery and MRL counterparts, released a well coordinated ripple of shock and awe onto enemy positions like the climax of some macabre fireworks display lasting a good three or four minutes.

As the forest fell silent once more, I opened the cupola and locked it in the 90 degree 'up' position before poking my head into the open to assess the target area ahead. It seemed quite a lot of forest foliage beyond our immediate tree line had been stripped clean, creating a sort of 'no-man's land' clearing across which opposing forces could face each other.

A minute later all 12 crew commanders' headsets sparked back to life with Cloete's unwelcomed command, "Charlie Squadron, move out in formation… may God be with you all."

An instant later I relayed that order to my crew

'Okay boys this is it… let's move out. Herb, prepare to fire'.

Today, after 20 months of training, preparation, lesser battles and small skirmishes against the enemy, all the pieces of that monstrous mechanised jigsaw puzzle finally dropped into place. The stage had been set for The Battle on the Lomba.

We resumed our slow and controlled forward movement in flat formation with about 30 metres separating each vehicle. Troop Two (32) arrayed to the left-front, Troop One (31) at the centre and Troop Three (33) on the right. Anything that happened behind us warranted no further consideration. With my field of focus now reduced to the 180 degree arc in front, I kept visual contact with at least one vehicle on either side of me.

The tree line obscuring our view of the contact area was now close, just 20-30 metres ahead; the area beyond seemed comparatively sparse following the earlier artillery ripples. Once we moved into this area we'd be fair game, visible to enemy positions with precious little cover.

Ratel crews were trained to manoeuvre and 'jockey' their vehicle into new firing positions to frustrate enemy targeting, but with such little cover it was imperative that the back, sideways and forward manoeuvre wasn't performed at too sharp an angle as this would expose the large soft flanks of the vehicle to enemy fire.

"Once more into the breach dear friends, once more…"

Fellow combatants, or those who've experienced severe trauma, such as a car accident, will know that during the traumatic event itself, time seems to slow right down. This happens because the brain speeds up so that things only appear to be happening much more slowly. While the rules of reality are suspended in this way, what seems impossible under normal conditions becomes quite possible in the heat of combat.

Autopilot kicked in at about 08:00. When it switched off eight hours later, we'd lost the life of Lieutenant Adrian Hind. His crew had been seriously injured; his Ratel destroyed by one unlucky shot. On the opposite side of the battlefield the 47th Brigade and TG1 had for all intents and purposes been completely annihi-lated and was no longer a credible fighting force. The survivors were beating a rapid and chaotic retreat. The remaining half-dozen T55s from their Tank Squadrons were in full flight, hundreds of soldiers lay dead or seriously wounded and an estimated 100 vehicles had been destroyed or abandoned. The bonus prize; they'd been forced to abandoned three of USSR's never-before-seen SAM-8's, although admittedly some were a little banged up.

[The 3 October battle on the Lomba was such a decisive and humiliating defeat for the FAPLA it resulted in severe reprimands for both the Cuban and Russian commanders who were replaced shortly afterwards; and it was rumoured to have cost the top Cuban general his life, although this was never acknowledged by the regime.

61 Mech inflicted such an overwhelming defeat on the 47th Brigade that some described it as a 'David v Goliath' miracle. Maybe it was, but probably the training and discipline so typical of the SADF was the decisive factor and, of course, a shed load of luck. Naturally, there were many contributory factors to the overwhelming victory that day and I've tried to set them out in the preceding

pages as honestly as possible, given my perspective on the Operation. But at this moment, I would like to give credit to Charlie Squadron and 61 Mechanised Battalion who stood on the shoulders of giants that day and achieved something extraordinary in the annals of military history.

It just so happens that I am very well placed to share my front-row-seat view of those dramatic hours.]

The very first moments of contact came as we approached no-man's land only seconds after the radioed warning: "All units be advised, enemy snipers have been spotted in the trees."

Before we could acknowledge the warning, the crackle of automatic fire ahead marked the start of battle and seeking out snipers became a secondary objective but they remained an ever-present and deadly threat.

In those early minutes the contact started tamely enough; staccato bursts from a number of light machine-gun emplacements with the odd crump of a high-powered weapon.

The enemy wasn't yet visible to me as we breached the last line of dense foliage before the field-of-fire opened up offering relatively uninterrupted views of the terrain 200-300m ahead. Here, in no-man's-land, the ripple bombardment had almost stripped the land of life, the few trees that still stood were devoid of foliage giving them a wintry appearance.

Then, as if on a single command, the forest at the opposite tree line burst into life with a ferocity we'd never before experienced. Charlie Squad suddenly came under a sustained barrage of small-arms, mortar and artillery fire, the sheer concentration of which would've been overwhelming were it not for our almost instinctive response borne from countless drills during training. Everything seemed unreal, dream like.

It seemed 47th Brigade were expecting us and had had sufficient time to deploy a sizeable force on their defensive frontline. But they were less well dug in to protective trenches than usual with enemy combatants kneeling or standing to fire on us from the cover of the trees on the far side of the no-man's land. Immediately ahead of us was the exposed area, a killing field which we'd have to cross if we were to make any significant progress today. As we entered this more open zone, we were now within 200 metres of the nearest identifiable enemy position.

Now it really was time for action. The fear I had felt on the approach suddenly melted away. The only way out this while still alive was to press forward – into the mechanised maelstrom. I was absolutely, coldly, prepared to unleash the most ruthlessly violent intensity of fire imaginable – anything to subdue and repel the enemy before he had opportunity to do same to me. I'm sure every crewman felt exactly the same, on both sides of the battle. The fighting was intensely, mercilessly, brutal

Zeelie and I were already working the turret machine guns hard in response to the incoming fire as we prepared to unleash our first HE round at the soft-target positions. Enemy soldiers were darting around within the tree line, the muzzle flashes of their weapons a beacon for my trusty, turret-mounted 7.62mm and Herb's 90mm cannon with its co-axially mounted Browning.

As we jockeyed positions, we gradually made incremental forward movement despite the enemy augmenting his lines. The silhouettes of harder targets started to appear in the background.

SOP recommended entering combat 'hatches-down', to close the cupola over my head, but target identification from within the turret was nigh on impossible. The periscope inside the turret offered limited views and the narrow, two-inch-thick glass ring surrounding the cupola was light-green in colour – quite unhelpful when hunting green-camouflaged targets amongst green undergrowth.

During earlier contacts we'd learned that the safest option, ironically, was head-out-turret when target finding only dropping down when hearing the pock-pock-pock, like a popcorn popping, of accurate incoming fire.

War is often punctuated by long periods of downtime, but the first hour of battle was the antithesis of that, it was like payback for the days we'd lazily loafed around in Angola while our contemporaries back in SA maintained camp drills.

The ground around us erupted with increasing fury as the enemy's artillery began to find our range. We were at the epicentre of the deadly, deafening cacophony of mechanised combat. The full might of FAPLA artillery and mortars were targeting both our frontline and support vehicles, their shells exploding in an almost unbroken thunder amongst us.

The artillery onslaught was unavoidable. We had no choice but to ignore the bombardment raining down on us and focussed only on maintaining drills and discipline – keep moving position…reload…replace machine-gun belts…clear the jam – concentrating only on those things within our control and doing it harder, faster and uglier than the opposition.

The battle soon became my most hard-core combat experience. It was more open, more intense and violent than anything I had previously encountered. This was the sort of large-scale battle Hollywood seeks, but mostly fails, to emulate when depicting war. In truth, the only way to prosecute this real-life gangbang was to get fucking brutal on the FAPLA boys; to that end 32 Alpha was working together in perfect harmony with Troop 2, sighting, aiming and destroying numerous soft and hard targets as they appeared. At the frontline there was no time to keep score or call in each destroyed target because the Squadron communications net was at times overloaded with chatter; we had much more pressing matters to deal with than taking audit.

On our right-front 33 Alpha, commanded by Troop Sergeant Stephan Rossouw, found himself within 30-40 metres of a trench bristling with men wielding AK47s and RPGs. The target was too close and too low to employ his 90 mil gun and the 7.62 was proving ineffectual against the emplacement – and there was no Infantry on the ground to silence the trench.

Rossouw realised his best available option was to lob a hand grenade into the trench. He stood up high enough in the turret to pitch the explosive ball in the face of a withering a hail of incoming fire.

He pulled the pin and pitched for his life.

The grenade fell short.

There wasn't time for another grenade. The angry hornet's nest he'd tried to disturb was emboldened; 33Alpha jockeyed vehicle position. Under intense fire, Rossouw ordered Driver Herman Ferreira to reverse 30-40 metres. Two RPGs narrowly missed the Ratel as its 12-litre powerhouse sent it roaring backwards towards the relative cover of a copse of trees.

Ten minutes later, after fighting their way forward once more to within 30 metres of the same emplacement, Rossouw tossed a second grenade. Again the restrictions of throwing out the turret from nipple-height saw his grenade drop metres short of the angry trench.

Rossouw's 33A was forced to withdraw once more and reposition once more under withering fire and this time the RPG and small-arms attack had been joined by a Russian BTR APC. A direct hit on 33 Alpha's turret then destroyed the gunsight, it would take an act of heroism by that crew to stay the battle without the ability to accurately sight their gun.

Half an hour after first engaging the trench, 33A finally got within range to throw a third grenade, this time plumb into the opposition position. By now, so caught up in the hellfire of war, Stephan Rossouw relentlessly pursued a single escaping soldier with his Browning 7.62, outpacing and then retracing the running man until Warren Adams, his gunner, suggested the job was done.

[Remarkably, Warren later told me he'd been unable to feel his legs at all during the day-long battle. They'd been numb the whole time which might be explained thus: a busy 90mm gunner has no real need for his legs, and his body, obviously realising the legs were unnecessary appendages at this time, rerouted vital resources elsewhere.]

Subconsciously I knew 61 Mech soldiers were ranged behind us, but I was physically oblivious of them or their actions. At best, during the course of battle, I could see the remaining two vehicles on my left and one or two vehicles on my right flank. That was the extent of the visibility. My focus was primarily my vehicle, my Troop and then the Squadron, and continually drawing mental maps about the position and status of my brethren from intel gleaned from radio transmissions across our front.

Then the first radio report of a T55 was called in.

That caught my attention.

The enemy MBT was targeting 31 Charlie somewhere near the centre of the Squad formation. There was nothing Troop two or I could do about that but Gunner Lance Corporal James Sharp on Three One (31), Martin Bremer's Ratel, almost choked on his radio mike as the T55 filled his gunsight at a distance less than 50m.

Sharp fired a round and missed, he'd never been trained to fire at moving targets from 50 metres – none of us had!

The T55 belched flame from its 100mm cannon, firing again on 31 Charlie. 31C was taking evasive action – the shot missed.

Bremer quickly loaded another HEAT round and this time the gunner made allowance for the target's movement. That shot stopped the Tank in its tracks. A third shot caused the T55's barrel to droop comically. A fourth shot, for good measure, marked the first of 18 enemy tanks scheduled for destruction at The Battle on the Lomba that day.

The arrival of Russian MBTs heralded a new, even deadlier phase as 47th began moving their biggest boys up onto the frontline, supported by more lightly armoured BTRs, BRDMs and Platoons of infantrymen .

The air thick was with the stench of burnt cordite; at times the plumes of earth thrown up by shells exploding nearby left clouds of dust hanging in the sky, reducing visibility to a few metres. We were in the midst of a continual explosive cacophony, the rattle of shrapnel and bullets on the steel body of our vehicle an almost constant reminder of the perilous nature of our predicament.

There was not a single moment of respite. We were under total attack. Absolutely focussed on the job at hand, we continued seeking and destroying targets as soon as they appeared, the quicker, the better; and as Rossouw demonstrated in 33A, in any way possible!

Retaining good linear form across the front, we gradually gained new ground, continually jockeying, a 20-30m reverse, then a similar distance forwards, never staying in the same spot longer than the time required to bring Zeelie on target, release one, perhaps two bombs and then give Corrie the order to move and reset. Whatever happened, we had to aim and shoot and be on the move again within 45 seconds so as never to present the enemy with a sitting duck for a target; the consequence of that was almost certain destruction.

Within the first two hours of battle, I noted fighter jets overhead, but they flew outside of target area. But this was no time to be concerned or distracted by them. I remained focussed on the targets ahead, occasionally snatching a glance to the left of our no-man's-land field of operations, looking for snipers in the tall trees. If something moved, the Browning at my right hand was quick to follow.

'Load HEAT! Tank 250, eleven o'clock. Fire when ready!' This was a close as my crew had been to a live Russian MBT.

The low-slung beast appeared initially as an apparition moving through the trees, hatches down, angling towards us. Herb quickly traversed the gun onto target and then…I saw the muzzle flash erupt from the MBT's 100mm cannon. He'd fired on us. Miss! We had less than 15 seconds before another round followed.

At such close range it took only moments for Zeelie to make sure of his aim.

"Do it Herb!" I was absolutely fucking praying that Zeelie would hold it together and make suitable allowance for the target's movement.

BOOM!

Before 32 Alpha had absorbed the recoil and settled back onto its suspension, I saw the HEAT round strike the T54's hull low, around the area of the tracks, creating only a small, almost imperceptible, white flash but instantly immobilising the 40-ton unit. But the T54's gun turret was still operational.

"Hit! You hit it! Fucking great shooting Herb. I'm loading another HEAT. Quick, let's finish it!"

Herb removed the spent shell. I slid another black-tipped antitank round into the open breach. The heavy breach block slammed up behind the bomb. Zeelie made a minor correction on the gun. BOOM!

"Driver reverse!"

It had taken less than eight seconds to release two rounds from the cannon, the second shot also hit true, this time higher up on the turret section of the T54, puncturing through the thick turret wall.

There was no time for triumphalism or celebration. We had killed our first MBT but we'd merely eliminated one of many threats to our lives – we had to *vok-voort* (push forward). The belts on both Brownings needed replacing. And there were more targets to find.

Herb reached down into the right-side door area, grabbed two more of our custom 'double belt' boxes of ammo before manually loading the first round.

Within minutes the next large target appeared in our field of fire, an APC, dark green, with what appeared to be corrugated iron-sides.

Corrie completed the jockey manoeuvre while I called in the location of the enemy APC. "Gunner, load HE. Target 250metres, twelve o,clock. Fire when ready." BOOM, the recoil concussion blast was like a punch in the nose, that familiar sensation from training of getting slapped in the face with a heavy wet towel – but now we welcomed it.

"Target eliminated! Driver reverse".

Across the line guys were increasingly encountering heavy mechanised resistance but we were really doing it – a Squadron of 90mm was taking on heavy armour, and doing OK!

It was at times slow going but gradually we inched our way further across no-man's-land, toward the line of trees that had been so heavily defended all morning.

Move forward, fire, reverse 20-30m then come back towards them from a cover position, or if no cover was available, simply perform the manoeuvre to try avoid incoming fire – this was how it was for Charlie Squadron during the morning, three hours of fluid fire-and-move action, a seemingly well-oiled machine on the chassis of 61 Mechanised Battalion Group. But we knew that it wasn't just the efficiency of 61's fighting force that would win the day, no, we needed a huge dollop of luck to survive the enemy's robust defence. There was just too much happening that was outside our control – sometimes mere millimetres separated life from death as projectiles and shrapnel fizzed continuously through the air around us. It was relentless.

Then the from the APC to my left, 32 Charlie (32C), Lance Corporal Bobby Robbello screamed over the Troop net, *"Ek kan nie skiet, ek kan nie skiet"* (I can't shoot, I can't shoot!)

What the fuck?

My first thought was that his gun or gunner had frozen, but how could that be… they'd just taken out an RPG installation. I later found out that accurate small-arms fire from another position had struck the crew commander's Browning, sparing Robbello from being hit – the near-death experience had momentarily rendered him incapable of command.

Robbello came back online, "Tank targeting me at my twelve o'clock, 60 metres!"

Standing nipples-high in the turret I couldn't immediately see 32C but knew we were nearest to them, on their right flank. I couldn't see the tank ahead either but called back, "OK Bobby, we're coming in…" still unable to envisage the scenario in his turret.

"Driver forward ten o'clock, 50 metres, fast!" I barked, "Gunner load HEAT!"

The manoeuvre was high risk, the angle of approach exposed our right flank to the enemy but no large-calibre weapons seemed to be targeting me just then, and there was no time to waste, three brothers' lives were at stake. The ball-grabbing, ear-biting squabble, between Bobby and I in the dust at Omuthiya was just an amusing anecdote from the past.

While the crew carried out my barked order, my every sense was hyper alert, searching for the deadly MBT targeting 32C.

As we angled in ahead and to the side of 32 Charlie's position, Gunner Wilco Brooks fired an HE round they had up the pipe. We deployed smoke grenades while the driver jockeyed left to avoid incoming fire. Many crews saved their hides by performing this rapid manoeuvre to spoil enemy targeting.

In the confusion Brooks continued to use his woefully inadequate Browning against the tank but the tracer fire, in an almost unbroken red line, pointed directly at the enemy tank.

I immediately joined him in pouring a continuous stream of fire from my mounted 7.62 machine gun with modified 400-round mag-belts, hoping to distract the T55 crew and simultaneously guide our gunner, Herb, onto the target.

"Gunner, follow my tracer rounds. Short range target. Fire now, fire now!"

BOOM! Bomb away and smack on target.

"You fucking beauty Herb, you got it, let's go again!"

It was unbelievable. The older T55 Tanks were not impervious to well-placed 90mm warheads, and it seemed we were more than capable of beating them in close-quarters combat by taking advantage of our manoeuvrability.

Selecting the Squad-net from the toggle switch at my chest I opened the radio channel and called the strike in, 'Three Zero, this is Three Two Alpha, threat neutralised!"

32 Charlie got herself together and we continued pushing forward with no let up in the intensity of contact while artillery elements on both sides of the battle raised the temperature of their pipes beyond normal operating levels.

On our left flank, Bravo Company were called into action to defend a significant tactical encirclement action by T55 MBTs supported by APC's in an attempt to open a smaller, second front.

This was by far our greatest single contact on Modular. No previous contact had lasted this long, nor had we ever been in clear striking distance of such an unrelenting number of high value targets. They had nowhere to run, they were committed to protecting their bridging area so when it seemed we'd knocked a tooth out the opponents mouth he quickly moved reinforcements to repair the gap with a new, even tougher tooth. They were highly mobile, appearing from rearward positions in deeper bush to move rapidly into frontal, offensive positions.

One moment, the area of denuded forest was clear as far as I could make out, and on the very next scan, a group of soldiers or rogue vehicle suddenly materialised to join the fray.

After three hours of non-stop frontal assault, Commandant Smit ordered a tactical withdrawal. 47th Brigade was a hardened, mechanised unit and their resilience had kept Charlie's crews busy and by now most of our turrets were running critically low on 90mm munitions.

The Squad continued attracting enemy fire for some time as we withdrew across the ground we'd gained at glacial pace during the morning.

We'd probably only made forward gains of 150-200 metres and as we moved behind that line to reach the relative safety of the deeper tree line behind which the morning's assault had been launched, a euphoric high flooded my entire body. The relief among the lads too, was palpable. We'd just survived the most unbelievable assault and the further we moved from contact and realised we were all still operational, the more the self-congratulatory we became. Once we completed our controlled withdrawal to safety – about 1000m from the front – our jovial mood was quickly extinguished when intel specialist Saunders informed us the Captain had been summoned to Commandant Smit's Battalion Command Ratel. Whatever they were discussing it was clearly not for radio channel chit chat!

There was immediate speculation that the cheese wanted to capitalise on the successful morning and send us back in for more of the same. It was hard to disagree with this assessment, battle conditions were the best they'd been since we'd arrived in Angola.

Crews across the battle group began refuelling and replenishing their vehicles, many of which bore testament to the narrowness of the margins between life and death at war. Black scars were evident on almost all the vehicles where a tank round or similar had struck at too shallow an angle to detonate, or penetrate, and had harmlessly slid down the side of the vehicle. And every one of our vehicles bore a myriad of little gouges in their armour; tattoos left by whizzing shrapnel.

Drivers replaced the bomb damaged run-flat tyres while gunners cleared thousands of spent 7.62mm bullet casings from their vehicles and prepared new 400-round belts while commanders discussed tactics.

The mood of the Squadron's men was actually quite ebullient; we'd all seen and targeted tanks, sometimes double-teaming them to good effect. Our Squadron was still intact and we felt very much in the ascendancy.

The early speculation turned out to be accurate. On Squad-net Captain Cloete conveyed the Commandant's commendation of our steadfast and heroic actions that morning before despatching us onto the frontline once more. Less than an hour after our withdrawal, 61 Mech started engines again and Charlie Squad returned to the head of formation, this time moving toward the target area more quickly and far more confident of the location and capability of 47th Brigade.

My Charlie Squad buddies were too deep on autopilot (or in shock) to have much emotional response to the risks of going back in. We were going in, end of story.

Unfortunately this wasn't the end of the story for the Battle on the Lomba because opposition forces hadn't been resting idly on their laurels during the hour-long lunch break, anything but!

These guys were in deep shit! FAPLA, it seems, had deployed TG1 and one of three armoured Battalion's during the morning but had demonstrated nothing like the mobility, rate of fire and accuracy brought to them by 61 Mechanised Battalion's well-trained SADF soldiers.

47th Brigade was cornered. They couldn't 'melt' such a large force into the forest behind them as they'd done when we encountered smaller enemy contingents during the previous two weeks. Their only escape was over the restricted river crossing but this could only safely handle a handful of vehicles per hour so they had to defend the position, their lives depended on it.

Clearly, there was an imperative that the valuable, and still secret, SAM-8 anti-aircraft technology and other key weapon systems were able make good their escape and not fall into enemy hands so FAPLA had no choice but to stand and fight, return maximum firepower and defend their position until such time as the Brigade could make safe egress.

59th Brigade was standing off five clicks on the northern side of Lomba and were called in to provide artillery support.

While we'd been brewing coffee and washing grime from our faces, 47th Brigade had reinforced their frontline with another Battalion.

As we moved back into no-man's-land the tempo of incoming fire quickly reached a deadly crescendo once more.

Rested and watered Charlie Squad adopted their drills, moving, targeting, firing, moving...

The afternoon session opened with more reports of direct action against T55s and BTRs.

Accompanied once more by the cacophony of battle, the crew of 32 Alpha picked up where we'd left off, as if the half-time break hadn't occurred, except now, turret replete with a full compliment of 29 bombs and thousands more Browning 7.62mm rounds, double belted and awaiting their call to duty.

Early afternoon offered even more high value targets than the morning as we squeezed the enemy back through their defensive lines towards the Lomba River. Consequently, the increasingly beleaguered 47th poured in ever more heavy-metal resources in a desperate attempt to hold us off until they could get across river.

Within two hours, 32A's turret ordinance was almost depleted once more, but this time there was to be no back-line reprieve which meant the inescapable spectre of having to break off contact to resupply.

The thought of leaving the other crews, my brothers, was unwelcome. The fear I'd felt before the commencement of battle had been supplanted by total commitment and dedication to the task and to my people. I had become so deeply immersed in the sensations of battle that I really didn't want to leave my Squad. It was with a nagging feeling of regret that I was forced to disengage from the fight but, unless we withdrew, 32Alpha would be defending itself with only 7.62mm rounds and the two remaining antipersonnel rounds.

"Herb, take the shot, David we're pulling back for resupply".

Opening the Troop net, I announced, "Three Two, this is Three Two Alpha, I'm withdrawing to replenish my turret!'

"Three Two Alpha affirm," was curt the response from 2nd Lt. Michael O'Connor, who was understandably focussed on his own field-of-fire.

David immediately began fast reverse. A Ratel driver has no rear-view capability; externally mounted side mirrors had no place in bush warfare, they'd be torn off within minutes, so the driver relied completely on someone else's guidance. With my head poking above the turret, I shouted instructions to David who skilfully manoeuvred the Ratel around obstacles, particularly large trees.

As we withdrew, Herb gainfully laid down a continuous stream of 7.62mm from his co-axially mounted Browning, only stopping briefly to reload a fresh 400-round belt. We had to keep the FAPLA boys' heads down as much as possible because they seemed to have an unending supply of RPGs.

I was uncertain how far we should reverse in order to replenish the turret 'safely'. I knew from experience during training that the reloading exercise required one of us to be exposed outside the vehicle for a few minutes but I also knew that the farther we pulled back, the longer we'd be out of line.

Bombs and bullets whizzing and pinging, branches snapping off trees, we'd only reversed 20-30 metres when inexplicably, David inadvertently tramped on the brakes slowing the Ratel dramatically. I shouted, "Keep going, keep going, the terrain clear!"

David Corrie responded immediately by flooring it again. Just as the 18-ton hulk's automatic gearbox gained pressure and our reverse movement resumed, I watched a huge explosion erupt less than four metres away on the Ratel's roof, inside the hub of the spare wheel locked atop the engine hatches!

Shielded from the blast by the thick steel cupola still locked in an upright position, my legs buckled beneath me, hardly believing I was still alive as the vehicle rocked under the force of what must've been a massive 82mm mortar round!

With a shudder, I immediately realised that David's momentary deceleration had altered the vehicle's location as the bomb struck…had he not slowed…. shit, that was another close call!

I forced myself to peer back out the turret and guide the vehicle safely as we continued reversing through no-man's-land. The area we were leaving, the area we'd fought over all day, resembled the apocalyptic Tunguska meteor event with its flattened and stripped-bare trees.

Two or three hundred metres back from the frontline, realising there was no place that would offer great cover or protection from the maelstrom, I halted the Ratel. "OK David stop here. There's no good cover nearby to do this. Open left door…let me know if anything changes at your twelve."

In a flash I'd unplugged the comm-jack from the channel selector, jumped over the top of the turret, landing cat-like on the ground. Before the pneumatic steel door fully opened I noticed new black streaks down the side of our vehicle, evidence of near misses.

Disregarding the nearby explosions, my attention was focussed only on selecting the appropriate ordinance, unlocking bomb catches and passing the heavy rounds up to Herb in the turret, one at a time.

Working at hyper speed, Zeelie slid and locked each bomb in place. Helpfully, David twisted around in his seat to clear a number of spent 90mm shells cluttering the turret floor area. SOP dictated that because loose casings could trap the turret mechanism, effectively jamming and delaying a turret traverse they should be manually ejected from the turret but in the madness of the preceding hours there just hadn't been opportunity to do so after every shot. To me it seemed we were taking forever to fully replenish the turret, but in reality it took no more than about three minutes.

I clambered up the side of the vehicle, back into the turret…tank helmet on… comm-check with crew. "David, close left door" and then, "Floor it!" The door slammed, locked, and we were racing back into the action.

"Three Two, Three Two Alpha, we're coming back in, I'll take up similar position."

Less than a minute later we returned to our position in formation, immediately coming under attack from a group of infantry at 200 metres, some of them still exiting a nearby APC and taking cover behind a large tree adjacent their vehicle. Then my attention was drawn to a black dot travelling toward us, almost in slow motion. Gradually, the dot grew larger and larger and until my brain finally fathomed that the dot was headed straight at me!

There was no time to move the vehicle, nothing I could do to change our fate. My legs gave way, I dropped back into the turret, looked up as the distinctive green tube spun lazily overhead, missing my hatch-cover by inches.

"Fucking RPG! God that was close!"

But this was not the time to dwell on the implications that would have followed a hit. "New target acquired! Gunner, load HE, large tree, 200 metres, follow tracer, fire now!"

BOOM! Recoil…slap-in-face sensation.

"OK, great shot, the tree is gone, let's take their vehicle, I'm loading HEAT, fire when ready!"

Without a flicker of emotion, the enemy Infantrymen no longer represented a threat, we moved smoothly on to finding the next target.

The Squadron was experiencing the ugly logic of warfare at first hand – kill or be killed. Across the frontline and on our left flank battle raged, 61 Mech continued bringing shed-loads of ugly to 47th Brigade who, for their part, were desperately clinging to their territory in defence of the crossing.

Then we started to lose vehicles from our own formation, not from enemy action directly, but from a technical issue with the 90mm cannons. The cannon recoil used internal gas chambers to return the gun to starting position after each round was fired. As part of regular maintenance the guns would be regassed but the toll of the long day's battle began to render a number of guns inoperable.

Troop 2 was one gun down when, in the fog of battle, Three Two (32) Commander Mike O'Connor opened comms on troop-net sounding panicked, "All units, I'm taking MBT fire but can't locate target!"

O'Connor had sensibly closed his hatch after catching shrapnel with his shoulder but operating hatch down made target discovery very tricky in the conditions,

Driver Van Niekerk on 32 jockeyed constantly, stalling for time, spoiling the enemy's aim while trying to pinpoint the tank.

By now, the crew of 32 Alpha and I were like a single organism working together in near perfect harmony. We'd survived five hours on war's insane stage, the number of close-calls and near misses impossible to calculate. Perhaps beginning to feel invincible, I was absolutely committed to the ruthless and immediate prosecution of the mission and the defence of my team. My response to the crew was instant, "Let's get this one!"

"Three Two, Three Two Alpha, we're moving forward from your three o'clock now."

Lesser targets temporarily forgotten, the elusive MBT became the primary target as we quickly moved some 60-80 metres diagonally down range, forward of 32's area of operation.

The forward rush gave me a different perspective on the terrain and almost immediately a large thick bush caught my attention, it looked an ideal size to shelter an MBT-sized lump, confirmed seconds later by a bright flash erupting from the bush. He was firing on the crew of 32, but just missed!

Within seconds of 32's urgent call, I'd spotted a section of 100mm barrel, obviously connected to a tank, protruding from the bush. Three Two had no more than 15 seconds before the enemy tank crew reloaded and reacquired the jockeying target.

The MBT's position in the bush meant the crew were blind to our rush from their ten o'clock position.

With a HEAT round already chambered, locked and loaded, David halted on my command. By now the back end of the T55 was visible and I immediately lit it up with 7.62mm tracers.

"Gunner new target, ten o'clock, 60 metres, follow tracers…"

In the seconds delay as he aimed, I silently willed Zeelie to make the shot count before the T55 released another round at O'Connor's Ratel. "Fire when ready."

Herb squeezed the firing button at his right thumb. BOOM!

Still pouring ack-ack fire into the bush, I ignored the slap in the face. A split second later a flash lit the T55.

I ripped the spent shell casing from the breach, slammed in another HEAT. Zeelie made sure of his aim before releasing the quick-fire shot. "Driver reverse!" Before we completed the jockey manoeuvre, a larger explosion ripped the turret clean off the tank's hull. It rose in the air a little, flipping over before toppling to the side so that it looked like a stranded turtle lying next to the stricken hull. "Three Two, this is Three Two Alpha, target eliminated."

In 1989 I was later awarded the Military Merit Medal (MMM) for 'services of a high order' in relation to 'bravery in combat' associated with this battle (but only learned this 25 years later). And such accolade must be shared with the crew and the Squad.

We saw that broken tank again a few weeks later, or at least, we saw a black and white photo of it on propaganda leaflets used against the FAPLA.

Our risky forward push to eliminate the T55 left me feeling like we could hold the additional ground we'd gained and within 20 minutes of fire and move we found ourselves moving deeper into enemy territory, past the stricken T55 turtle-turret. Now we were at least 500 metres nearer to 47th Brigade than we were at the start of the day. It felt as if enemy resistance was finally crumbling, certainly on the left front furthest from the river. Meanwhile Troop 3 and Troop 1 might still have been meeting somewhat heavier resistance due to being closer to the river and the bridging point.

From my turret it appeared we had exhausted the enemy's defence in our immediate area and we were finally able to enter the main tree line from which 47th had launched their stubborn defence during the whole of that afternoon.

Despite not knowing what lay behind the tree line we continued to make slow but steady progress deeper into enemy-held terrain.

The in-battle analysis was that Charlie Squad had destroyed dozens of hard targets including at least a Squadron of T55, 32 Alpha herself taking out three MBTs and a handful of armoured targets while our antitank boys on the left flank racked up a significant number of hard targets including some T55s. It seemed 61 Mech was unstoppable.

Then, just at that moment, as if to castrate my boyish triumphalism….

Someone once said that if you gave an infinite number of monkeys an infinite number of typewriters they'd eventually create the works of William Shakespeare. In our case, there were seemingly an infinite number of projectiles being hurled at us by any infinite number of humans (although, in fact, there were less than 2,500 men attached with the 47th and TG1), but countless thousands of the projectiles launched, or fired, on 3 October and each had sufficient kinetic energy to slice a Ratel open like hot knife through butter. Throughout the long hours of battle that day, there was not a second of silence, the never-ending, high-explosive soundtrack played endlessly on a loop and for any one of us, the music threatened to stop at any moment. [It is generally accepted –certainly from an SADF perspective – that the lads on the opposition team were less well trained, less disciplined and apparently less well nourished than us. Propaganda suggested many Angolans were fighting unwillingly against fellow countrymen, for a Communist-based cause they hardly believed in. Many willingly joined the army to improve their opportunities in life but nevertheless stories abounded of conscript snatching. It was also said that crewmen were limited to one cup of rice per day, and that tank drivers were shackled inside their vehicle to prevent them deserting during combat. Whatever the truth might be, I never witnessed dead drivers in shackles.] It was therefore little short of miraculous that by mid-afternoon on 3 October, 61 Mech had survived the maelstrom unleashed by 47th Brigade and TG1 without sustaining any real injury. Behind the opponent's frontline more than 70 enemy vehicles were already destroyed or abandoned due to direct and indirect action. Their number of dead was difficult to ascertain but must have been measured in hundreds.

On our left flank, the defensive shield made up of Bravo Company was holding rock solid, the eight 90mm crews of Seven One (71) and Seven Two (72) unequivocally earning their 'anti-tank stripes' that day.

If miracles do occur, they seemed to be occurring a whole lot more for us than for the guys on the opposite side – perhaps the commie-backed enemy had pissed off the God of Miracles. But the longer battle raged, the greater the chance of our enemy making a miracle of their own; of making their first kill shot. Lucky or otherwise, any FAPLA kill shot was not going to be 'much ado about nothing', not from our perspective anyway.

And then it finally happened!

Through the dense fog of war, a dreaded call came across the Squad net: Thirty Three (33) had taken a direct hit.

"Fuck! Adrian's vehicle, what's the situation, the crew?"

Saunders came back, "We're waiting to establish…" The command Ratel's crew was clearly stressed, "…the vehicle is immobilised." Then, "A crew member is sitting outside on top of the vehicle, he's a sitting duck!"

I'm imagining the next report will say 'and now he's been shot'. I couldn't understand what the fuck he was doing. The incident was playing out some 300m to the right of my position and, in the circumstances, too far away for us to get directly involved. Those closer to the stricken vehicle immediately sprang into action.

Gunner James Sharp on vehicle 31 was close enough to witness the incident unfold. He saw the gunner leap from his turret and run towards our back line. Moments later the crew commander staggered away from the vehicle, clearly wounded and confused as he walked laterally across the field of battle.

The whole Battalion twitched at the news.

Commandant Smit immediately ordered a full battle-group fire plan requiring all guns to unleash a barrage of continuous fire onto enemy positions to create a corridor for crew and vehicle recovery.

Charlie Squad and the 20mm guns of Alpha Coy launched a volley of fire in support of the recovery mission. I think we were all a little shaken by the news.

As Zeelie fired our second shot and I dropped back down into the turret to grab another round from its housing on the left side of the turret, I heard a loud 'CRACK'. At almost the same instant, a sharp pain stung the upper area of my back.

"Arggh!" I momentarily shat myself, thinking this was going downhill fast, "Fuck! I've been hit in the back!"

Zeelie's grimy face, brown eyes as wide as saucers, his skin beneath the grime white as a sheet, looked up at me from his gunsight, "*Wat gaan ons doen Korporaal?*" (What should we do Corporal?)

Corrie launched a blind reverse but after a long moment of total shitting myself, thinking, is this is how it all ends for me? I realised the pain was getting no worse. I turned in the turret so Herb could inspect my back.

"I can't see blood," said Herb.

That's when I realised I'd been lucky...again. "No wait, wait, I'm OK. Let's go!" We hadn't reversed more than twenty metres before halting, then moving forward once more and resuming our fire plan.

I'd just dodged a bullet, a sniper maybe. I was convinced the loud sharp 'crack' was the result of a bullet ricocheting and not bomb fragmentation, which makes a different sound altogether.

We were being fired upon but I couldn't see enemy positions or threats, they had to be dug in or sniping from up a tree somewhere. The crack sounded so loud and close it seemed the bullet had bounced off the upright cupola. Dropping into the turret a split second before the bullet's trajectory harmlessly bisected the space my head had occupied a moment earlier had possibly saved my life; only a tiny shard of it had ricocheted back off the cupola and found its way through my tank suit before coming to rest under the skin in the shoulder blade area.

[The flesh wound healed quickly, but the reason I never spotted the shooter was harder to pin down than a Platoon of well-trained infantry and took almost 25 years to discover.]

During the 30 seconds of shrapnel induced distraction, crew commanders nearest to Three Three (33) simultaneously launched smoke grenades, blanketing the area near Adrian Hind's Ratel with white smoke. An Alpha Company 20mm moved forward to within 30 metres of the stricken vehicle. Its doors opened and out poured the troops it was carrying, among them an old school pal, Rifleman Graham Green, sprinted forward under enemy fire towards the damaged Three Three. Graham was a good choice as runner – he was always quicker than me on the High School Cross-Country team.

The combined guns of 61 Mech continued laying down a heavy blanket of fire which continued for some twenty or thirty minutes while the recovery operation was completed.

Later that night, accounts of the event were somewhat confusing; some suggested Adrian had fired five shots at the oncoming T55 without jockeying once! Someone else suggested they'd 'seen' the projectile travelling toward the vehicle which suggest a slower-moving projectile, such as an RPG, but the extent of the damage indicated something more powerful.

A T55 MBT could quite easily pop a Ratel open with almost any sort of direct hit but it took them many hours of combat, and the loss of more than a Squadron of tanks, for the 47th Brigade to achieve this single direct hit.

Because we had a weaker cannon and thinner armour plate than the T55 so, to survive an encounter against one our gunnery had to be more accurate, we had to be quicker on the fire/reload cycle…*and* the shot had to count. A hit on the T55's track immobilised the platform but the ideal strike, on the seam between hull and turret, destroyed the tank. In these close-quarters encounters, the 90mm HEAT proved it had the power to punch through thick turret walls too. Sometimes the 90mm might require as many as 4 or 5 shots to completely suppress a T55 but if that many shots were needed they could not be fired from the same position. If the gunner missed with two shots, the crew commander had to reposition. Always!

Guys who saw the damaged 33 said the bomb must have hit the ground under its nose and then struck the suspension housing as it exploded upwards, through the hardened underbelly. As the blast entered the driver's cabin, it sheared the fingers off Glen Woodhouse's left hand on the gear-shift lever and destroyed the left side of his face before continuing up into the turret area, mainly into the crew commander's position on the left side.

Gunner Kurt 'Stompie' Oelofse, got lucky and only had some fingers torn off by shrapnel, but was in shock and instinctively opened the hatch above his head, evacuated the vehicle and sprinted to safety – he was later recovered by a support unit.

A design quirk of the 90mm cannon atop the Ratel body prevented the driver's hatch from opening when the cannon pointed forwards. SOP required a gunner to traverse his weapon 30-40 degrees to allow driver egress but, with Adrian mortally wounded, and Stompie making best speed to safety, Woodhouse, who was severely injured, was forced to reach back into the gunner's compartment and slowly traverse the gun before opening the hatch and extricating himself from the badly damaged vehicle.

The driver was so shell-shocked he simply sat heavily atop the turret, dazed and stared blankly ahead as the battle continued to unfold around him. Then, oblivious to the peril and believing he was sweating profusely, he jumped down from the vehicle to wash his face at the vehicle's water tank. He'd not yet realised that he'd lost an eye and a chunk of his face and that the 'sweat' he felt was fresh blood.

By now, Adrian was barely clinging to life, staggering, falling then picking himself up again to continue stumbling across our frontline before falling once more. The storm of steel shards inside the Ratel had peppered his body causing grievous internal injuries that would end his life in minutes. RIP.

Hind had not been at the top of his game that day suffering from a bout of *gyppo guts* (diarrhoea) most of the night, I learned later that he'd taken a number of pit-stops on final approach during the morning. It's very likely that by mid afternoon he was dehydrated. This might account for the less than optimum decisions taken in the turret on that fatal day which would otherwise remain inexplicable.

Graham Green reached the mortally wounded Adrian's and carried his near-lifeless body back to the safety of the support vehicle. Graham Green was later awarded the Honoris Crux for his courage and bravery under fire.

While listening to reports of the recovery operation, still hoping for the best outcome, two other issues came to my attention. Firstly, our blanket-fire plan, in support of 33, was rapidly depleting our remaining turret ordinance, and secondly, Corrie warned me that the engine was starting to overheat.

We were well forward now, totally embroiled in the madness of war and upset at the loss of 33 when Cloete piped up, "All units break off contact, we're pulling back."

My immediate emotion was one of frustration – we were so close to breaking enemy lines. One more push and we'd overrun them. I wasn't ready to stop, not now. It was only when we withdrew from the frontline that my whole body seemed to relax in a great sigh of relief. It was almost 16:00.

Medics attending the wounded called for blood group matches. Major Laas's was a match for Gunner Kurt Oelofse's and he later recounted his conversation while blood flowed directly into him from the Battalion 2IC. The Major offered Oelofse a cigarette, which he lit before offering it to the gunner (quite a rare honour for a Trooper). Oelofse then pleaded with the Major to provide him with a new vehicle, *"Majoor, die tenk het vir my Luitenant fokken dood geskiet, ek wil terug ingaan en vir hulle opfok, sal Majoor aseblief vir my crew commander wees."* (Major, a Tank fucking shot dead my Lieutenant, I want to go back in and fuck them up, will you act as crew commander for me please?)

The remaining operational vehicles of Charlie Squad drew together, adrenaline was flowing strongly as crews shared their relief at having survived the exhausting hours of intense non-stop combat but this was mixed with genuine sadness at the news of Adrian's sudden death and the dreadful injuries to his crew.

Despite this we were incredulous that so many of us had survived unscathed and never gave much thought to the scale of human tragedy wrought upon on the 47th Brigade and TG1. They were enemy targets, nothing more. Estimates of their losses by day's end were that 500 had perished or were seriously injured during The Battle on the Lomba. The scale of human suffering amongst the enemy had little emotional value for me at that time.

While we were catching our breath, discussing possible next orders, radio reports started coming in from intel sounded almost jubilant, "The enemy seems to be retreating, some are abandoning their vehicles and fleeing on foot... There's guys sitting on a hill out there just crying..."

Charlie Squadron boys were elated by the news; 61 Mech had hammered a much larger opponent and the 90mm crews had rewritten the book on mechanised warfare – they'd confronted and pulverised more than a Squadron of tanks into submission.

After enduring eight hours of hard defence, we later learned that the intensive fire-plan action we threw down, during the recovery of 33, was the final straw that crushed the spirit of FAPLA's beleaguered 47th Brigade. They managed to score one painful blow against 61 Mech, but when the Battalion twitched in response to that blow we snapped any lingering resolve they might've had to stand and fight.

The nature of their retreat was best exemplified by a Tank commander who, in his desperation to reach the north bank, ordered his driver to build up speed and launch the 40-ton beast across the river at its narrowest point.

He made it. To about half-way!

Then, a second tank commander steered his T55 onto the body of the stranded tank and tried using his stricken comrade's turret as a bridge. That didn't work and a second Russian MBT ended its career in the Lomba.

The remnants of the destroyed Brigade couldn't get away fast enough.

Shortly after reaching the draw-back positions, Cragg the Medic cut the shrapnel out my back.

O'Connor's wound was similar but had penetrated the deltoid muscle and was less easily treated in the field. He was offered the opportunity of casualty evacuation for a surgical procedure to remove the steel splinter.

Photo 38 Ops Medic and his tool kit. (Barry Taylor)

Before O'Connor left, he pulled me aside to thank me for saving his crew from the T55 – he was in no doubt that the actions of 32 Alpha had been decisive in the contact. Despite this accolade I have to admit a small part of me was regretful that my wound hadn't been severe enough to warrant cassevac (casualty evacuation), I was sure I'd get so lucky next time, despite this I happily returned from the ambulance to resume my role as Troop Sergeant of Troop 2, which otherwise faced losing both Troop leaders in a single day. That would have been as another knock to morale – I'd like to think so anyway!

Five minutes later a request was issued from Battalion Command seeking a posse of the remaining, fully functioning vehicles from Charlie Squad to join an expeditionary force made up of Bravo's Coy's ATK 90mms and an entourage from Battalion HQ.

The expeditionary force was to move forward once more, mop up any remaining resistance, evaluate the battlefield, record abandoned equipment for recovery by UNITA and, hopefully, locate a SAM-8 missile system for recovery to the USA.

By now my bloodlust had abated and fear began to resurface at the thought of going back in for a third time despite knowing the target area had been softened up like an overripe box of tomatoes dropped off the back of a Samil truck travelling at 120kms per hour on a tarred road.

We returned to our bomb-streaked vehicles to prepare and immediately noted four or five perfectly round puncture holes in the rear of our vehicle 32 Alpha. We didn't give it too much thought at first because we now noticed only one of the six massive Ratel run-flat tyres was still inflated, the remainder were pancake-flat – we needed a tyre change.

The spare tyre on the roof above the engine compartment hadn't fared any better after the direct hit from the 82mm mortar.

Corrie jumped back in to the driver's cabin but found he was unable to get the engine to fire up, the earlier over-heating issue had clearly worsened and on closer inspection we discovered some of the neat round holes in 32A's rear-end had entered the engine compartment and punctured the radiator. We couldn't see how deep into the engine they'd burrowed, but the radiator was repairable in the field by 61 Mech's well-equipped mechanics – just not immediately which excluded our participation in the final assault.

Some had tried to explain the bullet holes as if we had at some stage turned our back on the enemy – which never happened. One of the puncture holes in the rear cabin exit-door offered an explanation as to possible cause of the shrapnel in my back. It seemed possible we'd been hit by friendly fire. But, others said, if this were true we'd not have survived the 20mm tungsten-tipped round bouncing around inside cabin area. In the context of all that had happened during the day, this was a minor non-issue and put aside.

[25 years later, a crewman from the 20mm Ratel in the formation behind Charlie's frontline area of operation acknowledged the event: 32 Alpha had made good forward progress on the left flank and had got quite far forward of the Alpha Coy vehicles on that side of the front, then an unsighted and twitchy 20mm gunner, or perhaps the crew commander, had momentarily mistaken our Ratel for an enemy vehicle and fired a single burst on us – one of the rounds had pierced the rear-door and entered the cabin.]

The expeditionary force departed back to the frontline for the third time, quickly moving through no-man's land and beyond the final tree line I'd been hoping to breech. They met little resistance and in the end restrained themselves from slaughtering the almost defenceless groups of FAPLA boys fleeing across the river, mostly on foot.

The commandant's vehicle followed closely behind the advancing force during the final assault and a rumour emerged later that the *Dominee* (Church Priest or Minister) had hitched a ride into the 'action' and had insisted that Smit order his men to "finish off the survivors". This led to a falling-out between the two men. It may also explain why the Battalion got a new *Dominee* a week later.

In retrospect, I regretted not being able to drive through that final treeline and have got to see the objective we'd risked our lives for but, as it transpired, my vehicle's war was drawing to a close. Mechanics established that the damaged engine was not going to be repairable in the field after all. We'd lived in her on-and-off for ten months, the three of us were loath to give up our pink-barrelled 32A with her familiar engine whine. She'd not only shielded us from thousands of bullets and countless bombs, she felt like an integral part of our crew. We almost loved the thing, but she was fucked and we had to source a replacement.

The expeditionary force returned about an hour and a half later then the exhausted battle group withdrew about 10 clicks from the contact area before setting up camp for the night.

We were exhausted and, further than that, I have no recollection of the evening.

The following morning, against normal protocol, the three 'Troop Sergeant' Corporals of C-Squad were invited to Smit's Battle Group conference which was normally reserved for officers and senior NCOs only.

We wondered if we might cop some shit over the 33 affair – some said the recovery was a little chaotic – but I was more concerned that my unsanctioned push up the left flank might've been noticed. But it was nothing of the sort. Instead, it was a brand new experience. Battalion 2IC Major Laas, himself a former Tanker, strode forward as we approached. He seemed to be electric, his eyes blazing as he took my hand in both of his tug-o-war hardened paws to shake my whole arm like a piston. For the first time in my career in the army, I experienced genuine, heart-felt respect from a superior officer – a burning, deep admiration from a man I greatly admired. One of the most memorable moments during National Service.

Standing next his command vehicle, Bok Smit said some prayers for the guys of 33 and then took a long look at the magnetic board on which hung the tactical map of the area around Lomba. It had on it the location of four nearby FAPLA Brigades, each denoted by a different coloured magnet. Smit looked over his shoulder at us with an expression that bordered on disbelief, then he swept his hand dramatically over the black magnetic marker representing the 47th, casting it onto the ground as he said the immortal words: "Men! As of last night the 47th Brigade ceased to exist – they no longer represent a credible military force!"

Fucking hell man! Smit's words brought an attack of goose-bumps, we knew we'd done well but it was stunning to discover we'd effectively annihilated a heavily Armoured Brigade. We were blown away!

The remaining 47th combatants, some of whom were forced to swim to make good their escape across the Lomba, headed north to be absorbed into the 59th Brigade. Only a small percentage of materiel made safe crossing while more than 150 vehicles were destroyed or abandoned by the close of play.

To the troops, 3 October had been something of a blur, a day during which we'd fought for our lives, never considering retreat, pushing an immovable force so hard that we had shattered it. From a personal point of view I summarise the day thus:

32 Alpha – three mismatched boys who worked so well together, unflinching and resolute when it mattered most, apparently setting a record for most 90mm rounds fired in a single battle.

Troop 32 – overcame great challenges and finished the day strongly having made gains through enemy positions on the left-front.

Charlie Squadron – together we were the frontline that day, we faced and destroyed more than a Squadron of tanks and dozens of hardened vehicles! While incurring some casualties, we confronted a far greater force than had ever been envisaged when the Ratel 90 was conceived and we triumphed – a real-life David and Goliath epic!

But none of this could've worked without the formidable might of 61 Mechanised Battalion Group including the 90mm APC Platoons on our left flank and those providing direct and indirect support behind the frontline.

[Hundreds of enemy combatants died and I pay tribute to their sacrifice and of course to my brother-in-arms Adrian Hind who might not have been best suited to warfare, but the man, and his crew, showed extreme courage. When the chips fell, they were always right up there, leading Troop 3, facing the bombardment, never flinching from their task of targeting and eliminating enemy forces in defence of our country.

In standing up to the mighty 47th, Adrian, Glen and Stompie had shown immense bravery under fire and deserve an equal share of the plaudits for 61 Mechanised Battalion Group's achievement on 3 October, 1987.]

17

Mission Accomplished

The stunning and overwhelming victory on 3 October had caught everyone including our people off guard but it also raised the spectre of a major shift in tactics by FAPLA which in turn meant SADF big cheese needed to take pause to review our strategy.

Would FAPLA send the 59th on to join the 21st, would the 16th Brigade quickly be brought into theatre, were the 66th on the move?

In our deadly game of chess, we'd taken their queen, and only sacrificed a pawn. It still hurt though.

I never saw the crewmen of 33 again. O'Connor took the same cassevac flight out of Dodge City, leaving me in temporary command of Troop 2.

Two days after the monumental battle, a delegation of big cheese was escorted by Troop 1 to evaluate the battlefield. They were quite astounded at the scale of destruction and the potential value of abandoned equipment, particularly to UNITA who gained six second-hand MBTs (all with only one previous owner) and to the Yanks who scored some new hi-tech toys including the SA-9 and the much anticipated SAM-8! Not one, but three of the secret weapon systems including loader, launcher and control vehicle were captured.

The battlefield resembled an arms dealer online catalogue, everything from MRLs 'Stalin Organs' and hand-held rocket systems to BRDM and BMP tracked vehicles bristling with fearsome weaponry.

[The delegation recovered the 47 Battalion bell which had been used for signalling. This later became known as the Lomba Bell and formed the centrepiece of the Hind Memorial at the Johannesburg Military Museum to commemorate the fallen of 61 Mechanised Battalion Group, a clear sign of the significance of the battle in the history of a unit linked to many of the largest operations conducted in Angola.]

The arsenal of weaponry and materiel destroyed or discarded underscored the achievement on 3 October. It also proved unequivocally how extremely well the 47th Brigade had been equipped.

The events of 3 October cost Adrian Hind his life but in the harsh extremes of war, and when contrasted with the comprehensive battering we dealt 47th Brigade, this was a minor but nonetheless deeply tragic loss. We, the survivors, acknowledged our good fortune at having lived through that momentous day.

I don't really remember feeling much emotion then. Somehow it was easier to focus on the dangers ahead rather than dwell on the loss of 33. I hadn't seen Adrian die, or the extent of Glen's wounds, and for that reason perhaps they had less of an emotional impact on me, or maybe that's just the nature of war.

Losses and injuries aside, we needed to prepare for the next contact on 6 October, this time against the 21st Brigade which was still loitering at the river crossing.

I'd finally get to lead Troop 2 in combat, but only if we had a working Ratel.

In the days after The Battle on the Lomba, 32A was dragged by a monster tow truck from temporary base to temporary base as we moved back east toward the 21st Brigade.

A replacement vehicle was ordered up from god-only-knows-where and was promised to be with us in 'two or three days', which became increasingly significant when we learned of the impending contact on the 6th.

Waiting for the replacement Ratel was unbearable, I sincerely did not want the already depleted Squadron to go back into battle without me. We were a unit, a team, a crew and although I knew we weren't invincible, that battle on 3 October was the most adrenaline-filled, super high imaginable. And I had survived it almost unscathed.

But it wasn't because I'd morphed from beach-bum lover-boy to some Hollywood 'Top Gun' adrenalin junkie that I desperately wanted to return to the battle field – I was now bonded to my brothers-in-arms, prepared to stand shoulder to shoulder with them until the very end.

On the night of 5 October, 12 hours before contact, 32 Alpha's crew was still without a fighting vehicle. I was pestering the *Tiffies* to get me sorted.

"Ja, Ja ons sal vir jou nuwe voortuig voor die oggend he" (yes, yes, we'll have a new vehicle for you by the morning).

I felt like asking, "Do you *okes* not know the pre-battle rituals I have to go through?" Nevertheless, we were impressed that they'd managed to call up a reserve vehicle so quickly. Aside from my own preparatory rituals, there were other, more critical tasks to perform; transferring and mounting the brace of Brownings, 'sighting-in' the 90mm gunsight and loading almost a ton of ammo and personal effects/ration packs.

The gunsight was a sensitive piece of kit and easily damaged, so it was designed to be interchangeable. When housed, the sights require calibration to ensure they point at the same place as the cannon. Normally this involved a trip to the shooting range and a target whose distance is precisely known, ideally 1,000 metres. A good gunner should 'sight-in' and require no more than three shots before locking the gunsight into position.

Our overnight hop on the 5th had brought the Battalion within relatively close proximity of the 21st meaning the Squadron was enjoying an unusually late start on the morning of the 6th.

We finally greeted the arrival of our new Ratel 90 as the sun broke over the horizon but by now it was 06:00 and Charlie Squadron was making final preparations for departure.

We parked the new, unfamiliar Ratel next to its predecessor, and hurriedly transferred ordinance, personal kit including my 3 October souvenir and Troop 2's surplus rat-packs.

Half an hour later, after some assistance from mechanics, we mounted up and departed to chase down the Squadron which had already departed.

Without satellite navigation, roads or map for guidance, we relied on Charlie's fresh tyre tracks in powder-soft sand to direct us. I was anxious to close the gap, "Let's just get there! It's probably a 20-30 minute drive to the contact area. If we hammer it we can catch up with them before the shit goes down."

David floored it and gave the new Ratel 32A a thorough induction – our radio whip-antennae probably last felt such wind resistance before we came off tarmac roads, five weeks earlier.

Turning my attention to the radios, I tuned the two sets and followed the familiar pre-battle build-up on the Squad net. Ten minutes later, Cloete ordered Charlie to make a 90 degree right turn and deploy in combat formation facing suspected enemy positions 800m into the forest.

Under-strength Troop 2 had been on the tail of the convoy which would place them onto the right front, meaning all I needed to do was look out for the first tracks bearing right. We were now surely less than 2 or 3 clicks from their position.

After advising Cloete that we would soon be joining them, I radioed Fouche and Robbello, the Troop's remaining crew commanders, to advise them to expect us to drop in from behind when Zeelie piped up *"…maar Korporaal ons het nog nie die 90 ingeskiet"* (but Corporal we haven't calibrated the 90's gunsights!)

"Fuck, more time lost! Herb, you're going to have to 'sight-in' the gun on the move."

"Nee, Koporaal dit kan nie so gedoen nie." Which loosely translates as… "No Corporal it can't be done, you're nuts!"

Zeelie, by now a battle-hardened veteran and accomplished 90mm gunner knew as well as I did that the Ratel 90 is not designed for fire on the move. The gun couldn't track a target like more modern turrets with electronic 'stabilisers'.

Without 'stabs', the tiniest pitch or yaw over terrain is greatly magnified a mile down range, but we didn't need that degree of accuracy, we weren't expecting contact with the enemy at a range greater than a few hundred metres.

"Okay then, I'll do it. David don't stop, just slow down a little."

Zeelie unclipped his headset, jumped out onto the roof of the moving Ratel so we could swap places in the turret. "Just don't be getting too comfortable in the crew commander's chair," I quipped.

Grabbing the gunner's hand wheels, I traversed the turret through 75 degrees to aim at a single large tree about 400 metres away at our ten o'clock position. We'd be firing live rounds but the tree was in the opposite direction to Charlie Squad who were just starting to attract small arms fire from enemy positions.

I began the unorthodox calibration, shooting two rounds, each time making adjustments to the sight and cannon position as we moved relative to the target, then I called, "Gunner, load HE. Driver stop. Fire!"

Photo 39 31 Charlie 'shooting in' her gun-sight the proper way near Mavinga.
(Martin Bremer)

From a stable firing platform the third round took out the tree. Job done, I traversed the turret, jumped out of the gunner's chair and gave Corrie the order to drive. I reported our readiness to the Squad. "Three Zero, this is Three Two Alpha, we're a few minutes out"

With guidance from Saunders in the command vehicle, we moved quickly through the forest toward the frontline, safe in the knowledge our boys had just cleared through the area minutes earlier.

The contact was getting pretty hot ahead of us, so it was with a mixture of fear and pride that a few minutes later I opened comm again. "Three Two Bravo, this is Three Two Alpha, I'm dropping into line adjacent your position."

The morning contact in dense bushy conditions made target acquisition incredibly difficult so we were mostly reduced to firing at muzzle flashes rather than visible targets.

Sometimes, opposition forces were so well dug in we'd be forced to withdraw however, on this occasion, elements of the 21st had been on the move until they met a wall of Charlie Squad resistance and within half an hour they simply melted back into the deep forest.

FAPLA radio intercepts betrayed new-found respect for the 90mm fighting platform, a factor which might've swayed their decision to withdraw before the contact built up a head of steam.

It seemed like we had FAPLA on the back foot, evidently unable to get past us. October had started badly for them and now time was running out before the impending 'wet season' rainfall. They appeared to be running out of options which raised the appealing prospect that the worst of the fighting was behind us.

From a SADF perspective, it was a job well done that morning. We'd contained the 21st Brigade, as BG's Bravo and Charlie had done during September, continuing to starve them of the vital territory they needed to create a pocket for the 59th Brigade to move in to on the south bank of the bridgehead.

At the same time rumours began to spread that enemy forces were possibly preparing to move en masse, pathfinders were believed to scoping routes, heading away from us, due north! It was far too soon to be certain, but it seemed that the battering they took on October 3rd had been decisive.

With TG1 and the 47th out of the equation, the 59th was no longer on the offensive and the 16th was seemingly going nowhere. The only other immediate threats were the battle-weakened 21st and the by now almost non-existent TG2 which together had gainfully defended the bridgehead for five long weeks under almost constant SADF Artillery bombardment and frequent ground-force battles. And finally, it seemed, even the hardy warriors of the 21st were to be withdrawn.

The mood in the laager that night was fairly jubilant, however any notion that our war was coming to an end was to be obliterated in dramatic fashion less than 36 hours later. An unheralded and unplanned second phase of battle for the men of Operation Modular was about to begin, a phase that was destined to destroy my naïve sense of invincibility and have a profound and lasting impact on Charlie Squadron's morale.

Photo 40 Pretorius enjoys rare feast of wet rations.
(Len M. Robberts)

18

Floats like a Butterfly, Stings like a Bomb!

The type of Corporal that was our role model during JL's was a hand-picked, alpha male, bawl-in-your-face type.

When deciding which route to take through training I didn't 'connect' too well with this Corporal stereotype, considering myself better suited to the 'we don't get our hands too dirty if we can help it' ranks of the officer class.

My eviction from officer training left me little option but to take the second-choice outcome but it made my year as a Corporal somewhat challenging. It could be argued that before entering Angola I struggled to motivate the erstwhile hard-arsed Troopers. Some guys were naturally more compliant or respectful and willing to follow orders, but others required additional incentivising. This however did not hold true in Angola. When it came to digging foxholes, they didn't need coaxing – self-preservation was the greatest motivator of them all.

Digging into soft Angolan soil was normally quite easy. For some guys foxhole digging became something of an obsession. Sometimes they'd spend an inordinate amount of time vying to design the most ergonomically engineered and strategically well-placed foxhole. To me it mattered not how neat the thing was; what mattered most was how close you were to the fox when it was required.

MiGs were a constant annoyance, an almost daily presence during the entire Operation. We likened them to the malaria-carrying mosquito buzzing around just far enough out of reach to swat, and normally nothing more than an irritation. We'd all been issued anti-malaria drugs in advance of our sojourn into the subtropical area of operations because malaria was unfortunately still quite common. However, what we didn't have nearly enough of were anti-MiG tablets in the form of modern warplanes or anti-aircraft installations, so when the MiGs swooped and we got bitten, there were invariably deaths that followed.

Our best defence against the ever-present danger posed by the Russian aircraft was Mother Nature herself. The mature forests typical of the area offered good cover from air reconnaissance and, unless we were on the move or caught in

Photo 41 61 Meg – Ops Moduler 87 – Foxhole. (Len M. Robberts)

open Shona, we grew increasingly confident of our cover under the leafy blanket of forest canopy. Crews soon became adept at selecting the trees best suited for sheltering their steel limousines.

When arriving at a new location it was important to find a decent tree and a decent locale in the laager. We might move locations more than once in a 24-hour period, or we might not move for a few days. Crew commanders guided their drivers to the most suitable trees, seeking out ones with sufficiently thick canopies and preferably overhanging branches so that the camo nets were easier to spread over the Ratel.

Hooked up on a branch, the net created an artificial roof which blended seamlessly into the natural surroundings – at least when viewed from 20,000ft. And the longer the operation went on, the more refined the camo-net arrangements became evolving often into spacious areas under which we'd cook and commune.

The intensity of battle contrasted starkly with days of downtime and it became easy to dismiss the perilous state of our existence, dismissively living on the edge of danger and potential death. We joked that some people shelled out thousands

Photo 42 Storey, Pretorius and du Toit chilling under camo following a full night
in the saddle. (Len M. Robberts)

to experience the raw African wilderness while we were getting paid a few extra Rands per day for it. The additional danger experienced by soldiers at the front (by comparison for example, to a soldier chilling-out at a 'hotel command' on Durban's beachfront) was valued at R150 (£10 at today's exchange rate but in '87 more like £40 per month).

As nights got warmer, before the rainy season, my preferred place to sleep was on a flat section of Ratel roof behind the turret, an area that is 'all business' with various hatches and the huge, spare wheel cluttering her back so at first this might not seem a promising place to sleep but by traversing the turret to 90 degrees, a single-bed sized section of perfectly smooth steel was exposed. This sleeping arrangement was only possible if the overhanging camo-net was well clear of the turret so it didn't snag as it was rotated.

Lying there, on the bed atop the Ratel in the relatively tranquil surroundings of our wild safari game lodge, I read and frequently reread the beautifully penned love letters from my girlfriend, written on paper impregnated with the most sensual perfume imaginable. However, it is fair to point out that by this time I was so grubby that even a cheap toilet spray would've pleased my sense of smell.

David, my driver, preferred sleeping under the Ratel on the velvet-soft Angolan soil. Although it offered quite a comfy sleep it was my third choice of sleeping options because of the quantity of sand that found its way into my sleeping bag. But for the rest of us, David's choice was just fine given the frequency of his wet-dreams. Who knew war was an aphrodisiac? The number of such occurrences during the night became a standing joke. In the morning he'd crawl out with a broad grin on his face, look over at me, and offer a choice of numbers between one and three.

Herb mostly stretched himself out on the long, hard-rubber bench along the right side of the rear cabin, which could be used by up to half-a-dozen sweaty foot soldiers in a combat zone.

The 90mm crews made the most of the extra space we had compared to our Infantry comrades. Among our kitbags in the rear cabin, we'd built up a reserve of spare cartons of the 10-box rations along with thousands of rounds of 7.62mm ammo boxed in their 200-clip belts – and then there was always room for the odd alcohol 'still' fashioned from a bomb canister.

Using the two turret machine guns, it was quite normal to run through ten or fifteen belts (2-3,000 rounds) of ammo in a single contact; multiplied by four vehicles this is around 10,000 rounds, or 50 belts. As Troop Sergeant and responsible for food and firepower it was quite acceptable, prudent of me even, to build up a healthy stock of 7.62mm ammunition.

Despite the great distances and inherent hazards faced by the Logistics Corps guys, they maintained good supply lines.

Weekly armed convoys, laden with ammo, rations, cigarettes, *Dankie Tanie* (thank you aunty) gift parcels and letters from home, ran the gauntlet of a 1,000 click round trip, sometimes with the close attendance of Russian fighter jets so the occasional truck got whacked, once even by our own air force.

Like warfare the world over, days of searing intensity were often punctuated by lazy days with very little to do. Operation Modular was no different and we spent such days killing time, plane spotting, prepping and cleaning equipment, resting – or decapitating shoelaces.

Unless we knew the enemy was very close, or attack imminent, evenings in our forest camps were often pretty chilled.

In addition to the technology at their disposal, intel boys relied heavily on reconnaissance and info harvested from POWs.

Just prior to Operation Modular, a small band of Recces with eyes on the main bodies of the FAPLA forces had combined with UNITA forces to communicate

Photo 43 Willemse, Coetzee and Linde *bak bal* (bake balls - chillin) in the Angolan bush. (Martin Bremer)

key coordinates and enemy movements, including aircraft sightings (known as 'Victors' back to SADF high-command). In addition, our air force's early warning radar systems detected flights as they popped up from the nearest airbase about 80 clicks north of us at Cuito Cuanavale or further north at Menongue. Intelligence officers would then broadcast 'Victor, Victor' alerts meaning *vyandelike vliegtuig* (enemy aircraft) incoming.

When close to enemy positions at night we were dark – lights off, no fires and very little noise – but at other times, when the enemy was farther away, we'd get together as a group to share stories, tell jokes and generally take the piss out of one another. During these get-togethers each guy contributed a number of rat-pack tins to make a great big 'tasty' *potjie* (pot) for the evening's 'banquet'. This far from home, at our Safari lodge, the banquet always tasted really good no matter what was tossed into the pot, even though boys often brought the least popular tins for *potjie* and why Mrs Ball's Chutney, dried herbs-n-spices and salt were such treasured commodities.

The rat-pack burger was another favourite; it was made by inverting a foil-lined cereal sachet then carefully inserting a sandwich made from thick dog biscuits (there were two types of dog biscuit: thick – which was nice – and thin – which was dry/shit). These biscuits were found only in rat-packs # 1, 3 & 5. To make the filling, the contents of a *Cheesie got* spread onto the biscuits and a few slices of *vark-piel* (Pig-dick, or mini Vienna – only available in two varieties of Rat-pack) added and, when available, a slice of fresh onion. After adding 5ml water, the resealed the bag was cooked over an esbit (fire-tablet) for about 90 seconds, turning once. If the water level was correct, the swollen, hot biscuits and melted cheese made an extremely tasty treat – the Angolan Mc Donald's Zero Pounder. Just as tasty as the real thing, and at a fraction of the calories, it left plenty of space for a bowl of milkshake-flavoured cereal or rum-n-raisin energy bar.

Members of the 'Angolan Game Lodge' who enjoyed getting on a bit of a buzz, made a fruit-based, puke-coloured alcoholic stew, fermented for days in a recycled 90mm bomb transportation canister – suitable because of their screw-cap seal. Yeast required for the fermentation process was occasionally trucked in along with 'wet' rations (ostensibly for making bread – or dough fried in oil); rat-packs provided the tinned fruit and sugar. Water and heat were on tap – most of the time – and within a week we'd have an alcoholic fruit drink that had less punch than my preferred Castle Lager. Since beer was an extremely rare commodity deep in Angola, and the Owambo Mohungu Juice now far behind, our improvised 'Mavinga Moonshine' was better than nothing. Some creative types cut 90mm bomb canisters into coffee/moonshine mugs, cleverly melting plastic handles onto them.

Four days after The Battle on the Lomba news from intel was increasingly bullish.

59th Brigade was moving two of its Battalions north, their ranks swelled by survivors of the 3 October battle. The 21st were drawing back to the opposite bank of the river, it seemed, in preparation for a full scale retreat.

If this was accurate, it surely meant they were walking away from their main objective; to wipe out Jonas Savimbi's strategic base at Mavinga and ultimately reach Jamba.

It didn't require a University Degree in Warfare to recognise this was a major turning point in the war. The November rain would soon make conditions diffi-cult and by December the terrain would be almost impassable to heavy weapons.

This really bolstered our belief this presaged the imminent cessation of hostility following which we would be withdrawal from conflict and sent for an early bath back on base at Omuthiya.

At about the same time we heard reports that 4 SAI (South African Infantry), AKA 62 Mech were being called up to the front to join us. This didn't really

Photo 44 31 Alpha – crewmen Dries Rheeder, Cpl Sievert Wiid (who replaced Venter) and charismatic driver Gert Niemand. (Martin Bremer)

make sense given that the Operation was a success and war was over, but it was reasonable to assume that the unit had been mobilised before the game-changer on 3 October. But, we supposed, as they were *en route*, why not bring them in for insurance? We were even told: "4 SAI is on the way to give you guys a break from the frontline." However, rumours that four of them had died *en route* didn't augur well.

The boys were pleased with the idea of a break, but (slightly arrogantly) uncertain about the experience of 4 SAI green-horn warriors if they'd already lost four guys before even hitting contact!

The South African Government had now given up its diplomatic charade and finally committed overtly to military action which at last included the Olifant Squadron from School of Armour, Echo Squadron.

E-Squad makes for quite an entourage, and would've made the 4 SAI columns look even more potent than 61 Mech as it travelled through South Africa and SWA, but only at night, for security reasons.

The Tank Squadron came equipped with its own compliment of support, maintenance and ammo trucks. The large tow trucks that dragged our damaged vehicles 500 clicks out of Angola may've been monsters, but when it came to recovering a 55-ton tank, they needed something super-sized – E-Squad mechanics' recovery vehicle looked like an *Olifant* on steroids.

It was about fucking time too, these lads had been living like kings at School of Armour and it was high time they got some combat dirt under their nails!

SADF MBTs hadn't been deployed in a full scale conventional setting since World War 2 – those big beasts of the Defence Force hadn't killed an MBT in conflict for 40 years. They must've been itching to get in on the action, particularly now the boys of 32 & 61 Battalion had notched more than 40 killed or captured MBTs on their Armoured bedpost.

The word around camp was that we would soon be deploying in integrated formation with Elephants.

"Fuck! Imagine going in with a Squadron of Olifant MBTs alongside us! If those Russian Tanks took a pounding from the Ratel, they'll get annihilated by the *Olifant* boys! Bring it on!"

A retreating enemy and a rejuvenated and hardened SADF – it seemed our war was all but over. I was more than happy to hear that the fresh-legged 4 SAI and the slightly arrogant Tanker boys would be taking the lead. We didn't yet realise it would be three-weeks, or more, before reinforcements arrived on the frontline. We were still due some pain.

8 October started unremarkably enough, a pleasant day at war with no contact scheduled nor 'Victor Victor' alerts. The air was cool and crisp, warming early on, and the sky light blue and cloudless.

Still deep in the hot-zone, Charlie Squad was assigned to escort a convoy of supply vehicles to 61 Mech's new forward operating base, a sign of increasing confidence against what appeared to be a retreating enemy.

Our relatively small group of about 20 vehicles had been on the move since 23:00 the previous night. The Squad itself wasn't at full strength. Captain Cloete was travelling with the command circus while Bremer was sent to collect 2nd Lt. Kobus Boshoff (from 202 Battalion at Rundu who'd been flown into Mavinga to replace Hind) and Gawie Combrink, a Tank commander who had previously been assigned to command vehicle Zero Bravo (0B) who replaced O'Connor.

I seem to recall that Squad command was handed to Lt Robberts (30A) but unsure who was responsible for navigation on the mission in the absence of Three Zero (30).

Nine Ratel 90s were available for the task, more than adequate to safely deliver a convoy of about ten logistics vehicles to 61's FOP.

Scheduled completion of task, 05:30, no later than 06:00, after which time we'd been given the rest of the day for R&R. This would be the first time 61 Battalion would be together since the 'morning after the day before', on 4 October and since the scale of our victory had been made clear. Charlie Squad lads would be able to hold their heads up pretty high when moving about the laager during R&R. We were heroes to a man!

During the night of the 7th a few vehicles developed mechanical problems, then, at some stage our navigation got screwed up.

Blokes are notoriously shite at stopping to ask for directions, but as sunrise approached we became increasingly concerned by the arrival of deadly Cuban mosquitoes for breakfast, and by the time the sun crested the forested horizon, we were behind schedule and starting to cut things a little bit fine.

There was no doubt in anyone's mind we had to be camo'd before Mozzies started buzzing around us. Despite this we were fairly confident we had some time to spare before the Cuban pilots started their pre-flight checks.

After five weeks of fairly relentless but unsuccessful harassment from Russian fighter-jets our Squadron might've been a little gung-ho in travelling by daytime; perhaps the trucks we escorted were needed urgently at the 61 Mech FOP. Whatever the reason, we pushed on despite the risk secure in the knowledge that radio alerts would warn us if enemy sorties had departed their Cuito Cuanavale airfield.

The convoy, having resolved the mechanical and navigational issues, was moving at a relatively brisk pace, partly due to its small contingent size but mainly because it was daylight and risk of attack from the air ratcheted up by the minute. We reassured ourselves that we'd reach 61 Mech before long, maybe 30-60 minutes

Other than the minor navigational and mechanical niggles, there was very little to trouble the crews that morning. The route now was mostly open shona, clear of trees and obstacles, making for very easy driving and a relaxed atmosphere on Squad-net.

Lance Corporal Wayne Mills was bitching down the radio, "I'm fucking exhausted! What's the first thing I'm doing when we arrive? Grab some sleep man!"

During the dark hours of early morning, turret crew on 'low risk' actions like this could take turns to snatch a little broken sleep while seated upright, head resting – and bumping off – the ironmongery. Drivers could expect no such luxury.

By 07:00 we were still not within striking distance of 61 FOP and the aerial risk had risen quite sharply. Thankfully, the blue African sky remained satisfyingly clear of Mozzies and our radios reassuringly silent – no 'Victor Victor' warnings.

Travelling at heady speeds of about 30kph, our convoy generated a sizeable dust plume of dust in its wake, but speed was the priority. At the rear of the column, the crew of 33 Charlie munched on dust kicked up from 32A (the 2nd) and both these vehicle crews ate 33 Alpha's dust. The remaining six Ratels were interspersed front and centre.

Herb was snoozing next to me on the right-hand side of the turret. When he stirred, the perennially cheerful, freakishly buck-toothed gunner smiled to reveal his trademark 'travelling brown' front teeth. Normally, his teeth were pearly white, but because his parents never got them straightened when he was kid they protruded some way out his mouth. Even when his lips were closed and his teeth always attracted a thick coating of dust, like a swarm of flies on an exposed *bos-kak*. The guy had already endured a shed load of abuse on account of his teeth so I avoided making too many jokes at his expense but this quirk of nature was a source of frequent banter and I couldn't resist poking a little good-natured fun at him on the troop-net that morning. We were having a giggle with the usual stuff like, "Herb, you could eat an apple through a tennis racket", or, "With tusks like that, don't let the elephant poachers catch sight of you!" He knew I loved him like a brother so he accepted the banter in good humour. But the happy exchange soon gave way to increasingly nervous chatter, all of it concerned with the exponentially increasing risk from above as the sun crept higher into the sky…"How far to go?…why are we are not there yet… who's leading this thing?"

We'd never previously had so much difficulty reaching an overnight objective before sun up but clearly, on 8 October something had gone wrong.

The radio-waves were still clear, but then someone chirped up, "Guys we really need to think about taking cover."

Enemy observation posts could easily plot the convoy's progress as the dust storm thrown up by our vehicles rose like a brown scar across the clear blue sky.

Shortly before 08:00, we finally agreed the risk was too high so we performed our usual *visgraad* (fish rib) manoeuvre, spreading out under cover of a fairly dense copse of trees at our three o'clock position while those in charge sought further clarification from Battalion command.

The *visgraad* manoeuvre was billed as a short pit-stop to determine whether we should press on or hunker down for the day. On this occasion, the general consensus was that we were quite close to our objective and therefore likely to be asked to complete the task before resting up for the day.

The convoy slowed and, at an agreed signal, simultaneously performed a hard right-turn to drive away from the track for about 80 metres until we entered the nearby tree line. After continuing for 50-70 metres deeper into the forest, we stopped under the protective canopy of some large Ficus trees. It seemed to us that the area offered the convoy reasonable cover, the tallest trees standing about 20 metres tall and a similar distance apart.

If we did receive an order to *hang-bal* (hold tight) for the day we'd probably move a couple hundred metres deeper into the forest to ensure our security from airborne attack.

David steered our Ratel in tight, the left flank almost touching a good-sized tree as we pulled in for the temporary stop. By virtue of the distribution of the surrounding flora, the three Ratels on the convoy's tail loosely adopted a 'U' formation when parked: 32A on the left, 33A on the right and 33C completing the underside of the 'U'. Both 32 Alpha and 33 Alpha turned again and faced the direction of travel; 33 Charlie remained facing in the three o'clock direction we'd left the track from. The remainder of the convoy were scattered loosely in a 50-metre-wide stripe spread some 300 metres or so up-range, parallel to the track we'd been travelling on.

We expected to receive a rapid reply to our urgent call for instructions. Within minutes we would either be on the move again toward FOP, or looking for a safe haven. I thought there was no need to spread the camouflage nets or dig a 'foxie'; we'd simply hold cover for a few minutes and then respond to the order.

The orientation of the vehicles under the trees was dictated mainly by the direction of the larger of the lower-hanging branches. There were no ground-attack threats in the area – all enemy forces were believed to be north of the Lomba – so my friend from Durban, Wayne Mills, who commanded 33 Charlie, an experienced and extremely capable commander, guided his tired driver, Frikkie De Jager, directly into the tree line where they found suitable cover under a large tree on his vehicle's right flank and about 15-20 metres diagonally behind 32A's rear end.

After many hours in the saddle and with a few minutes to kill, the guys got out to stretch their legs, share a smoke and maybe brew a coffee or catch up with the news from mates. Understandably everyone was a little unhappy about the "fucking delay" and the breaking of the "do not travel during the daytime" rule.

Wayne Mills decided to forgo the nap he'd promised himself and kindly relinquished his place on the rubber bench in the rear cabin to his exhausted driver,

Frik De Jager. Cigarette in hand, he ambled over the soft sand to 33A, a distance of around 30 metres, to catch up with his pal, Warren Adams.

The minutes ticked by. Some crews started to set out camouflage nets, others dug foxholes to pass the time…we were beginning to get a little agitated. We had hoped to be underway again without too much delay. About 20 minutes after leaving the track, I was still no clearer about our next move.

"Jeeeezuusss!" I instinctively ducked.

A split second after the sighting an almighty gut-rending roar tore through the air, as if the sky had been ripped apart by Zeus himself. In a few milliseconds a pair of MiGs had shot directly overhead our position, almost brushing the tops of the trees, disappearing as quickly as they had appeared, obscured by the canopy of trees.

Hardly able to hear my own voice above the ringing in my ears, I turned to Herbie, "Did you see that?" This was a rhetorical question!

The jets' flight path had perfectly bisected the long stripe of brown-painted steel lying in the forest beneath them, the pilots hugging the treetops so closely their cockpits were less than 40 metres above us. Even in the fraction of a second they were directly overhead, a red Cuban star was clearly visible on the pilots' helmets; even their faces were identifiable. The jets were so close, small print on the fuselage was visible and a few of us even saw a pilot's lips moving as he communicated with his wingman! Well, that was the banter directly afterwards. And they weren't Angolan pilots, though that was largely irrelevant at that instant. There *was* one thing we did all agree upon – we fucking-well shat ourselves!

There'd been no 'Victor Victor' warning from intel, which made no sense but the most disturbing aspect of this incident was that we'd not even heard them coming. This had never happened before – we'd always heard the fighter-jets diving in from altitude on bombing runs. This time they were out-running the sound of their own engines. A disturbing thought crossed my mind; *they can hit us without us even knowing about it.*

We weren't certain they'd spotted us. The morning had gone from good to ugly in a single heartbeat.

We weren't in great camo readiness but the convoy's dust cloud had settled. The MiGs had flown so fast and low there was a slim chance the pilots hadn't seen us. Maybe we just happened to be on a flight path toward some other target further down-range and parallel with the track we'd been using earlier.

We all remained on hyper alert in those electric moments after the dramatic fly-by, the adrenaline flooding our bodies faster than the fuel pumps feeding the afterburners in the MiGs' Mach 2 Tumansky twin-spool turbojet engines as they'd screamed overhead.

… 15 seconds

We were shocked to say the least. None of us had been this close to a MiG despite weeks of them seeking us out. We'd grown quite accustomed to watching them cruise at high altitude. Typically, bombing raids were launched at a range above our 20mm air-defence capability; or like a hawk they'd dive in steep and fast directly onto an identified target, drop bombs and regain altitude as quickly as possible before hightailing back to base. Mostly they missed their target, but not always. So far Lady Luck had looked after Charlie Squad.

We listened for the familiar crump of heavy ordinance exploding. It never came.

Some guys hurriedly started digging foxholes; others preferred to believe the enemy fighters wouldn't be back.

Perhaps it is the nature of the conditioning that comes with having lived in such dangerous and noisy situations that in 33 Charlie, Frik De Jager wasn't roused from his sleep by the din of the fly-by.

We couldn't hear the MiGs at all now. Nonetheless, a guy was despatched to climb a tree to try catch a glimpse of the warplanes and give us early warning if the nippy bastards came back.

… 120 seconds

Some guys were digging furiously; others called in the near miss on the radio net.

During Operation Modular, standing orders were to avoid wherever possible swatting at these annoying mosquitoes with our outdated, double-barrelled 20mm *Ystervaark* (Iron-Pig) anti-aircraft weapons in preference to letting the UNITA boys have a go with their American shoulder-launched Stinger missiles. Far as we knew, neither 20mm *Ystervark* nor guys with Stingers were anywhere near us that morning. We were on our own.

But then again, had the pilots really spotted us? They were long gone, weren't they?

We realised now that our deep tyre tracks must've been like a beacon in the sand to the jets' pilots, indicating the point we turned in for cover within the tree line but were unaware of a single vehicle travelling along the same bush track that our convoy had been using. Someone else was on our route just a couple clicks to our six, and still churning up dust.

Angolan radio intercepts later indicated that the two Cuban pilots flying the MiG 23s were indeed heading for the dust-churning target.

… 90 seconds

Rossouw, Adams and Mills were on the adjacent side of their vehicle deciding whether or not to crank up an *esbit* fire lighter and get back to making their coffee.

At 33 Charlie, Pearman-White stooped to take a drink from the right-hand water tank located between the two rear wheels.

David Corrie, my driver, was some way off chatting with friends at another vehicle. Zeelie and I stood some ten or fifteen metres to the right of our vehicle, near the centre of that little three vehicle 'U' formation at the tail of the *visgraad*, still ill at ease. Up the front of our *visgraad* formation, to our 12 o'clock, guys were busying themselves with camo nets.

Then it happened! Fast!

This time we spotted the MiGs slightly earlier than before because we were more alert.

One second.

We were transfixed, for what seemed an eternity. Two parachutes blossomed 50 metres above the ground and 200 metres directly ahead.

One point five seconds.

The canopies of the red and white panelled parachutes were as large as those used by our Parabats but that's where the similarities ended; each of them supported half a ton of high explosive and they were hurtling towards us at fucking high speed!

Detonation would be seconds after such a freakishly low-altitude release.

Two seconds.

Time slowed. We stared slack-jawed at the surreal scene unfolding in the patch of blue sky visible through a break in the tree canopy. I even had time for a quick thought: *Hey! We didn't get taught about bombs with parachutes attached to them, did we?"* Then again, maybe we did, and just hadn't been paying attention that day at the School of Armour.

Then the parachutes were less than 100 metres up-range, slowing rapidly.

There wasn't time for sight seeing but apparently my brain found time to mull over the new discovery: *bombs are deployed with parachutes and, moreover, the manufacturer has taken the trouble to design a chute with red and white silk panels for his Communist client.*

From the chutes' initial trajectory and velocity my brain, working at Cray super-computer speed, deduced that the 'thousand pounders' had been released too late and would cruise overhead before detonating harmlessly in the forest behind us.

However, as their chutes 'bit into the air' and the bombs' velocity bled off rapidly, it dawned on me that their trajectory was also altering. Gravity had taken over and began dragging the payload on a new heading, one which might very well lead them close to the spot where Herb and I were standing. My world, everything in it, shrunk down to those two bombs and me.

Two point five seconds.
They were headed right for us!

Three seconds.
As if waking from a dream, I grabbed Herb by the arm, sprinted over the heavy dune-like sand back to our Ratel. Other guys who'd seen the parachutes and bombs knew the danger we were in and frantically sought cover wherever they could. Guys further up the formation watched helplessly as the bombs shot past them just overhead.

Four seconds.
The right-side vehicle door had been left open. That was fortunate. I bundled Herb inside and followed immediately, dragging the heavy steel door shut behind us. Wide-eyed, we looked at each other as we waited for the impact...

Five seconds.
A flash lit up the inside of the Ratel. The concussive force of the explosion thumped our lungs, tugged at our skin, rocked the 18-ton vehicle and buckled all three steel engine-firewalls (though we only realised this later). 32A bucked as she bore the brunt of the explosion. A storm of shrapnel blasted her metal body. Our brains, overwhelmed by the ferocity of the onslaught of sound were in an instant overloaded.

Six seconds.
Everything was still, except for a loud, high-pitched ringing in the eardrums.

Seven seconds.
Stunned, shocked, disoriented, Herb and I stared at each other in utter disbelief. By some miracle we'd survived the gigantic explosion.

Eight seconds.

Our new vehicle, 32A the 2nd, had just earned her place on the team. She had saved us from the ton of high explosive that had just detonated only a few metres away from us and had sustained nothing more than a few bruises.

Nine Seconds.

"Help … help…"

The urgent plaintive cry sounding from outside snapped us back into action and on opening the door we could see how events had unfolded.

Ten seconds.

L/Cpl Mills' Ratel, 33 Charlie, some fifteen metres down-range of my position, had been perpendicular and directly in line with the deadly payload's trajectory prior to impact.

Eleven seconds.

The 18-ton Ratel had been blown askew liked a toy truck kicked over by a careless kid.

Photo 45 Gunner Mackinnon standing in one of two MiG-made craters at ground zero on 8 October. (Len M. Robberts)

Twelve seconds.

As we ran towards the damaged Ratel, the black splashes I'd noticed on Charlie's bodywork revealed themselves as hideous, misshapen holes, some larger than a clenched fist.

Massive chunks of shrapnel had torn right through 33C's inch-thick steel left flank.

The area immediately surrounding 33C was a scene of total devastation; foliage and bark had been stripped from the trees by the shock waves from the exploding bombs for about 40 metres down-range. And this was the reason we'd survived the cataclysm; the vast majority of force had radiated away from ground zero in a kind of 'V' shape. The point of impact was marked by two large craters a few metres short of 33C, not far from of the spot Herb and I'd had been standing seconds earlier. 32A was almost perpendicular to the point of impact, fortuitously outside the blast pattern.

Time was still moving super-slow but the rest of the day became something of a blur.

We later estimated the explosion shunted the 18-ton Ratel between 5 and 10 metres, sideways! Both MiGs had dropped a pair of 500kg bombs but one pilot had released his ordinance a second too late and it detonated harmlessly some 300 metres down range.

The targeted ton of high explosive that floated in like a butterfly stung the ground just short, and towards the rear, of 33 Charlie's left flank.

Our Ratel was on the side of the 'U' formation and was struck by significantly less energetic shrapnel. On the opposite side of the formation, Wayne Mills and Warren Adams had sought cover on the ground beneath their vehicle and had seen shrapnel take out one of their tyres but because they too were outside the 'V' shaped bomb dispersal pattern they came to no serious harm.

Only 33 Charlie was down range of impact well inside the 'V' blast pattern – the crew never stood a chance.

13 seconds.

Like shell-shocked holocaust survivors, guys nearby began emerging from their place of refuge while others, from the vehicles further up range, came running towards us.

Then we heard again that plaintive cry, this time clearly coming from the opposite side of 33 Charlie.

15 seconds.

As we rounded the rear of 33 Charlie the full horror of the MiG strike became clear. Two guys were lying prone on the ground next to the Ratel, badly injured.

We assumed they'd either taken refuge inside or behind the vehicle but this had offered too little protection against the two half-tonners. Even the steel door had been blown clean off its hinges; the boys were clearly in serious trouble!

It appears that Gary and Frik didn't know the bombs were dropping. In the seconds that elapsed from 'bombs away' to detonation, there was too little time to react, and if unsighted and relying only on the sound of the jets overhead would have given them perhaps a three-second warning but none whatsoever of the silent parachutes floating towards them.

The deadly butterfly bombs made no discernable sound as they floated in, certainly not enough to be heard over the rapidly receding roar of the MiGs.

It is probable that the two crewmen believed the second flyby to have been just that, another harmless over-flight. Having seen the MiGs flash over the roof of their vehicle and disappear behind the close horizon, they probably believed the danger was past and were thankful that the MiGs had not strafed us.

The silence betrayed them. With only three seconds to detonation, everyone was scrambling for cover – except them.

Frik De Jager sat, or lay, in the rear cabin while Pearman-White leaned into the water tap to take a drink, apparently oblivious to the impending danger.

At one second before impact, Herb and I assumed the foetal position inside our Ratel; while Gary and Frik were just chilling – and then their world erupted in a cataclysm of such magnitude I struggle to describe, or even imagine, their experience.

Sure, they were shielded from the full force of the blast by their vehicle, but even a Ratel proved woefully inadequate so close to ground zero and inside the 'V'. Chance had put them in the wrong place

Mill's earlier decision to visit 33A was the difference between helping his friends live, or being another one of our brothers lying in agony on the sand because anyone inside the 'V' would've been fighting for their life – unless they'd been in a deep foxhole.

Under Dion Cragg's guidance we began triage, initially tending their wounds right where they'd fallen next to the wrecked vehicle.

Someone got on the radio, called in the strike and requested immediate cassevac.

We moved our vehicles, distributing them more deeply into the forest.

Gert Niemand, Paul Storey and Dries Rheeder stood watch on the roof of a Ratel with their R4 machine guns at the ready, like a tin-pot anti-aircraft installation. Although a feeble defence against the MiGs, if they returned we had nothing to lose by using them; our stealth and cover had already been betrayed by the smouldering Ratel.

Pop, pop, pop…it sounded like the crackle of small-arms fire, a bit like the sound made when a bag of M&Ms (candy-covered chocolate sweets) are emptied onto a marble floor.

But the 'M&M' popping heralded a new and unexpected twist; 33 Charlie's ordinance was starting to cook-off – fires inside the cabin were growing in intensity and boxes of 7.62mm ammo were overheating and exploding.

We prepared to move Gary and Frikkie away from the vehicle on a stretcher ride that would sear itself into my memory.

As I helped carry one of the stretchers, I was horrified by the sight of a foot and leg bobble completely independently of each other. A three-inch section of Gary's lower leg was completely missing with just a strand of tendon connecting it to an otherwise intact foot. Gary was in agony, screaming for his mother, who I was sure had died some years earlier.

It seemed that as they were blown backwards along with the Ratel, shrapnel had reached Gary and Frik two ways. Firstly, it had travelled the open space under the vehicle, between the two rear tyres, as Gary stood drinking, taking with it a section of his lower leg. Secondly – and this was harder for us to accept at the time because of the implications for our safety – shrapnel had ripped through 33C's left flank like a stone thrown through a wet, paper bag. Some of the largest chunks had continued on unchecked to punch smaller holes through the right-hand wall but none passed through the area shielded by the huge engine – this probably spared Gary's life because his torso was shielded not only by the body-work but crucially, also by the Ratel engine.

Inside the cabin of the vehicle, Frik De Jager's luck ran out as a swarm of angry shrapnel continued through him downrange. He was deathly pale and uncommunicative.

Cragg hit the boys with morphine, tended the wounds and called for blood from guys with matched blood groups (we all knew our blood group; it was also written clearly on our web belt for moments like this).

First we'd been hit by the Mozzies, and then the flies came. Attracted by the metallic tang of fresh blood oozing from countless puncture wounds in Frikkie's body and around Gary's stump, they homed in for a feast! A small team of guys spent hours fanning the never-ending swarm of flies off their buddies' wounds.

Rossouw, mechanic Billy Hall Jones and a few others who were blood-matched took turns getting hooked up to feed blood directly into Pearman-White and De Jager's by now lifeless body. There would be no giving up on Frik De Jager but the grim truth was that there was no way to staunch the internal bleeding in the field. Other than the blood transfusion it seemed there was very little that could be done for Frik apart from making him comfortable and whispering big, white lies… "Everything's gonna be OK, you're gonna be fine, just hang in there buddy…"

Both guys urgently required medical assistance and surgery, but it wasn't coming. Not yet.

SAAF flights couldn't operate safely this deep in country during the daytime.

We were advised to sit tight as it wouldn't be possible for our Alhouette helicopters to cassevac in such hot conditions. They wouldn't even scramble Mirage fighters to cover us – the sanctions-limited stock of fighter jets was more precious than a few grunts on the ground.

We'd have to wait it out until dusk.

A second strike by the MiGs was extremely likely but we were unwilling to move until our wounded boys had been shipped off to safety so we dug foxholes and prepared our inadequate defences with some guys standing watch on the roof of their Ratel, R4 at the ready. The jubilant Cubans meanwhile, doubtless sped back to Cuito Cuanavale calling in their successful strike.

Some good news followed about 30 or 60 minutes after the strike. A Stinger missile was reported to have taken out one of the two planes. Quid pro quo motherfucker! That, we hoped, would keep the Mozzies off our backs, for a while at least.

However, the FAPLA commanders realised there was an opportunity to inflict yet further damage on our convoy and scrambled a Squadron of MiGs to finish the job.

Unknown to us at the time, the flurry of extra activity at Cuito Cuanavale had not gone unnoticed by forward UNITA and SADF reconnaissance teams who'd gone to ground near Cuito's AFB. As the enemy flight departed Cuito, a SADF *Ystervark* 20mm AA battery scored the first ever direct hit on a MiG, clipping its wing and prompting the four jets to return to base, one of them limping badly. This ended their mission before it began and in so doing, probably saved many more lives.

The ammo in the burning 33C was beginning to crackle and pop with alacrity, at times blending into an unbroken cacophony of explosions, like a large city's entire fireworks display accidentally firing off inside a shipping container. The internal fireball hungrily consumed the thousands of rounds of machine-gun ammunition in a chain reaction that eventually engulfed the 90mm ordinance.

When the 90mm rounds began to blow we maintained a safe distance for about half an hour until it seemed all 71 had cooked off, then Robberts and Sergeant Schidlowski – the only career soldier who'd been riding with the convoy of trucks – drove the Samil water bunker alongside the doomed Ratel in a brave attempt to extinguish the raging inferno.

While all of this was happening, we were unaware of the Fighter Squadron taking off and then quickly landing again at Cuito's AFB. Far as we knew, the smoke from the burning Ratel was a tempting beacon in the azure sky that was likely to attract another attack.

By midday the firestorm in 33C's belly was finally extinguished. It was astounding that the vehicle had been reduced to little more than a blackened, steel box; pretty much everything familiar in the turret, including the steel-tube turret chassis, had melted like a candle.

During the day we received an order from Battalion command to destroy 33C lest it end up in enemy hands.

Storm Pioneers attached to Charlie Squad, like Corporals Vorster and Briers, carried plastic explosives for when shit needed blowing up, but there wasn't much need for that, 33C was by now useless to all but a scrap-metal merchant.

The only personal item Mills recovered from the conflagration was his shrapnel pitted arm patch with the single stripe denoting his rank.

When we discovered there'd be no cassevac until dusk – that would make it almost ten hours after the attack – we were more than pissed off! Regular doses of morphine kept the wounded boys comfortable until the barely conscious Frikkie finally slipped away from us, long before the helicopter arrived. His shrapnel-riddled body had ballooned to more than twice its normal size, a consequence of massive internal haemorrhaging. His death before the evacuation was extremely hard on the boys. RIP Frikkie.

Learning of a comrade's death on the battlefield was painful enough, but watching that death slowly unfold over many hours took a far greater toll on morale, most especially for the lads who'd shared a bungalow with Frikkie and Gary at 2 Special Services Battalion, and later a tent at Omuthiya.

Photo 46 1000 yard stare already evident among Charlie's boys after the loss of Frikkie de Jager the previous day. (Len M. Robberts)

Crew Commander Wayne Mills was devastated and probably never recovered from the loss of his crew – the 'survivors guilt' scenario so typical in wartime. We'd never been so vulnerable, and though we understood and respected the difficulties faced by the air force, because they'd lost pilots to the enemy's advanced anti-aircraft capabilities, we also thought: "so, we spend months putting ourselves in the direct line of fire against superior weapons, for friend and for country, but when we get whacked you don't wanna risk sending a fucking helicopter in?"

That shit is kinda hard to swallow at any age, let alone aged 19!

We'd all heard the word about a MiG getting whacked that morning: "so why not take the risk man?"

In the cold light of day, I knew Frikkie's wounds were not survivable and a rapid evacuation would not have altered the final outcome for either him or Gary. But just like with the Labuschagne accident earlier in the year, you don't give up on your guy, even if it seems all is lost.

After a long tense day we cleared a landing area for the Alhouette, said our final farewells and loaded the boys on to the chopper.

Once the helicopter lifted off we mounted up and moved off into the early evening to complete the disaster-plagued task of escorting the convoy. Within the hour we reached our FOP and went through the motions of setting camo and digging foxholes.

The joy of surviving 1,000kg of explosives which floated in like butterflies, and stung like a motherfucker, was hollow. There was little room for celebrating surviving our close call when the Squad has been so well and truly hurt.

Charlie Squadron never felt quite the same after that day; the illusion of invincibility had been blown away in five deadly seconds, our innocence shattered forever.

Later, on the night of 8 October, some lads in Troop 2 approached me with a mini-revolt. They really didn't want to be asked to go into contact again, a sentiment I secretly shared but despite that, I encouraged them to push on and honour our fallen comrades by continuing to take the fight to the enemy.

What the fuck did I know?

A few tears were shed and for the first time during Modular I found myself needing to cajole some of the guys to hold firm and stay the course. We'd been through so much together without flinching, but somehow the violence of the MiG attack had shocked us deeply – this is what it felt like to lose at war.

It would be nice to say I delivered some heroic William Wallace (Braveheart) rabble-rousing speech from atop my Ratel that night, but instead I spoke gently with my guys, reminding them we were still a proud team and very close to achieving our personal mission – to get home…alive.

If Troops One and Two had issues of lowered morale, Troop Three must've been totally fucked up! They were now at half-strength having lost a second crew in the space of five days.

There were scary days that followed but I recollect very little of the following two months before returning home. Perhaps the 'shield of Armour' I'd been growing to protect the kid inside since basic training had just grown about eight-inches thicker.

Waiting for us at the FOP that evening were the two Lieutenants sent to replace Charlie's missing officers. [I have no recollection of the replacement officers joining Charlie Squad. In my bomb-scarred memory of the remaining seven weeks on Ops Modular, I retained responsibility for Troop Two and Rossouw retained control of Troop Three. I mean no disrespect to either man but it's remarkable that I have no memory of this change. I've come to realise that very few memories survive from the period at war after 8 October 1987, but I shall recount the few I have retained].

19

The Rumble in the Jungle (Tank Ambush of the 16th Brigade)

The war had become a lot more personal, some of us seemed inured to the idea of killing more enemy combatants. It was easy to believe that, somehow, their lives didn't count as highly as ours. Perhaps that was the point of training; it was mental and physical conditioning intended to produce human weapons capable of ending a life without hesitation, without compunction.

Violence and death can be compartmentalised, locked away in dark places deep in the recesses of a human psyche; this might explain why some cultures and societies are more bloodthirsty than others. I this is known as 'environmental conditioning'.

Charlie Squad had become conditioned to the violence of warfare, even if we didn't like that concept.

Before sunrise on the 9th we were on the move again, this time only moving a few clicks east of the FOP. The journey was uneventful and safely navigated.

Overnight the replacement Battalion *Dominee* (Church Minister) joined Charlie Squad for a few days to offer prayer and support to the bereft lads.

The civilian priest had just begun a one-month Reserve Citizen Force 'Camp', part of the legal requirement imposed on all former National Servicemen. Camps didn't always run as long as a month and very seldom threw participants right into the cauldron of conflict. This was his first full day on the job and he was understandably eager to help the broken-spirited boys of Charlie. He kindly offered to perform a Memorial service for Adrian Hind and Frikkie De Jager and all the other boys so badly wounded.

Sergeant Schidlowski and his echelon support crew, set about preparing a makeshift pulpit in a clearing about 80 metres from the Squadron's laager and, perhaps given the events of the previous day, dug a good sized foxhole right next to the pulpit. Normally a Sergeant would assign an underling such a menial task, but perhaps helping prepare the 'facilities' for the memorial service gave Sergeant Schidlowski a deeper sense of control of the event – a profound contrast to the situation 24 hours earlier. Or perhaps this was just his way of saying goodbye to Frikkie.

The Memorial service was scheduled for 14:00 and as we ambled towards the Sergeant's carefully prepared 'Church' the sky was ripped apart once more!

One second.
The deafening roar of supersonic jets at treetop height spiked the adrenaline as we hit the ground with our eyes searching for incoming ordinance.

Two seconds.
The minister was next to react – he dived into his newly carved foxie, swiftly followed by six or seven guys who nearly crushed the poor bloke.

Five seconds.
Still hugging the ground, tight as possible.
    Silence.

Six seconds.
Just as we're thinking: "Groundhog Day, they're coming back", a laugh erupts. Someone realised they were a pair of our Mirage fighters. Much later, radio contact with command confirmed the situation to us on the ground.

Bit fucking late, mate! The Mirage had been on final approach to bomb 59th Brigade just over the river from us.

We normally got 'heads-up' whenever friendly aircraft were passing through but again the warning system failed, although this time the painful consequences of an airborne attack were experienced by the opposition team.

To his credit, the Minister pulled himself together and gave a moving tribute to our lost and injured brothers.

Just as the Memorial service was being wrapped up, the familiar whistling of incoming projectiles getting louder warned of incoming rocket fire. The swooshing sound made by a swarm of Stalin Organ Multiple Rocket warheads streaking through the sky was unmistakeable.

Five seconds.

There was a good chance the FAPLA's artillery would miss. They usually did. As yet it was impossible to pinpoint their precise trajectory, but they were definitely heading somewhere near us.

Four seconds.

"No, fuck that! Take cover!"

We were still near the 'Church' and our fucking foxholes too far away to reach and there was only room for so many in the rapidly repopulated Sergeant's excavation.

They were much closer now.

Three seconds.

We sprinted to find anything that resembled a ditch or hole to throw ourselves into – for the second time in two days we found ourselves under enemy attack without foxholes.

The swooshing was louder, closer.

Two seconds.

It was always hard to tell where the missiles would strike. Those of us without a ditch, knowing the music was about to stop, launched ourselves into tyre-ruts in the soil.

"They're about to hit!"

One second.

Still frantically digging, squirming, trying to push ourselves deeper into the soil like a giant earthworm performing 'eyelash excavations'.

The thunder-like rumbling of high explosives detonating in the nearby forest for about ten seconds rolled across the sky. More than 50 rockets had detonated 2-300 metres east of our position. We later learned this was the first time chemical weapons had been deployed against us but fortuitously, the rockets struck downwind of our position. As soon as the rumbling died down we returned to our vehicles and relocated the Squadron post haste.

The day after this attack, 2nd Lt. Bremer gathered the Squad together to prepare us for chemical warfare. Gas masks were issued which we practised putting on during a mock gas attack –using real tear gas.

The enemy were clearly getting desperate if they were resorting to using chemicals.

Intelligence was now confirming the wholesale withdrawal of FAPLA forces.

On the ground, there was still uncertainty as to whether SADF would chase the retreating FAPLA or allow them to run home tail between legs. It was thought amongst our lads that the latter was the more likely scenario.

However, the dramatic turn of events on 3 October presented new opportunities for the big cheeses. The imminent arrival of the 'fresh as daisies' 4 SAI, and E-Squad Tanks would more than double our mechanised presence in theatre. It must've been tempting for them to imagine that the phenomenal achievements of 61 and 32 Battalions, with the light Infantry support of 101 Battalion and UNITA, would be overshadowed once the heavyweight Olifant tanks came into play. These forces now offered the potential to inflict permanent damage on the wider communist threat in the region. With the original brief of repelling the enemy achieved, this might have become the new objective, the big prize.

The wider geo-Political situation at the end of '87 would surely have been influential in the decision to extend the objectives of the war. Castro's forces, despite the assistance of their powerful allies, were 'all-in', defeated, and the white-minority government in South Africa were seeking to strengthen their internationally unpopular grip on power.

It certainly wouldn't help the provincial situation if five or six enemy Brigades were to garrison at Cuito for the wet season – they'd be banging on UNITA's front door the moment the ground started drying out in February/March '88. This threat was real and perhaps too serious to ignore.

Two days after the MRL gas attack, new orders confirmed our suspicions – the goalposts were being shifted. The temptation to cause the FAPLA lasting damage had proved too great for the big cheese to ignore. Our new mission: chase the retreating FAPLA forces, frustrate their progress while reinforcements (4 SAI) moved into theatre. The plan, it seemed, was to prevent retreating forces from crossing the Cuito River and thus stop them from reaching the relative safety of Cuito Cuanavale.

For almost two weeks our battle group engaged in a deadly cat-n-mouse chase with 59th Brigade while plans were drawn up to confront the remaining four enemy Brigades in the area south of Cuito. This was a period of strict night-time disciplines and disconnection from supply lines.

16th Brigade, who'd been dug in some 30 clicks NNE of the Lomba crossing, were at the vanguard of the Eastern corridor and moved northwards to hold a

Photo 47 Trying our new gas masks for size. These were delivered after intelligence reports warned of further chemical warfare attacks. (Len M. Robberts)

strategically useful position in support of the retreating 21st Brigade. To achieve our recently extended objectives in the conflict, this tactical move by the enemy forces would have to be countered by the SADF, but with insufficient ground forces in the arena, plans were drawn up to insert a regiment from 1 Parachute Battalion behind enemy lines. This force would join with ground forces in disrupting and slowing the retreat of the 16th Brigade

The well-trained Parabats undertook a dangerous night-time jump from low altitude, close enough to enemy positions to be effective, but without running the risk of getting shot out the sky by anti-aircraft batteries.

As we chased the retreating 59th our supply lines became precariously stretched out over territory that until very recently had been the FAPLA's stomping ground. Now, landmines were added to the smorgasbord of threats.

Without access to logistical support we had to make do with our remaining supplies. I don't want to infer that we starved during this phase but rations ran low enough that even the least favoured foods were eaten. Smokers ran out of stocks too and in desperation a few of the guys tried smoking animal dung.

When the Sergeant finally caught up with us a fortnight later, we washed our foul bodies under the 'shower' from the taps of a brim-full water bunker, a cause for much celebration in the stifling heat of the early African Summer.

Threat levels remained stubbornly high but no-one died during the chase. Then, without warning, we were ordered to break off the pursuit and given four or five day's respite from the frontline.

4 SAI was apparently close enough to take up the chase while the battle-weary 61 Mech rested before the next phase – AKA 'The Chambinga Gallop' – began in earnest. This was in effect a race to gain control of strategic high ground in an area known as Chambinga, near the Cuito river. Dominance of this area would be a significant advantage to whichever side controlled it.

The SADF began the chase almost a week behind FAPLA and needed to slow them down – hence the planned 1 Para night strike and the ongoing harassment by our Artillery and ground forces. But Summer rains were imminent, and once the deluge began it would spoil the terrain for mechanised warfare. The race was therefore against two enemies – the FAPLA and the tropical wet season.

It never quite made sense to me that 61 Mech were granted time off from the chase but perhaps the cheese thought we were shell-shocked and needed respite if we were to be of further value.

After two solid nights in the saddle, we arrived at an old logistics base some 30-40 clicks south of the Lomba River. Captain Cloete immediately made a big noise about having a bath as soon as we arrived that morning and ordered the Sergeant to set about heating a drum of water. A bathing area was created near the rear of Cloete's command vehicle – a hole dug in the ground lined with a plastic bivvy; a perfect bush-bath in fairly tranquil surroundings. I'm sure the Captain deserved the treat given the hardship he'd endured on the frontline.

The Squad Sergeant was one of the most *rustig* (chilled) Permanent Force guys we ever encountered but we'd not spent much time together during the operation as he was normally ferrying in and out with a convoy of supplies.

Soon after arriving at the logistics base/holiday camp, Sarge called Charlie's Troop Sergeants together and ordered, nay, compelled, the three of us, to urinate into the drum of water he was heating for Captain Cloete's bath.

By now, so well-conditioned to obeying orders, we complied unquestioningly, putting every last drop of effort into the task. Unwittingly, we may even have helped raised the temperature of Captain's bathwater. Unfortunately, the Captain also shaved and brushed his teeth using the same water.

Photo 48 2nd Lt Bremer enjoying the luxuries afforded us on our break from the frontline. (Len M. Robberts)

[I'm not sure I'm proud of this revelation, however the insight is interesting in context.]

During the day NCOs and officers received a 'formal' invite to dine with the Captain at his vehicle. The three of us wondered if we'd been found out. Captain Cloete would've been a little pissed-off had he learned the truth about his bush-spa's secret, anti-aging ingredient, but I'm not entirely sure what kind of punishment he would've meted out in the situation.

When we arrived for the dinner party later that evening, Cloete looked fresh and rejuvenated, even youthful, for a 25 year old. He'd secured some quality wet rations and I felt a bit like Oliver Twist arriving at an all-you-can eat buffet.

During our three-day stay at the holiday camp we had a pep talk from Army Chief, General Jannie Geldenhuis. I only recall one phrase from this rousing speech: "…the battle on 3 October, causing the destruction of 47th Brigade on the Lomba River, represents the single greatest battle victory in the history of SADF!"

Fuckin-hell bru! We thought we'd done something pretty special on 3 October and here, three-weeks later, the really big cheese was singing about it. However, by this stage we cared less about major victories than the loss of our friends and we were scared that this could happen again, a prospect that was all too real now that the SADF was committed to further overt action.

A few days later, rested and clean(er), we prepared to mount up and return once more to the frontline. At about the same time 1 Parachute Battalion was making final preparations for their risky night-jump into battle.

Two more days of hard driving later, we arrived near the advance SADF units including E-Squad Tankers who'd stopped because they were lost. As David navigated 32A between the stationary tanks, I was looking for one call-sign in particular, Five Zero – my mate Greg had been the gunner on Echo Squadron's command tank last time I heard. When we drew up alongside Five Zero (50), I pulled off my helmet, jumped out the turret and clambered onto the Olifant.

With broad grin on my face, I whispered to the major to hop out the turret so I could surprise my mate who, it was confirmed, was sitting in the gunner's chair, deep in the bowels of the beast.

I leaned down into the turret hatch and startled him by slapping his helmet.

Despite retaining so few memories from this period of my time at war, I always retained this one, partly I think because the shocked look on Hodges clean face was so memorable – it took him several long seconds to work out the identity of the wild-haired and dirty creature looking at him – and partly because seeing South African Tanks for the first time boosted our morale. These powerful machines promised to give us a real advantage on the ground.

It had been 40 years since South African tanks had killed enemy MBTs in combat and the Echo Squad boys were, they said, primed and ready to break the drought but, unsurprisingly, the tankers were somewhat less willing to engage in dialogue concerning the number of days it had been since their weaker cousin, the Ratel 90, had killed enemy MBTs.

Pride – it's a motherfucker man!

Our two circus's moved on to different objectives and it would be two weeks before my mates from Echo Squadron would meet us again, this time under very different circumstances.

About a week later, Bravo Company was leading the battle group as we 'stalked' up behind elements of the 59th Brigade.

32 Alpha *gereed* (made ready), not so happy, but ready.

I made my usual pre-fight preparations: put on clean, army-issue underwear, Tank-suit, checked weapons and psyched up the crew.

After an early morning start the convoy made steady progress over easy terrain – scraggly trees and sparse grasses – following the distinctive tracks of a T55 which disappeared into what looked like a solid wall of foliage. The guys were concerned about entering the forest without knowledge of what lay ahead but we pushed on nevertheless, into the unknown.

The formation went in two by two with the antitank detachment from Bravo Company up front.

Guys were chattering on comms. At driver eye-level, visibility was less than five metres. Herb opened his hatch to take a peek at the weird surroundings. "How thick is this wall of frikkin bush Corporal, it's much darker than usual."

My mind began to play tricks. I imagined us to be very near to enemy forces but unable to hear them above the noise of our machines. Were they there, just ahead? My eyes searched for signs of enemy soldiers I could not see. We rolled slowly forwards until we became totally ensconced in the densest, most unusual flora we'd encountered on tour. I was uneasy, nervous, but made every effort not to let this show in my voice as I exchanged radio messages with the other crews. The uneasiness in their voices made it clear that they too were anxious to emerge from this bizarre 'Honey I Shrunk The Kids' scene in which our battle group had been shrunk to the size of a toy army lost in a neglected overgrown garden.

After fifteen minutes of slow progress the visibility was, I convinced myself, a little worse – we were so totally enveloped, completely blinded by what is best described as a forest of five-metre-tall timber fingers with the appearance of giant Twiglets (a wheat-based snack that looks like a knobbly twig). Everything was brown and dead-looking and even the harsh African sun was barely able to penetrate into that deep gloom where millions of these strange 'fingers' were so tightly clustered together that we could see no farther than the tip of the 90mm barrel.

Our powerful Ratel had no difficulty flattening the strange plants as we crept forward, twigs snapping easily before disappearing beneath the angled, armour-plated nose to leave a clear passage for following vehicles.

Every second seemed to last ten, and the feeling of being in imminent danger from an unseen threat was akin to scuba diving in the murky waters off Natal's coast, visibility near zero, when you know a dozen sharks are circling just out of view.

The vehicles to our right were out of sight but, by standing high in the turret, I could see 32 Bravo's whip-antennae alongside. The following vehicle, travelling in the path our Ratel had just cleared, was about 30 metres behind.

Half an hour after entering the gloom we'd only made about 500 metres progress.

BOOM!

A single, powerful but unseen explosion erupted nearby. My adrenaline level spiked.

The radio crackled. Cloete was angry. "All vehicles halt! Who fired that round?"

A flurry of negative responses came from the crew commanders in double-quick succession.

Had Bravo Company's lead vehicles tripped a land mine, or provoked an ambush? They were in two-up formation with no clear targets, or room for manoeuvre in the deep bush, and it seems they had little choice but to withdraw.

In response to the threat, Cloete immediately ordered a number of the Charlie Squad guns to provide a defensive cordon covering the withdrawal.

Immediately, I ordered Corrie to push out to the left flank and move forward toward the unseen danger. With no small serving of trepidation we cut a line through some 30 or 40 metres of dense shrubbery, absolutely bricking it, maintaining close lateral formation with the adjacent vehicle.

32 Alpha held the left flank across a narrow 200-metre front. We were blind, and a sitting target.

BOOM! A second shot rang out.

We'd approached a killing zone blind, unable to retaliate against an invisible enemy who might be anywhere. Meantime, the boys at the centre of Charlie's defensive cordon reported seeing the Bravo boys rushing backwards 'pale in the face'. Whatever they'd encountered couldn't have been very pretty.

We waited for what seemed an age for an order to shoot or retreat. Zeelie had a round up the spout, obviously. We were primed and prepared to shoot, but even if that order was given we'd be firing blindly into the spaghetti of twigs and branches. And in this thicket there was always the chance we'd start shooting each other. We waited, expecting another enemy shot, or volley.

Finally the order came: "pull back in overlapping jumps."

Once Charlie began its withdrawal we pulled back in coordinated 50 metre jumps in concert with Bravo until we reached the edge of the forest of twigs where we swung through 180 degrees and hightailed out of there, unscathed.

There were obvious questions but few clear answers following the near-disaster in the forest of twigs. We were told we'd driven blindly into an enemy tank ambush. A Squadron of T55s was formed in a 'U' shape just ahead of our position. The two speculative shots fired served as an early warning which undoubtedly saved lives – the weird forest had both hindered and shielded us. Both sides went home unscathed.

There were repercussions from our failure to engage the 16th Brigade. Commandant Bok Smit and others were relieved of their posts, a process that rippled on for months and which may even have had a significant impact on the outcome of the war. Battalion commanders were unhappy at being forced to the engage enemy with mechanised forces in such heavily forested terrain.

On that same night, not far from our position, SADF suffered its single biggest setback of the Operation, certainly in terms of lives lost. The action to drop Para's behind enemy lines and create havoc was a total fuck-up! The boys were inadvertently inserted directly overhead the Brigade they'd been sent to torment.

Unsurprisingly, the 16th Brigade did everything they could to neutralise the threat. Guys were being shot in their harnesses on their descent, survivors forced to fight their way out of the LZ while supporting wounded comrades.

That any of the men, including my school pal Carl Robberts, survived the self-inflicted ordeal is testament to the quality of our soldiers, their training and the innate human desire to survive against the odds. But that disastrous escapade cost more than fifteen SA soldiers their lives, including that of a school mate, Hughes De Rose, and another alma mater member from the year above, Raymond Light – young lives extinguished far too soon. RIP.

20

The Day of the Elephant

Echo Squadron Tankers finally got the call to arms and began shipping out of the School of Armour about the same time that 61 Mech was shipping 47th Brigade into the Lomba River on 3 October.

I knew many of the Tankers from our time together in Bloemfontein. Some of the guys like Clint were also from Durban and we'd occasionally hit the bars together on a weekend pass. I probably would've liked to have become a tank crew commander but then again I'd never have had the honour of serving with 61 Mech.

Over the coming weeks, 4 SAI and E-Squad formed the primary strike force while 61 Mech was mostly used to harry and divert enemy fire before the fresh-faced warriors went in to earn their own scars. Even with the addition of the Olifant Squadron, 4 SAI didn't have it all their way. As combat moved into the heavily mined Chambinga Heights area, 4 SAI endured some of the heaviest battles of the Operation against well-reinforced, dug-in enemy Battalions, notably on 9 and 17 November. During the course of a battle, FAPLA only managed to disable a single Olifant tank, by shooting out the track. This must've been something of a morale boost for the retreating force which by now, had sacrificed more than 100 MBTs of their own. More poignantly however, the 4 SAI men endured a number of KIA. In the most costly engagement, a Ratel was torn up by 23mm ZSU 23 anti-aircraft fire. The ZSU 23 was designed as a vehicle-mounted, quad-barrelled, anti-aircraft weapon but the enemy discovered that by elevating the vehicle's rear end, they could aim the ZSU 23's high-velocity projectiles at ground troops. At close range, the ZSU 23 was easily capable of tearing new portholes in the flanks of a Ratel; only the reinforced nose plate was just about thick enough to survive direct hits.

By now we were within spitting distance of Cuito. The enemy forces holed up there had paid dearly but still had sufficient reserves to continue defending the garrison town.

In combat the Olifant Squadron was unparalleled. I only recall integrating once with Echo Squad in an attack which included a close quarters, frontal assault against a number of T55s. This relatively brief contact was prosecuted

232

at a quicker tempo than in earlier battles and often at ranges of less than 200 metres. Initially, the enemy Tanks burst through a thicket ahead of our position, to charge towards us. The Olifants were like bodybuilders on an alcohol-fuelled 'road-rage' and quickly stopped the enemy Tanks dead in their tracks.

Corporal Mark Alexander's tank was 30 metres, on my right flank. Johnny Purnell's 50-ton unit equally spaced on my left. The speed with which they flattened trees as we crossed terrain, simultaneously firing on the move, would have been breathtaking had I not been totally focussed on sharing the workload that morning. Their 105mm stabilised guns fired rapidly and to devastating effect, often only needing a single shot to destroy a T55 before moving onto the next target.

It was insane. The speed they could reload and fire using a dedicated loader gave them a real advantage over the Ratel 90. Mark's gunner, Don Munro, never missed at such close range, each 105mm warhead doing immense damage, quickly disabling the target.

The contact was in a different league. We were smashing into the enemy's Squadron so hard and fast I felt confident enough to call Alexander on our shared channel: "tell Don to leave some targets for us. It's no fun picking off your sloppy seconds *bru*!"

The Olifant represented a major boost to our offensive capability and they were called on to either lead or integrate with the 90s during the significant battles of November. But the enemy had achieved a territorial advantage near Cuito Cuanavale and increasingly frequent rain began to undermine the effectiveness of the heavyweight giants.

My mate Corporal Paul Gladwin from 4 SAI (who would've swapped places with me for a border tour), with nothing but a 7.62 Browning for defence, narrowly escaped a one on one encounter with a T55 he happened upon when transporting a Ratel 90 with damaged cannon. Gladwin's driver reversed his vehicle in blind panic over the stump of a large tree, beaching it before jumping out. Gladwin was forced to enter the cabin and drive the vehicle free while being targeted by the T55. Fortunately, his heroics were not punished. He and the vehicle lived on to fight another day.

There are countless other stories of scrapes, incidents and accidents but these are not my stories to tell.

Toward the end of November, Charlie Squad received our final orders of Operation Modular: move off the frontline and provide security to the G6 (155mm) battery who were now within striking range of Cuito Cuanavale and her airstrip.

Photo 49 Hanging out with (protecting) G6 cannons at the end of our tour in Angola. They clearly weren't firing at this moment! (Len M. Robberts)

Enemy aircraft remained a constant threat but they never found Charlie again, nor did we endure further direct enemy action.

The G6 gunners noisily went about job hurling air-burst and other deadly ordinance onto targets identified by our forward observation posts (OPs). These OP guys were the sort they make movies about, the types who *bos-kuk* into plastic bags, eat slugs and grubs and most probably scared the shit out of their pre-school teacher.

A standing legacy of Angola's long war meant it boasted some of the mostly densely mined areas in the world, the price of which included a generation of limbless children and civilians picking up the tab for the folly of war. Over the years, SADF also lost many lives and limbs to landmines.

On one of our final days as 32 Alpha (the 2nd) we had a close encounter with a landmine, probably the last incident I can recall at war. We were inside a narrow cordon cleared through a minefield. It all seemed rather routine, no immediate threat but Zeelie's hatch was shut and the gunner was in the turret at the ready. I was standing waist-high in the turret when, without warning, a blast erupted violently from the ground at our three o'clock position, about ten metres from the vehicle.

The resulting shock wave rocked me sideways, shrapnel angrily peppered the Ratel's bodywork – no ill effects whatsoever, nothing to report.

It is debatable that the vibration from a convoy of Ratels would have tripped a twitchy mine at that distance. Another possible explanation is that the explosion was an artillery, or mortar strike of some description but that too is unlikely because a single speculative artillery round didn't make much sense either and there been none of the tell-tale whistling usually made by incoming ordinance. In any event the incident was laughed off as an amusing anecdote. It was a close call but no big deal, we were at war after all.

As Operation Modular drew to a close and a new containment operation began, 20 Brigade mustered a contingent of Citizen Force and national servicemen to prepare to replace the combatants in the field. By now UNITA had been re-equipped from captured materiel including a Squadron of Russian tanks, armoured personnel carriers and over 100 logistics vehicles. And then there were the big prizes like the SAM-8 and SA-9 missile systems which were apparently of great interest to the Americans.

At the end of November, Operation Modular formally ended. Operations Hooper and Packer started, but these actions belong to other brave men in whom the ultimate sacrifice was sought and it is their history for the telling.

61 Mech, 4 SAI and 32 Battalion were withdrawn from the frontline in preparation for the end of our two-year call of duty, but not before the offer of a 'generous' financial incentive to stay in Angola and continue the fight.

One evening, Trooper Roderick van der Westhuizen noticed the unusual addition of UNITA security around the laager. His curiosity piqued by the arrival of an incoming helicopter, he grabbed his R4 and leopard-crawled through the bush to within 15 metres of the great rebel leader himself, Jonas Savimbi.

Savimbi, van der Westhuizen later reported to us, was in conference with our battle group commanders, requesting that the current contingent of soldiers be forced to stay the war rather than being replaced with young bucks without the hard-won experience of the departing forces.

Fortunately the law only required two years of army service and surviving even this length of time had tested our good fortune to the maximum. There was no way we would volunteer to take more of that shit.

Even though the SADF was unquestionably the more potent force in the conflict, we'd learned that any contact can lead to casualties, no matter how well prepared or strong we were.

Just outside Mavinga, and on our way home, we were happy, no, relieved, to be relinquishing our Ratels to youngsters coming through from the '87 intake. Time would tell that theirs wouldn't be an easy ride either and the new soldiers of 61 Mech and Charlie Squad would lose brothers of their own in the months ahead as the enemy hunkered down at Cuito Cuanavale.

Embarrassed by the hammering his forces and investment had taken at the Lomba River, Fidel Castro reacted by deploying thousands of his best soldiers and hundreds more MBT and by February '88 had opened a new front in south-western Angola.

The communists were willing to press on with the war, death toll be damned, but the SA government was less willing to sacrifice so many of its young men. Ultimately, a form of diplomacy, inextricably linked to a changing world order, determined the final outcome of the bloody Angolan Bush War.

Charlie Squad arranged a little welcome party for the greenhorn replacement soldiers. As their transport trucks pulled through the bushes to our camouflaged positions we stormed the trucks yelling loudly and brandishing sticks – the poor lads shat themselves!

We didn't tell them about the horrors of war but they were understandably shaken by our appearance and by the state of our bomb-scarred vehicles.

I couldn't imagine being thrown into this hell on our first week after arriving at Grootfontein a year before without having had the advantage of all the extra training together as a unit, Squadron and crew. These new crews deserve much respect.

We wished them well, donated our overstock of rat packs and bade them God speed.

32A (the 2nd) got a fond pat on the cannon and then we were bundled onto Troop transport aircraft at Mavinga, bound for Rundu, then shipped by truck back into Angola, to a secret, temporary rehabilitation camp to complete our demobilisation.

Our rancid army clothing was replaced unquestioningly – a first in the army!

Ice cold beers were bought. A band played a cool tune we'd never heard, appropriately called 'Johnny Come Home' by Fine Young Cannibals. Apparently it was a big hit on the music charts, but we'd been out of circulation for some time.

That first night I drank 23 cans of Castle Lager and woke with no ill effects, however, I recollect nothing whatsoever of the following ten days after our plane touched down at Durban airport. An outline of our activities from that missing fortnight has been provided to me by others who have some recall of that period.

Photo 50 61 Mech boys enjoy the live music and first female sighting at demobilisation. (Len M. Robberts)

Photo 51 First day of demobilisation – I look somewhat worse for wear in the centre of the image. (Len M. Robberts)

Photo 52 Coming back over the Okavango river near Bagani in the Caprivi strip after Ops Modular. Gert Niemand has the biggest grin on his bearded face – he certainly earned it! On the left of the shot Len Robberts can be seen taking the last in his series of war photos with his contraband camera. (Martin Bremer)

Photo 53 Crossing over the border for the final time. Departing demob camp returning to Omuthiya for pass-out parade. (Len M. Robberts)

Four days after arriving at demobilisation camp we crossed the border at Bittersweet and departed Angola for the very last time. Back at our Omuthiya base, we were strangers in a familiar environment. The unit conducted the final full-Battalion parade where we were issued with the unique 61 Mech dagger *balkie* (badge) in recognition of our cross-border actions.

Later we were despatched to Grootfontein AFB which involved a three day lay-over for our flights home. During this period there was, it is alleged, copious consumption of alcoholic refreshments. Adams and Mills claim they took care of me during a violent bout of sickness, apparently the after-effects of a few drops of alcohol.

Looking around the flight on the way home, the missing men, the thousand-yard stares told their own story of the year on the border. Three months at war had taken a particularly heavy toll, not only in terms of lives lost but also in the damaged and scarred psyche of soldiers about to become civilians.

In the army we'd earned respect, as a unit we'd learned to trust each other like brothers and together in battle we'd triumphed against the odds.

Then, we were heroes.

But that was then, and that was there.

Away from SA, the world really didn't give a fuck. We were on a fast track back to zero, no thanks, no credit. No backup.

We said final goodbyes to our brothers and I thought the Angolan war, for me, had ended.

I never looked back, nor followed the half truths printed in the government controlled press. The door to that part of my psyche was generally locked shut but the odd account leaked out when I was drunk, one time even leading to a brawl at Gold

Photo 54
Sisters Carol and Jenny pleased to get their bro back from the war.
(Elizabeth Mannall)

Reef City, near Johannesburg, when three blokes refused to believe I'd fought in the war.

Landing at Durban airport was a low-key event, no state-sponsored fanfare, no brass band, but being reunited with my family was the highlight. They asked me for information on the war. "We were in some big battles Dad," was about all I could say.

Society at large was uninterested, and the government seemed equally so, unless it was to call us up for Citizen Force duties in the form of a three-month 'camp'. Though worse was to come when a few years later political upheaval would push the plight of SADF veterans much further down the political agenda. It felt as if we'd been discarded, left to find our own way, young men abandoned to make sense of a world without the high octane, high-stakes adrenaline-fuelled camaraderie and candour we'd become accustomed to in just 90 days at war, for many the experience would resonate deeply, even shaping our outlook on life forever.

Some prospective employers placed no value on the skills and leadership we'd learned at such high cost. Courage and commitment counted for little.

My mother, like many other moms, knew her son hadn't returned unaffected. She read about the – at that time – little-known PTSD but despite her best efforts, it took me twenty-four years and her 7-month terminal battle with MND to begin to heal from my 'war within'.

Losing my Mom was devastating, but her bravery and courage was astounding, compelling me to begin the reconciliation of my post-war trauma and share this story of 61 Mech's participation in Operation Modular 1987 and in particular, honour the courage of SADF Ratel 90 crewmen who defied the odds, repeatedly, in battle against Squadrons of Russian main Battle Tanks.

Together, these forces repelled a tsunami of weaponry and in so doing, changed the course of the Angolan War, and maybe even with it, the course of South Africa's history at the end of the 20th Century.

SALUTE.

Appendix I

Charlie Squadron 1987 – 61 Mechanised Battalion Group

NOMMER	RANG	NAAM	AANST	BL GP	BOEK NO
71219240PE	Maj	E.K. Pienaar	Eskn Bev	A+	DD-001
81147308PE	Lt	G.J. van der Walt	Eskn 2IB	A+	DC-002
83325324BG	2Lt	H.M. Bremer	Tp Bev	B+	DC 003
84340157BG	2Lt	A.H. Hind	Tp Bev	O+	DC-004
79624565BG	2Lt	M. O' Connor	Tp Bev	A+	DC 005
81259814BG	2Lt	L.M. Robberts	Pt Bev	O+	DC 006
76321462PE	S/Sers	R. Slabbert	Esm	A+	DC 007
82534942BG	Kpl	P.J. Delport	Tp Sers	O+	DC 089
84429877BG	Kpl	D. Mannall	Tp Sers	O+	DC 008
83511394BG	Kpl	S.S. Rossouw	Tp Sers	O+	DC 009
81115222BG	Kpl	J.H.C. Venter	Tp Sers	A+	DC 010
83227082BG	Kpl	A.B. Vorster	Pt Sers	A+	DC-011
83208398BG	Kpl	F.W. Briers	Sek Bev	O+	DC-012
83384198BG	Kpl	D.W. Brown	Span Bev	A+	DC 013
83341404BG	Kpl	D.S. Cragg	Medic Ops	AB+	DC 015
83344150BG	Kpl	J. Coetzee	Span Bev	O+	DC 016
81092306BG	Kpl	F. Fouché	Span Bev	O+	DC 017
83566157BG	Kpl	W.A. Fraser	Span Bev	O+	DC 018
84283738BG	Kpl	R. Rebelo	Span Bev	A+	DC 023
83379164BG	Kpl	B.W. Saunders	I00	A+	DC 024
82387390BG	Kpl	D.B. Taylor	Span Bev	O-	DC 025
83462333BG	Kpl	R.P. v/d Westhuizen	Span Bev	A+	DC 026
83559492BG	Kpl	D.R. van Vuuren	Sek Bev	A+	DC-013
84207521BG	Kpl	S.C. Wiid	Gnr	O+	DC 027
83462192BG	O/Kpl	J.G. du Toit	Beheer Bdr	A-	DC 042
85202794BG	O/Kpl	L. Fritsch	Eskm	O-	DC 019
83389675BG	O/Kpl	D.L. Kolm	Sek 2IB	B+	DC-020
83584029BG	O/Kpl	W.J. Mills	Span Bev	A+	DC 021
82386772BG	O/Kpl	T.G. Pretorius	Sek 2IB	O+	DC 022
83473975BG	O/Kpl	J. Sharp	Gnr	O+	DC 070
84440627BG	O/Kpl	M.L. Storbeck	Klerk	A+	DC 072
84396704BG	Kav	W.J. Adams	Gnr	A+	DC 028
81014102BG	Kav	J.C. Botha	Dwr B	O+	DC-029
82376534BG	Sktr	M.E. Bradwell	Mag 2	A+	DC 030
83421529BG	Kav	W. Brooks	Gnr	A+	DC 032
84426965BG	Sktr	N.V. Buckley	Gnr	B+	DC-033
83487155BG	Sktr	P.R. Burger	Radio/Gnr	A+	DC 034
84264498BG	Kav	J.C. Chester	Dwr B	O+	DC 035
85203651BG	Kav	R. Clark	Dwr A	O+	DC 036
83338459BG	Sktr	C.J. Coetzee	Sktr	AB+	DC 037

NOMMER	RANG	NAAM	AANST	BL GP	BOEK NO
~~71219240PE~~ 7830525 PE	~~Maj~~ KAPT 30	~~B.K. Pienaar~~ P.J. Cloete	Eskn Bev	~~A+~~ A-	~~DD-001~~ DC 002
~~81147308PE~~	Lt	G.J. van der Walt	~~Eskn 2IB~~	~~A+~~	~~DC-002~~
83325324BG	2Lt 31	H.M. Bremer	Tp Bev	B+	DC 003
~~84340157BG~~	~~2Lt~~ dood	~~A.H. Hind~~	~~Tp Bev~~	~~O+~~	~~DC-004~~
~~79624565BG~~	2Lt	M. O' Connor	Tp Bev	A+	~~DC-005~~
81259814BG 78567534 PE	2Lt 30A SERS	L.M. Robberts R.O. SCHIDLOW-KIO	Pt Bev	O+ A+	DC 006
~~76321462PE~~	S/Sers	R. Slabbert	Esm	A+	DC 007
82534942BG	Kpl 30A	P.J. Delport	Tp Sers	O+	DC 089
84429877BG	Kpl 32A	D. Mannall	Tp Sers	O+	DC 008
83511394BG	Kpl 33A	S.S. Rossouw	Tp Sers	O+	DC 009
81115222BG	Kpl 30	J.H.C. Venter	Tp Sers	A+	DC 010
~~83227082BG~~	~~Kpl~~	~~A.B. Vorster~~	~~Pt Sers~~	~~A+~~	~~DC-011~~
~~83208398BG~~	Kpl	F.W. Briers	~~Sek Bev~~	O+	~~DC-012~~
83384198BG	Kpl 31C	D.W. Brown	Span Bev	A+	DC 013
83341404BG	Kpl C/9J	D.S. Cragg	Medic Ops	AB+	DC 015
83344150BG	Kpl 31B	J. Coetzee	Span Bev	O+	DC 016
81092306BG	Kpl 32E	F. Fouché	Span Bev	O+	DC 017
83566157BG	Kpl	W.A. Fraser	Span Bev	O+	DC 018
84283738BG	Kpl 32C	R. Rebelo	Span Bev	A+	DC 023
83379164BG	Kpl 30	B.W. Saunders	IOO	A+	DC 024
82387390BG	Kpl	D.B. Taylor	Span Bev	O-	DC 025
83462333BG	Kpl	R.P. v/d Westhuizen	Span Bev	A+	DC 026
~~83559492BG~~	Kpl	D.R. van Vuuren	Sek Bev	A+	~~DC-013~~
84207521BG	Kpl 31A	S.C. Wiid	Gnr	O+	DC 027
83462192BG	O/Kpl 30A	J.G. du Toit	Beheer Bdr	A-	DC 042
85202794BG	O/Kpl	L. Fritsch	Eskm	O-	DC 019
~~83389675BG~~	O/Kpl	D.L. Kolm	Sek 2IB	B+	~~DC-020~~
83584029BG	O/Kpl	W.J. Mills	Span Bev	A+	DC 021
~~82386772BG~~	O/Kpl	T.G. Pretorius	~~Sek 2IB~~	O+	~~DC-022~~
83473975BG	O/Kpl 31	J. Sharp	Gnr	O+	DC 070
~~84440627BG~~	O/Kpl	M.L. Storbeck	Klerk	A+	~~DC-072~~
84396704BG	Kav 33A	W.J. Adams	Gnr	A+	DC 028
~~81014102BG~~	Kav	J.C. Botha	Dwr B	O+	~~DC-029~~
82376534BG	Sktr	M.E. Bradwell	Mag 2	A+	DC 030
83421529BG	Kav 32C	W. Brooks	Gnr	A+	DC 032
84426965BG	Sktr	N.V. Buckley	Gnr	B+	~~DC-033~~
~~83487155BG~~	Sktr	P.R. Burger	Radio/Gnr	A+	DC 034
84264498BG	Kav	J.C. Chester	Dwr B	O+	~~DC-035~~
85203651BG	Kav 33B	R. Clark	Dwr A	O+	DC 036
~~83338459BG~~	Sktr	G.J. Coetzee	Sktr	AB+	~~DC-037~~

NOMMER	RANG	NAAM	AANST	BL GP	BOEK NO
71219240PE	Maj	B.K. Pienaar	Eskn Bev	A+	BD-001
81147308PE	Lt	G.J. van der Walt	Eskn 2IB	A+	DC-002
83325324BG	2Lt	H.M. Bremer	Tp Bev	B+	DC 003
84340157BG	2Lt	A.H. Hind	Tp Bev	O+	DC-004
79624565BG	2Lt	M. O' Connor	Tp Bev	A+	DC 005
81259814BG	2Lt	L.M. Robberts	Pt Bev	O+	DC 006
76321462PE	S/Sers	R. Slabbert	Esm	A+	DC 007
82534942BG	Kpl	P.J. Delport	Tp Sers	O+	DC 089
84429877BG	Kpl	D. Mannall	Tp Sers	O+	DC 008
83511394BG	Kpl	S.S. Rossouw	Tp Sers	O+	DC 009
81115222BG	Kpl	J.H.C. Venter	Tp Sers	A+	DC 010
83227082BG	Kpl	A.B. Vorster	Pt Sers	A+	DC-011
83208398BG	Kpl	F.W. Briers	Sek Bev	O+	DC 012
83384198BG	Kpl	D.W. Brown	Span Bev	A+	DC 013
83341404BG	Kpl	D.S. Cragg	Medic Ops	AB+	DC 015
833441508G	Kpl	J. Coetzee	Span Bev	O+	DC 016
81092306BG	Kpl	F. Fouché	Span Bev	O+	DC 017
83566157BG	Kpl	W.A. Fraser	Span Bev	O+	DC 018
84283738BG	Kpl	R. Rebelo	Span Bev	A+	DC 023
83379164BG	Kpl	B.W. Saunders	IOO	A+	DC 024
82387390BG	Kpl	D.B. Taylor	Span Bev	O-	DC 025
83462333BG	Kpl	R.P. v/d Westhuizen	Span Bev	A+	DC 026
83559492BG	Kpl	D.R. van Vuuren	Sek Bev	A+	DC-013
84207521BG	Kpl	S.C. Wiid	Gnr	O+	DC 027
83462192BG	O/Kpl	J.G. du Toit	Beheer Bdr	A-	DC 042
85202794BG	O/Kpl	L. Fritsch	Eskm	O-	DC 019
83399675BG	O/Kpl	D.L. Kolm	Sek 2IB	B+	DC-020
83584029BG	O/Kpl	W.J. Mills	Span Bev	A+	DC 021
82386772BG	O/Kpl	T.G. Pretorius	Sek 2IB	O+	DC 022
83473975BG	O/Kpl	J. Sharp	Gnr	O+	DC 070
84440627BG	O/Kpl	M.L. Storbeck	Klerk	A+	DC 072
84396704BG	Kav	W.J. Adams	Gnr	A+	DC 028
81014102BG	Kav	J.C. Botha	Dwr B	O+	DC-029
82376534BG	Sktr	M.E. Bradwell	Mag 2	A+	DC 030
83421529BG	Kav	W. Brooks	Gnr	A+	DC 032
84426965BG	Sktr	N.V. Buckley	Gnr	B+	DC-033
83487155BG	Sktr	P.R. Burger	Radio/Gnr	A+	DC 034
84264498BG	Kav	J.C. Chester	Dwr B	O+	DC 035
85203651BG	Kav	R. Clark	Dwr A	O+	DC 036
83338459BG	Sktr	G.J. Coetzee	Sktr	AB+	DC 037

Appendix II

The History of 61 Mechanised Battalion Group

Combat Group (CG) Juliet was formed as a distinct Battalion Group in February 1978, led by Commandant Joep Joubert, with the specific remit of providing a mobile reserve force for the South West African Territorial Force and conducting lightening cross-border strikes against South West Africa People's Organisation's (SWAPO) military wing who maintained training camps and strategic operational bases across a vast swathe of Southern Angola.

The unit needed to be available to strike into either east or west Angola at short notice, so it established the beginnings of a permanent base at Oshivello in central northern SWA, above the Etosha National Park. The area around the base was later renamed after a local river 'Omuthiya' in 1979 by Commandant Johan Dippenaar when the base was formally established as the primary operational launch pad for operations conducted during the South West African and Angolan military campaigns.

CG Juliet was an evolutionary step in the military's response to the increasing security threat on the SWA/Angola border and with the mobile and versatile Ratel Armoured Fighting Vehicle (AFV) at the core of its fighting force; CG Juliet was well suited to combating the light-infantry, guerrilla-style tactics employed by SWAPO.

SWAPO was well supported by the Angolan Government and their army got involved in cross-border military incursions into SWA.

CG Juliet proved its versatility, evolving over a number of years to also counter the increasingly conventional threat posed by Brigades of Angolan government forces, the FAPLA (People's Armed Forces of Angola – Forcas Armadas Popular de Angola).

Both SWAPO and FAPLA were supported by Russian and East German military advisors, augmented by Cuban ground and air forces.

Commandant Frank Bestbier was appointed second commanding officer of CG Juliet. Under his command the unit prosecuted Operation Reindeer in May

1978 with the aim of disrupting the main forward operational headquarters and training camp of SWAPO for Southern Angola.

Objective Bravo, AKA 'Vietnam' by Angolan SWAPO, was a network of six bases in the vicinity of Chetequera, 30 km over the border and also provided a vital logistical springboard for insurgents into SWA.

Objective Bravo was attacked and destroyed by Combat Group Juliet on 4 May 1978 which led to the establishment of 61 Mechanised Battalion Group on 1 January, 1979.

The decision to commit fully to a pre-formed battle group marked a formal change in strategy for the SADF and "61" was promulgated by Chief of the Army's Operations Order Number 1/79, dated 6 February 1979. This order was issued by the then serving Chief of the Army, Lieutenant General Constand Viljoen.

In June 1980, 61 Mech successfully participated in its first joint operation – Sceptic (AKA Smokeshell), under Commandant Johann Dippenaar.

During the ops, 61 Mech was tasked with destroying SWAPO command, control and logistic structures in Angola on 10 and 11 June 1980, in the vicinity of Ionde in Southern Angola. The attacks were followed by two weeks of mop-up operations against dispersed insurgent groups.

Commandant Roland de Vries assumed command of the unit in January 1981. The operations conducted during his 2-year command included Protea, Carrot, Yahoo, Makro, Daisy and Meebos.

Operation Protea, launched 24 August 1981, became widely recognised as one of the most successful large-scale, conventional actions in Africa since WW2.

Ops Protea was a targeted pre-emptive strike against conventional FAPLA units and formations at Humbe, Peu-Peu, Xangongo and Ongiva. Each target was to be attacked simultaneously by one of Task Force Alpha's four mechanised combat groups.

61 Mech was designated as Combat Group 10, the force that attacked Humbe from the western side of Kunene River.

This large-scale conventional operation was a portent of things to come. The war in Southern Angola was escalating, FAPLA and SWAPO insurgents fighting side by side while the FAPLA modernised their mechanised capabilities, air power and air defences. SWAPO insurgents were also fighting side by side with FAPLA and Cuban conventional forces.

By 1987, the unit had gained a fearsome reputation and went on to prosecute Operation Modular under Commandant Bok Smit, bringing about the destruction of an enemy tank-hardened, mechanised Battalion to earn itself the distinction of winning "SADF's greatest battle victory achieved in a single day".

The unit was never defeated on the battlefield. The commanders and soldiers of 61 Mech were highly trained and extremely adept at fighting fast moving offensive actions on the hoof.

61 Mech was disbanded on 18 November 2005 at Lohatlha and merged with 8 South African Infantry Battalion at Upington.

The last serving commanding officer was Lieutenant Colonel Etienne Visagie.

In the post-war period, 61 Mechanised Battalion Group was one of the South African units singled out by the Cubans for their professionalism and military prowess in prosecuting military campaigns in Angola.

Commendation by the Cuban delegation negotiating the peace treaty in 1989, serves as a tribute to soldiers of 61 Mech, most of whom were young national servicemen.

Former members of the unit have established a veteran's organisation to honour the memories of the unit, its soldiers and fallen.

Extract © Maj Gen (Ret) Roland de Vries, SD, SM, MMM – former Officer Commanding 61 Mechanised Battalion Group from 1981 to 1982 and 61 Mech Battalion Group Veterans' Association.